THE SHC

D0626655

The Short Story

An Introduction

PAUL MARCH-RUSSELL

EDINBURGH UNIVERSITY PRESS

© Paul March-Russell, 2009

Edinburgh University Press Ltd
22 George Square, Edinburgh

Typeset in Ehrhardt
by Servis Filmsetting Ltd, Stockport, Cheshire, and
printed and bound in Great Britain by
CPI Antony Rowe, Chippenham and Eastbourne

A CIP record for this book is available from the British Library

ISBN 978 0 7486 2773 8 (hardback)
ISBN 978 0 7486 2774 5 (paperback)

Contents

Acknowledgements

I would first of all like to thank the editorial team at Edinburgh University Press, in particular the commissioning editor Jackie Jones, for their help and enthusiasm. I would also like to thank the anonymous readers whose comments helped me to reshape the original proposal. Past and present colleagues at the University of Kent have aided me with advice, encouragement, insights and the loan of books, among them Maggie Awadalla, David Ayers, Jennifer Ballantine-Perera, David Blair, Keith Carabine, Agnès Cardinal, Stefania Ciocia, Patricia Debney, Brian Dillon, Alex Dolby, Rob Duggan, Lyn Innes, Julian Preece, Dave Reason, Caroline Rooney, Elizabeth Schächter, Martin Scofield, Florian Stadtler, David Stirrup, Scarlett Thomas and Sue Wicks. I remain grateful for the continued support of my PhD examiner Robert Hampson, while I am also indebted to timely conversations with Ailsa Cox and Toby Litt. Part of Chapter 10 was presented in a different form at the J. G. Ballard conference at the University of East Anglia in 2007: I am grateful to the organiser, Jeannette Baxter. I would also like to thank my many students in English, American and Comparative Literature for partaking (suffering?) seminars in tales, short stories and popular fictions. Lastly, I would like to thank the love and support of my far-flung family: John and Virginia in Oxford; Brandon, Lucy and their children in Somerset; Zahra in the Isle of Man; and Isabella and Kirit in Canterbury. This book is dedicated to the memories of Pamela Russell and Colin March.

Copyright permissions: I would like to thank the Estate of Donald Barthelme for allowing me to reprint an illustration from Donald Barthelme's 'The Flight of Pigeons from the Palace' in *Forty Stories* (1989), and Iain Sinclair for permitting me to reprint a page from his story, 'The Griffin's Egg' (1996).

Illustrations

Preface

The aim of this new introduction is two-fold. First, it introduces the development of the international short story from its folktale origins to the present day, and second, it relates the short story to cultural debates that will also introduce the reader to areas of critical and theoretical discussion. To achieve this aim, the book is structured in twenty chapters that work thematically rather than chronologically. Consequently, although I have strived for inclusion, I have not sought to be comprehensive. There are regrettable omissions – some of which I allude to in the text – while some notable writers are reduced to passing comment. Equally, other writers, too often overlooked by the narrow focus of short story theory, receive greater prominence. This decision has been influenced by the argument that underwrites the study, namely, that the making of the short story is central to an understanding of modern literature and that the short story can be best understood as a type of fragment. Like the literary fragment, the short story is prone to snap and to confound readers' expectations, to delight in its own incompleteness, and to resist definition. These qualities not only mean that the short story has been of service to experimental writers but that they also relate the short story – and, in turn, modern and contemporary literature – to the mutability of the oral tradition. Since one (late Marxist) strain in critical theory sees modern culture as irrevocably split, the short story is of particular use in understanding the relationship between art and modernity, and in particular the development of popular fiction. Greater space is devoted to popular sub-genres, and their relationship to literary fiction, than in previous introductions. Critical attempts to gloss the short story as a 'well-made' structure omit not only these areas but also the irreducible complexity of the short story form: this is one reason among many why I sound a cautionary note about the enduring legacy of formalism within short story criticism. Furthermore, at no point do I attempt to define the short story. To make an astronomical allusion, the short story can be likened to a black hole. Although unobservable, its presence is detectable by its radial effect. In this study I explore the effects of the short story on its surrounding contexts so that it becomes a catalyst for investigating and inter-relating a 'constellation' (in Walter Benjamin's terms) of elements drawn from art, literature, culture and history. To this end, I ultimately regard the short story as a dissident form of communication.

Origins: From Folktale to Art-Tale

The *Oxford English Dictionary* dates the earliest recorded reference to the term 'short story' to 1877. Anthony Trollope, in his *Autobiography* (1883), mentions writing 'certain short stories' but, as he suggests elsewhere ('It was a short story, about one volume in length'), he is referring to prose fictions that are simply shorter than his usual narratives (Trollope 1950: 136, 160). Wilkie Collins, likewise, referred to his shorter fiction as 'little novels'. In the United States, despite their apparent advance upon the British, the term only gained currency during the 1880s. Nevertheless, as Raymond Williams indicates in his book *Keywords* (1976), the coinage of a word or phrase implies the need to represent in language a cultural change, a shift in consciousness or society. The neologism of the 'short story' signifies a redefinition of literature towards the end of the nineteenth century; how it is produced, received and consumed. Consequently, the making of the short story acts as an index to the invention of modern fiction and its relationship to changing social, economic and cultural contexts.

Yet, writers did not immediately embrace this new term. British writers, such as Thomas Hardy, Rudyard Kipling and Robert Louis Stevenson, adhered to the older designation of the tale, while E. M. Forster referred to his short stories as fables. Joseph Conrad made no clear distinction between his longer and shorter fictions – to him they were all 'stories' (Fraser 1996: 25). Contrary to popular critical belief, American writers were not any more helpful. Henry James rejected the distinction of novel and short story, preferring instead the non-equivalent French terms of *nouvelle* and *conte*. Mark Twain's satires and tall tales also fail to fit the dictates of the modern short story as prescribed by pioneering critics such as Brander Matthews. Yet, as the title of Matthews' *The Philosophy of the Short-Story* (1901) indicates, even he was uncertain as to how this new form should be spelt. During the last years of the nineteenth century, there was much debate and confusion surrounding the nature of the short story (see Barr et al. 1897).

For many writers of the period, 'tale' and 'story' were used interchangeably, and no clear distinctions were made except by the editors of periodicals that encouraged, and thrived upon, the late nineteenth-century boom in short stories. Even though the term 'short story' implies a plotted narrative, written as opposed to recited, writers tended to regard themselves as producing the modern-day equivalent of the folktale. H. G. Wells, in particular, took delight in the variety and elasticity of the form: 'Insistence upon rigid forms and austere unities seems to me the instinctive reaction of the sterile against the fecund' (Wells 1914: vii). In other words, to understand the artistic appeal of the short story, it is important to trace, first of all, the prehistory of the form, for that was the tradition in which many early short storywriters felt they were working.

The tale can be traced back to the earliest surviving narrative, *The Epic of Gilgamesh*, written in the third millennium BCE. In the following overview, five sub-genres of tale will be considered: parable and fable, the Creation myth, novella, fairy tale and art-tale. The most notable aspect is that, despite its printed versions, the tale is a *spoken* form that, consequently, implies a speaker and a listener. The context for the tale, however, may vary widely, from a parent talking to a child to a religious speaker instructing a congregation to a teacher addressing a class to a storyteller performing to an audience to friends swapping stories. Not only is the tale oral, it is *context-sensitive* to a degree that reading is not. The context will affect the type of tale, its purpose, delivery and reception, nuances of style and presentation that are omitted from a printed account. Furthermore, there is an intimacy of address, which is lost within printed literature. I may never meet the author of the novel I am currently reading; in fact, meeting a favourite author can be a slightly eerie experience. Reading in the era of mass-production is a more alienated activity. I can describe to friends the novel I'm reading but I am unlikely to retell it (the survival of Mikhail Bulgakov's *The Master and Margarita* as an oral piece, in the context of Soviet oppression, is a rare exception). But the tale rests upon the physical encounter of speaker and listener, in which the presence of the listener shapes the tale being told. The listener participates in a tale to an extent that a reader does not. Not only is the tale mutable, changing from context to context, but the positions of speaker and listener are also variable. A listener can become a speaker by choosing to relate the tale: the authority for tale-telling is itself transferable from one participant to another. In this way, the wisdom contained within tales is passed on from one generation to the next. Yet, in different historical circumstances, a storyteller who performs a well-known tale badly or gives offence could, at the very least, be attacked or criticised or, worse, be imprisoned or executed. Both instances are extreme forms of audience participation that re-emphasise the importance of the *co-text*: the manner and technique with which the tale is presented. The recitation of Ares and Aphrodite from Book Eight of Homer's *Odyssey* is a revealing example of how a tale might have been told in the classical period. The gods within the tale act as a kind of stage audience; their amusement parallels the pleasure that the storyteller gives his listeners. Within the unspoken pact of speaker and listener, the tale is an open-ended or *dialogic* form.

Parable and Fable

Parable and fable are closely related forms. The former is a type of storytelling that operates by analogy. While the narrative may be fictional, its aim is to instruct the reader according to a higher religious or moral purpose. Fable is similar, but its chief differences are the endowment of animals and other natural elements with human qualities, a generalised sense of setting or place, and the use of irony. Aesop's *Fables*, for example, rely upon stock characters, such as the ass, the lion and the fox, and despite occasional reference-points, the location is non-specific. This lack of detail allows, instead, for an ironic humour that complements the violence of the fables. So, in one tale after the ass has divided the kill 'into three equal parts', the lion is 'enraged' and eats him. The fox, quite sensibly, then divides the spoils, leaving only the smallest amount for himself, adding 'I learned this technique from the ass's misfortune.' While the appended moral claims that 'we learn from the misfortune of others' (Aesop 1998: 157), the fox's grim joke loads all the meaning of the fable in the final line. The grimness of the humour often unsettles a consistent or overarching morality, so that in another tale, after the fox has ensured the ass' capture to save himself, he is eaten by the lion which saves 'the ass for later' (Aesop 1998: 201). Aesop's characterisation is simple but not reductive. In some contexts, it is better to be a fox; in others a lion (or even a mouse). The ass, though, is the eternal victim.

In other words, whereas Christian parables such as the Good Samaritan have a clear and instructive meaning, Aesop's *Fables* are more ambiguous, especially the shorter fables that are scarcely more than epigrams. Consequently, while short stories such as Franz Kafka's 'Before the Law' (1914) appear to have a parabolic structure, in that they seem to portend some deeper meaning, the narrative form is closer to that of the fable. The stories of Bertolt Brecht, written in exile from Nazi Germany, can for instance be read as political fables. Brecht's locations, although real, are merely sketched-in; his characters are often anonymous figures, while the precise meaning is unclear. Like his nineteenth-century predecessor, J. P. Hebel, Brecht wants his readers to think but he does not instruct them on *what* to think. Similarly, the apocalyptic ending to Flannery O'Connor's 'Revelation' (1964), a parabolic story laced with irony, calls into question the insight of its central character.

The Creation Myth

Creation myths occur throughout the world from the Norse sagas to Native American tales to Ancient Egypt, Judeo-Christianity and Greco-Roman culture. The Creation myth is a type of parable, but although conceived within a religious framework that considers the events to be fundamentally true, the myth describes not only in terms of moral order how the world came to be. Creation myths are the cornerstone of a culture's cosmology, of how it regards itself in relation to the universe. They describe humanity's perennial concern with origins: the search for identity.

In *The Epic of Gilgamesh*, the Creation myth is presented as a tale within a tale, which is told to the eponymous hero by Utnapishtim, the immortal survivor of the divine Flood that reshaped the world. Gilgamesh has pursued Utnapishtim into the underworld in search of everlasting life following the death of his soul-mate, Enkidu. In other words, the tale that Utnapishtim recalls is connected to Gilgamesh's own quest for self-knowledge. The senseless actions of Enlil, the warrior god who summoned the Flood, prefigure the foolish hopes of Gilgamesh to secure immortality. While Utnapishtim's tale records how the present world came into existence, it also comments upon mankind's need to accept the inevitability of death. Gilgamesh, like his audience, only realises the wisdom of the myth once his search has ended in failure. It is the encounter though between Utnapishtim and Gilgamesh, set within the literal shadow of death, that contributes to the myth's extraordinary power.

In contrast, the Flood narrative recorded in the *King James Bible* is written with confidence and authority. It bears witness by emphasising details, times, names and places. The writing is inscribed with the narrative's oral use: its delivery from a pulpit by a single speaker. By way of a further contrast, the Flood narrative from Ovid's *Metamorphoses* struggles with his stated aim of spinning 'a thread from the world's beginning/down to my own lifetime, in one continuous poem' (Ovid 2004: 5). If, in one sense, Ovid's text is an attempt to justify the Roman Empire by locating its origins within the divine actions of gods, then the text also has to negotiate the misdeeds recorded by the myths themselves. Jupiter demands for the world to be destroyed due to the evil of men. The other gods are dismayed but Jupiter quells their protest by promising to create an improved human species (which he singularly fails to do). Unlike the biblical God, Jupiter opts for a flood as an afterthought. The ensuing description of devastation is rich and evocative: it functions not as a parable but as drama. Although Jupiter subsequently blesses the lucky survivors, Deucalion and Pyrrha, it is they who have to create a new human race through one of the poem's many transformations. Ovid's final comment, 'And so our race is a hard one; we work by the sweat of our brow/and bear the unmistakable marks of our stony origin' (Ovid 2004: 25), imposes a moral shape upon a set of spoken legends that are altogether more unruly. In this sense, the Roman Creation myth acts more as a portrait of human, rather than divine, society and less as a piece of religious instruction.

Novella

In its modern usage, the term 'novella' refers to a short novel, which in the nineteenth century was called a 'novelette'. Up until the end of the fourteenth century though, 'a novella was a story that could be true or fictional, new or simply unusual, written or recited' (Clements and Gibaldi 1977: 5). The tale collections of the Middle Ages, such as Giovanni Boccaccio's *Decameron* (1349–50) and Geoffrey Chaucer's *The Canterbury Tales* (1387), harness these contrasting definitions. Their form, though, was indebted equally to Roman texts, such as Apuleius' *The Golden Ass* (written during the second century CE), and Eastern collections such as the *Panchatantra*, written in Sanskrit sometime in the fifth century CE, and circulating in various translations at the time of Boccaccio. Ovid's *Metamorphoses* offers an even earlier model for the novella through its use of interpolated tales, such as Pan and Syrinx (Book One), and the tales told to one another by the daughters of Minyas (Book Four). *Metamorphoses* is travestied by *The Golden Ass*, a rambling narrative that tells the story of Lucius, a naïve student of folklore, who is transformed into a donkey. Lucius' plight, passed on from one master to the next, allows for a miscellany of tales to be strung together, such as the story of Cupid and Psyche which may have been derived from a Hittite text of the second millennium BCE (Anderson 2000: 63–9). The novelty of the tale lies not in its newness but in its strangeness, a description that can also be applied to the narrative's framing device and point of view, in which readers see the Greco-Roman world from the estranged perspective of Lucius. Apuleius' use of scatological comedy is mirrored by Petronius' *Satyricon* (written in the first century CE), which features a series of bawdy and sensational tales told by a group of party guests.

Boccaccio uses a similar strategy in *The Decameron*. Ten Florentines escape the plague-ridden city to the countryside. Over ten days they each tell ten tales: the purpose is to distract themselves and, in effect, their readers from the horrors of the Black Death. The tales are not original; they all hark from earlier sources such as Books Eight and Nine of *The Golden Ass*. Nevertheless, Boccaccio revolutionised European literature by mixing serious and comic modes, such as the court romance and the *fabliau*, while also parodying pre-existing forms, such as the saint's legend and the *exemplum*. At the same time as drawing his readers' attention to certain kinds of writing, Boccaccio brought a new sensitivity to the use of everyday speech: his characters' vernacular is clearly delineated, a success also achieved by Chaucer in his use, for example, of regional accents. The use made of the novella by both Boccaccio and Chaucer is, at once, self-consciously literary

(Chaucer's insertion of himself into his tales) and embedded within the oral tradition: the reciprocation between tales, for example those told by the Miller and the Reeve or in Boccaccio and Chaucer's rewriting of the same tale in Petrarch as the source of Patient Griselda.

Fairy Tale

The popularisation of the framed narrative by Boccaccio and Chaucer influenced collectors of folktales such as Giovan Francesco Straparola and Giambattista Basile. (The influence of *The Thousand and One Nights* upon Western literature did not occur until Antoine Galland's translation between 1704 and 1717.) Straparola's *The Delectable Nights* (1550–3) has a similar structure to the *Decameron*. Thirteen ladies and gentlemen flee political persecution to the island of Murano near Venice. Over thirteen days they tell each other seventy-five stories, fourteen of which are tales of wonder, including the earliest literary version of 'Puss-in-Boots'. Though the tales are either European or oriental in origin, Straparola rewrote them within the Italian vernacular and framed them so as to capture the readers' attention. Riddles were also added to the end of each tale rather than a didactic message. Although the tales may feature moral observations, they do not function as parables. Wit, low comedy, tragedy and sexual frankness exist alongside one another.

Basile's *Il Pentamerone* or 'The Tale of Tales' (1634–6) features a miscellany of recognisable fairy tales such as 'Cinderella', 'Sleeping Beauty' and 'Rapunzel'. During the course of civil service both in Italy and overseas, Basile overheard and recorded folktales from his servants and other members of the lower orders. Later, he elaborated these tales in a baroque literary style that made use of the Neapolitan dialect. Basile wrote for an aristocratic audience, so while he drew upon folk culture, he combined these references with a parody of elite culture, including canonical texts such as the *Decameron*. The structure of *Il Pentamerone* consists of fifty tales, including the frame-story that opens and closes the collection, related by a group of hags summoned by the Princess Zoza. Like Straparola, the tales are comic, violent and sexually explicit, but marked by Basile's own form of rhetorical play.

Although the tales of Basile and Straparola were circulated among an aristocratic readership for their own amusement, the stories were still linked to their folk roots. Charles Perrault's *Stories and Tales of Times Past* (1697) took pre-existing fairy tales – the term *conte de fée* was popularised in the same year by Mme d'Aulnoy – and rationalised their structure for French aristocratic readers. Perrault's fairy tales are less explicit than his predecessors, the narratives are smoother and more ordered, the magical elements are more logically explained, and the protagonists conform to emerging notions of gender and sexual conduct. Unlike Basile's 'The Cat Cinderilla', Perrault's heroine is passive, pure and generous, even to her stepsisters, an ideal model of grace and beauty for the girls of aristocratic families. With Perrault, the fairy tale enters a growing discourse surrounding modernity and enlightenment, most problematically displayed in 'Blue Beard'. The tale becomes a vehicle for moral and social instruction, a medium through which children are taught how to be civilised. In the process, the fairy tale is gradually removed from its folk origins.

This displacement can be seen most clearly in the work of Jacob and Wilhelm Grimm. The rise of nationalistic movements in the wake of the Napoleonic Wars encouraged a new interest in folk culture including, in Germany, *Volksmärchen* or the folktale. Between 1812 and 1857, the Grimms assembled tales from oral and printed sources under the collective title of *Kinder- und Hausmärchen* (*Children's and Household Tales*). As the title indicates, these tales were addressed towards the domestic space associated with children and their mothers. Like Perrault, the Grimms streamlined the tales but inculcated the narratives with the austere beliefs of Protestantism. Whereas Perrault's Cinderella is kind-hearted, the Grimms' Ashiepattle avenges herself in the form of the doves that peck out the sisters' eyes. Unlike the playfulness of Basile, the violence of the Grimms is directed towards a didactic message based upon punishment and proscription while sexuality is either repressed or denied. (It is for this reason that psychoanalysis becomes such a useful tool in decoding the hidden meanings within Perrault and the Brothers Grimm. Before then, psychoanalysis adds little to a story such as Straparola's 'Incestuous Designs of a King'.) Instead of Perrault's enlightened modernity, the Grimms use the fairy tale as a means of introducing a strict and regulated social order. In other words, despite the academic interest in folk culture, the fairy tale is slowly appropriated, in this case for the services of the German bourgeoisie.

Art-Tale

The Grimms introduced in the course of their collecting the notion of *Kunstmärchen*, the artistic or literary fairy tale. Hans Christian Andersen is the most famous exponent of this form, either writing original tales such as 'The Steadfast Tin Soldier' (1838) or adapting tales, such as 'The Little Mermaid' (1837), from popular ballads. Andersen's earliest tales are adaptations from traditional folktales, but even these are invested with Andersen's own characteristic style – colloquial language, irony, commonplace references, realism juxtaposed with magic. In tales such as 'The Red Shoes' (1845), the element of transformation allows for spiritual and metaphysical insight: the step into other worlds.

Throughout America and Europe in the nineteenth century, many art-tales were composed. The fairy tale was a popular and accessible form for readers, while its motifs, especially that of magic, allowed writers to comment upon and transform the observable world. Though fairy tales can be read in terms of social comment, art-tales are written with an expressed artistic or political purpose in mind. The art-tales of, for example, Washington Irving ('Rip Van Winkle'), Charles Dickens ('A Christmas Carol'), Nikolai Gogol, J. P. Hebel and Oscar Wilde ('The Happy Prince') introduce a level of self-consciousness absent from the earlier fairy tale collections. Two stories, Gogol's 'The Nose' (1836) and Hebel's 'Unexpected Reunion' (1811), are exemplary of the sub-genre. Gogol's tale is a fantastical piece in which, for unexplained reasons, a self-important official, Kovalyov, loses his nose. The nose, though, reappears dressed in government uniform, and proceeds to lead an active life around St Petersburg. Unable to persuade the nose that it is not an individual person, and unable to rejoin it to his face, Kovalyov's identity begins to disintegrate for 'lacking a nose, a man is devil knows what' (Gogol 2003: 315). In the final section of the story, the nose magically returns to Kovalyov's face, and normality is restored, except that Gogol's narrator struggles to accept the reality of the story he has just told: 'And then, too, are there not incongruities everywhere?' (Gogol 2003: 326).

Hebel's 'Unexpected Reunion', one of the most moving stories in the German language, also presents an unlikely event but, characteristic of its author's style, relates the incident in a realistic and understated manner: 'When however, before the feast of Saint Lucia, the parson had called out their names in church for the second time, "If any of you know cause, or just hindrance, why these persons should not be joined together in holy Matrimony" – Death paid a call' (Hebel 1995: 25). The bridegroom dies in a mining accident and his body is lost. Years later, the corpse is rediscovered, petrified in ferrous vitriol, so that the body has not decayed. It is the former bride, who has spent the rest of her life in mourning, who identifies the body:

> The hearts of all those there were moved to sadness and tears when they saw the former bride-to-be as an old woman whose beauty and strength had left her; and the groom still in the flower of his youth; and how the flame of young love was rekindled in her breast after fifty years, yet he did not open his mouth to smile, nor his eyes to recognize her. (Hebel 1995: 27)

Through a chance occurrence, bordering upon magic, two separate times are brought into relation with one another. In-between, though, Hebel relates an extraordinary chronicle of miscellaneous events – wars, natural disasters, political upheavals – that proceed without apparent consequence upon the lives of the common folk. Instead, the confusion of history is offset by the turn of the seasons and the rhythmical pattern of agrarian labour. In the story's final paragraph, the groom's miraculous return prefigures the Day of Judgement when the dead will rise again. To quote Walter Benjamin, who elsewhere praises Hebel's story, the conclusion is 'shot through with chips of Messianic time . . . the strait gate through which the Messiah might enter' (Benjamin 1992: 255).

In other words, as the fairy tale was gradually removed from its folk roots to become an instrument within the civilising process of young children, so writers such as Gogol and Hebel found within its resources a medium for social and philosophic thought. The art-tale, then, is an important development since it bridges the gap between the folktale and the modern short story. From this brief survey, it is possible to draw some preliminary conclusions. First, while tales often feature moral messages, they are not innately didactic, though they have subsequently been used for moral purposes. Second, while narrative elements reoccur, tales are mutable: they alter according to their retelling but these changes are not sudden. Tales are slowly transformed over time and within social contexts. Third, the mutability of tales runs counter to the fixed arrangement of the printed page. The success of Boccaccio was to write in a literary style that highlighted the framing and perspective of narration, while also displaying sensitivity to the spoken voice. Chaucer and Basile recapture a semblance of the oral tradition through their respective use of rhetorical play: the mixing of modes and registers. Fourth, despite the rationalisation of the tale as an instrument of social conduct in the eighteenth and nineteenth centuries, writers addressing an adult audience realised in the tale a capacity for artistic and social purpose. These observations, in varying degrees, are relevant to the development of the short story. Yet they are prefigured by the ending to *The Epic of Gilgamesh* when the hero, who 'was wise . . . saw mysteries and knew secret things', returns from his epic quest and engraves 'the whole story' onto stone tablets (*Epic of Gilgamesh* 1960: 117), in effect, the cosmology of his people and the story that, as readers, we have just read. Gilgamesh is transformed from the warrior to the storyteller, who explores uncharted territories, converts his experience into art and establishes his authority through the wisdom he has accrued. In effect, Gilgamesh becomes a model of both the storyteller and the pioneering artist, who writes not only themselves but also their relationship to their readers into their art. This deeply self-conscious notion of the artist will also be important to an understanding of the short story.

Further Reading

For a useful sketch of the short story from its ancient origins, see Chapter 2 of Ian Reid's *The Short Story* (1977). On the folktale and the fairy tale, see respectively the influential formalist study by Vladimir Propp, *Morphology of the Folk-Tale* (1968), and the psychoanalytic account by Bruno Bettelheim, *The Uses of Enchantment* (1976). Jack Zipes has edited an excellent critical anthology, *The Great Fairy Tale Tradition* (2001). Although there is little critical literature on the art-tale, see Kari Lokke, 'The Romantic Fairy Tale', in Michael Ferber's *Companion to European Romanticism* (2005). On the subject of genre, see Jacques Derrida's difficult yet rewarding essay, 'The Law of Genre', in *Acts of Literature* (1992).

2

Riddles, Hoaxes and Conundrums

The art-tale, which prospered throughout the nineteenth century, was an important bridge between the folktale and the short story. Its immediate and accessible form allowed writers to comment upon the attitudes and organisation of modern society. The role of magic, in particular, gave writers the opportunity of imagining different kinds of relationship, especially different ways of feeling and perceiving reality. If earlier fairy tales tended to be one-dimensional, for example the moral didacticism of Charles Perrault and the Brothers Grimm, then the art-tale tended to be multi-layered and ambiguous. Washington Irving's 'Rip Van Winkle' (1819), for instance, can be read either as a demand not to sleep through one's life, as Rip does, and thereby miss the chance of personal and political freedom, or as a critique of the post-revolutionary settlement, in which Rip's laziness embodies a spirit of individualism that contrasts with the political fervour and crowd mentality of the new Republic. Either response can be supported by a reading of the text, an interpretative split which is precipitated by the draught that sends Rip into his twenty-year sleep, and which argues for the new American democracy to be composed of disputatious voices rather than a monotone.

The ambiguity of the art-tale, though, echoes a much earlier form of wordplay: the riddle. The interruption of lifelike scenarios by magical or uncanny events, for example in the stories of Nikolai Gogol and J. P. Hebel, casts the reader's recognition into doubt. Readers are presented with an intriguing puzzle so that the art-tale can be regarded as a riddle concealed within a narrative. Riddle stories were widespread throughout the nineteenth century. Two very popular examples in America were Thomas Bailey Aldrich's 'Marjorie Daw' (1873) and Frank R. Stockton's 'The Lady, or the Tiger' (1882). Both stories deliberately withhold information; in Stockton's case, he suspends the narrative and poses the unanswerable question as to whether the hero is about to encounter either the lady or the tiger. Since the interest of the story rests upon this final conceit, the narrative is nothing but a riddle. Yet, the story's popularity was entirely due to the spirit of sport and jest in which it was written.

Riddle stories became part of the bedrock of short fiction, for example in the tall tales of Henry Lawson, Stephen Leacock and Mark Twain and in the development of the detective story by Edgar Allan Poe and Arthur Conan Doyle. The riddle story is, arguably, one of the most influential sub-genres within the history of short fiction. Yet, it has often been neglected by short story critics since, by its very nature, the riddle story tends towards plot rather than characterisation. Its structure is an anathema to that kind of short fiction often described by academics as 'lyrical': the stories, for instance, of Anton Chekhov, A. E. Coppard and Katherine Mansfield. Furthermore, the riddle story has traditionally thrived within the competitive world of the mass market as opposed to the more precious realm of the small literary magazine. To understand the development of the short story, though, it is necessary to rethink the role of the riddle and to decline from segregating short stories according to professional taste. The aim of this chapter is to argue that an early form of modernist short fiction emerges, precisely, out of the riddle rather than in opposition. Two other sub-genres, the hoax and, following Brander Matthews (1901: 70), what I will term the conundrum, will also be discussed. I shall focus upon the following stories: Nathaniel Hawthorne's 'Rappaccini's Daughter', Poe's 'The Balloon-Hoax' (both 1844) and Henry James' 'The Figure in the Carpet' (1896).

The Riddle: 'Rappaccini's Daughter'

One of the best insights into the rhetorical use of riddles comes from Aristotle: 'the very nature of a riddle is this, to describe a fact in an impossible combination of words', adding that 'a good metaphor implies an intuitive perception of the similarity in dissimilars' (Aristotle 1954: 253, 255). The language of a riddle is metaphorical, since it describes an object as if it were something else, as if two non-identical things were the same. By the same token, the riddle story reveals a secret in a manner oblique yet suggestive of an underlying pattern. In other words, despite the surface confusion, the false trails that may blind the reader and the story's protagonist, there is a causal logic that ultimately connects the narrative and explains the plot.

Nathaniel Hawthorne inherited two contradictory ideologies. On the one hand, he was the descendant of Puritan settlers; on the other hand, he was a beneficiary of the Enlightenment project that underscored the American War of Independence (1775–83). The Puritans were devout Protestants, who fled England in the early seventeenth century because of their fears surrounding persecution and Catholic insurgency. Both rational and sceptical in their beliefs, the Puritans distrusted the rituals associated with Catholicism, and in particular doubted the Pope as God's representative on Earth. For the Puritans, no human being could fully understand the ways of God since that would suggest that humanity was on a par with God. Instead, God revealed Himself through signs and wonders that demanded interpretation upon the part of His believers. Consequently, reading and the precise attribution of meaning were fundamentally important facets of Puritan culture. This sceptical approach was true also of the Founding Fathers of the American Constitution (1787) such as Benjamin Franklin and Thomas Jefferson. Yet, whereas the Puritan community was rigid and hierarchical, the *Declaration of Independence* (1776) defended personal freedom and individual happiness. Both movements were rational in their beliefs, but they disagreed over the type of society they sought to create. Hawthorne's writing belongs to a hinterland, refusing to align itself to either the Puritan legacy or the new American Republic, but equally refusing to let go of its own rational scepticism. His fiction tends towards allegory: 'a neutral territory, somewhere between the real world and fairy-land, where the Actual and the Imaginary may meet, and each imbue itself with the nature of the other' (Hawthorne 1990: 36).

'Rappaccini's Daughter' is framed by a preface that is, in itself, a riddle. It claims that the following story is a translation from the work of M. de l'Aubépine (French for 'hawthorn'). The preface introduces a note of playfulness that at the same time undercuts Hawthorne's own authority. The reader is not necessarily sure of the story's provenance and, therefore, its authenticity. The opening itself echoes the familiar introduction to a fairy tale while the exotic, Italian setting is drawn from the Gothic novels of the British writer Ann Radcliffe.

Other allusions occur: the student and hero, Giovanni, is a Quixotic character who has consumed legends and romantic fictions; the object of his desire, Beatrice, recalls Dante's ideal of feminine grace from *The Divine Comedy* (c. 1308–21); the poisoned garden in which they meet carries overtones of Eden; while Beatrice's father, the homeopath and designer of the garden, Rappaccini, is a mixture of Faust, Prospero and Frankenstein. As the preface indicates, Hawthorne's tale is wholly inauthentic: its characters and settings are derived from other sources. In that sense, to allude to the title of Hawthorne's most famous collection, the tale is *twice-told*; its elements are culled from narratives that its readers have either read or heard of before. The tale's self-referentiality not only breaks with any attempt at lifelikeness but also establishes the idea of the narrative as a conceit for the telling of a riddle.

Though the narrative is written in the third-person, it is told through the eyes of Giovanni. It is his function to decipher the events that are occurring around him. Yet, Hawthorne demystifies the Puritan faith in the reading of signs by showing the sign to be unstable and the reader to be subjective:

> But . . . it seemed to Giovanni, when she was on the point of vanishing beneath the sculptured portal, that his beautiful bouquet was already beginning to wither in her grasp. It was an idle thought; there could be no possibility of distinguishing a faded flower from a fresh one at so great a distance.

Giovanni distrusts the evidence of his eyes and is, instead, subject to 'the wild vagaries' of his imagination, 'the lurid intermixture' of his emotions, and his passion for Beatrice resembling 'a wild offspring of both love and horror' (Hawthorne 1987: 296–7). Giovanni's unreliability means that the readers themselves have to decipher the mystery so that, in that sense, the story is again twice-told. Initially, it is told through Giovanni's perspective and then it is retold as the readers piece the clues together. Reading is shown to be an ambiguous but necessary activity in which the responsibility for interpretation is passed from the author to his readers.

Yet, while the central mystery is solved, another riddle emerges. Is Beatrice really the beautiful murderess referred to in the preface or is she the victim of both her father's machinations and Giovanni's objectification? To Giovanni, it matters not 'whether she were angel or demon; he was irrevocably within her sphere' (Hawthorne 1987: 300), but to the reader it does matter since Beatrice's characterisation is central to the moral crux of the story. She protests her divine innocence, 'my spirit is God's creature' (Hawthorne 1987: 313), yet she has 'instilled a fierce and subtle poison' (Hawthorne 1987: 297) into Giovanni, both literally and metaphorically. Yet, it is Giovanni who treats Beatrice with 'venomous scorn' (Hawthorne 1987: 312). Consequently, the story is once more twice-told. As the main plotline is resolved, so a further irresolution is opened up, an ambiguity that only the reader can decide. In exposing the network of fictions which underpin not only his story but also patriarchal society, Hawthorne leaves open the possibility of transcending these cultural myths. The riddle story, allied to the art-tale, calls moral and social truths into question.

The Hoax: 'The Balloon-Hoax'

The tales of Edgar Allan Poe cover a wide range of forms, including Gothic horror, adventure stories, science fiction, detective fiction and parodies. Here, I have chosen to concentrate upon only one aspect of Poe's art: the hoax. The literary hoax has its origins in the classical period, in particular the Greek author Lucian, whose tale, 'A True Story', is the first account of interplanetary travel. Later examples include *The Memoirs of Martinus Scriblerus* (1741), a satire on academics composed by, among others, John Gay, Alexander Pope and Jonathan Swift. Scriblerus was an inspiration for Washington Irving's frame narrator of 'Rip Van Winkle', the pedantic historian, Diedrich Knickerbocker. Each of these hoaxes attempts to pass off as factually true a narrative that the authors know to be false.

Despite Poe's dissolute reputation, including his fascination with the violent, the perverse and the uncanny, he was ultimately a rationalist. As Poe shows in the stories featuring his detective hero, Auguste Dupin, he believed in the ability of the human mind to explain an incomprehensible universe. Dupin imagines himself into the mind of the criminal: 'the analyst throws himself into the spirit of his opponent, identifies himself therewith, and . . . sees thus, at a glance, the sole methods . . . by which he may seduce into error or hurry into miscalculation' (Poe 1998: 93). Dupin's analytical method is based upon speculation rather than empirical deduction. Poe believed that the virtues of Enlightenment thought – reason and logic – were too narrowly defined: they omitted any role for the imagination and, as a consequence, ignored the darker recesses of the human mind. As Poe writes in 'The Imp of the Perverse' (1845), the spirit of perversity is intrinsic to human nature since 'to indulge for a moment, in any attempt at *thought*, is to be inevitably lost' (Poe 1998: 286). To think is to go astray, to leave the recognisable path and to plunge into the forests of one's own imagination. Poe's fiction constitutes a necessary foray into this remote territory since, following the logic of Poe's argument, the Enlightenment project will remain limited as long as it denies these fundamental areas of human desire. Poe seeks to explore what has been deemed irrational – paranoia, murder, incest – so that many of his stories, such as 'William Wilson' (1839) and 'The Tell-Tale Heart' (1843), are narrated from the point of view of their perpetrators. In so doing, Poe's tales disturb social and moral distinctions between fact and fiction, good and evil.

In 1835, Poe wrote 'The Unparalleled Adventure of One Hans Pfall' largely in the form of a letter detailing a balloon flight to the Moon, although it might also be the description of a dream in which the eponymous Pfall escapes his creditors. The ambiguity is built into the story which concludes with the rumours and speculations that follow the letter's revelation. Poe's narrator, though, pre-empts the reader's derision by remarking that 'the over-wise even made themselves ridiculous by decrying the whole business as nothing better than a hoax. But hoax, with these sort of people, is, I believe, a general term for all matters above their comprehension' (Poe 1976: 57). If the story is not a hoax then what exactly is it? Poe's playful account grounds its realism in astronomical discoveries of the day while, at the same time, drawing upon a literary tradition of fantastical voyages to the Moon. Pfall's journey is no more implausible than these other adventures, but neither is it any more believable, since the story's allusiveness runs counter to the realistic tone of the narrative. Whereas the riddle story ultimately denotes an underlying pattern, the hoax resists a similar movement towards closure. It insists upon a final hesitancy towards truth; an ambiguous play surrounding categories of knowledge.

In Poe's case, though, matters became more complicated when he accused Richard Adams Locke, editor of the New York *Sun*, of plagiarising his story in a series of fake articles, 'Discoveries in the Moon'. Poe was unable to prove his accusation, but nine years later, he had his revenge. The *Sun* was a cheaply produced newspaper that specialised in scoops and sensational stories. On 13 April 1844, it ran an early morning 'Postscript', claiming that a balloon had crossed the Atlantic for the first time. A special edition, featuring the full story, was published later that day and quickly sold out. The following day though, when the story was reprinted elsewhere, it was revealed to be a fiction penned by Poe. 'The Balloon-Hoax' succeeded, because it pandered to the *Sun*'s taste for sensation and the American public's appetite for progress and adventure. Most especially, it blurred the boundaries between fact and fiction in what contemporary writers often refer to as 'faction' (for example, Truman Capote's *In Cold Blood*, 1966). The story mixes literary registers by commencing as journalistic prose but continuing in the form of a diary. Real-life figures, such as the aviator Monck Mason, the inventor William Henson, the novelist Harrison Ainsworth and the politician Robert Hollond, appear alongside fictional characters. Much of the technical information is derived from Mason's own work, while the journal features a pastiche of Harrison's melodramatic style: 'The immense flaming ocean writhes and is tortured uncomplainingly' (Poe 1976: 120). To further authenticate the narrative actual locations are used, but in what should have been a clue to the hoax, one of these place-names is Sullivan's Island, the setting for Poe's mystery story, 'The Gold-Bug' (1843). The combined effect of these strategies is to disorientate the reader; to persuade them that what is plainly false is actually true.

'The Balloon-Hoax' prefigures a characteristic development within avant-garde and postmodern culture: the use of simulated or synthetic representations in place of authentic experience. A notorious example occurred in 1980 when a group of political activists reprinted J. G. Ballard's story, 'Why I Want to Fuck Ronald Reagan' (1967), on official Republican Party notepaper, removed the title and sub-headings, and circulated the document – a pastiche of a psychological experiment – at the Republican Party Convention as if it were a genuine medical profile of the Presidential candidate. The delegates, apparently, accepted it at face value. Whereas the riddle questions the relationship between truth and falsehood, hoaxes such as those by Poe or Ballard doubt the very distinction itself. Hoaxes live vicariously within the world of mass media; 'The Balloon-Hoax' is no exception. Inspired by personal rivalry with another writer and editor, the story participates within an emerging culture of celebrity: its success was meant to garner fresh attention for Poe. Yet, hoaxes also reveal the superficiality of such a culture; their collapsing of the boundaries between truth and falsehood prompts their readers into greater scepticism. Part of this suspicion, though, may also involve a revelling in the text, a delight in its artifice, a sensibility that Jorge Luis Borges describes in 'Pierre Menard, Author of the *Quixote*' (1939): 'Menard . . . does not define history as an inquiry into reality but as its origin. Historical truth, for him, is not what has happened; it is what we judge to have happened' (Borges 1970: 43). Hoaxes transfer the responsibility of interpretation to their consumers, and in the process it is they – not the hoaxer – who are made to bear the weight of accountability.

The Conundrum: 'The Figure in the Carpet'

Henry James' story, one of a number that he published during the 1890s concerning the mass media, focuses on a young critic who attends a party in order to meet the author Hugh Vereker, with the hope of enhancing his own reputation. Vereker, though, criticises the young man's recent review of his work for failing to uncover 'the particular thing I've written my books most *for*'. He adds that 'this little trick of mine' extends 'from book to book' (James 1986: 365–6): 'It governs every line, it chooses every word, it dots every i, it places every comma' (James 1986: 368). Vereker persuades the young man of both the presence of this figure and the need for its detection: 'it's naturally the thing for the critic to look for . . . even as the thing for the critic to find' (James 1986: 366). The chase, though, comes to involve a fellow critic, George Corvick, and a female novelist, Gwendolen Erme. Corvick claims to have discovered the secret but makes its revelation conditional upon his marriage to Gwendolen, a union repeatedly frustrated by her mother. Corvick, Vereker and finally Gwendolen die before the figure can be revealed to the narrator, who closes his narrative sealed in his 'obsession for ever' (James 1986: 395).

James' enigmatic tale has puzzled readers since its publication. In more recent years, the story's pursuit of a sign whose appearance is endlessly withheld has come to resemble an exercise in deconstructive criticism. Tzvetan Todorov, for example, has argued that the narrative describes 'a quest for an absolute and absent cause' (Todorov 1977: 145). In Todorov's description of the story, Vereker claims that there is an idea that preconditions his work but which has so far gone undetected. This suggestion provokes the quest, but for the purpose of the search, the figure must be absent and unknown, yet always present, since its disappearance determines all that occurs in the rest of the narrative. In effect, the story redoubles the illusory figure that Vereker claims to be omnipresent, yet invisible, throughout his work. The contradiction of an absence that is simultaneously present is very similar to a hoax, since it appears to be what it is not. Since the cause preconditions the quest, from which it is nonetheless absent, revelation never comes. Where this enigma differs from the hoax, though, is that even if the reader denies Vereker's claim that there is a secret, the reader is no nearer to understanding his motivations in posing the dilemma. Whereas Poe's 'The Balloon-Hoax' can be shown to be untrue – it is a scandal, literally a trap, for the unwary – it is impossible to say whether there is a 'figure in the carpet', what it might be if it exists, or even what James' aim was in writing the story. This endless play of meaning constitutes what deconstructionists often refer to as an aporia: literally, a routeless route, a path that leads nowhere.

Stories such as 'The Figure in the Carpet', Joseph Conrad's 'The Tale' (1917) and Rudyard Kipling's 'Mrs Bathurst' (1904) can be best described as conundrums. They feature a riddle or a mystery, like 'Rappaccini's Daughter', and often seem to have a hoaxing quality like the stories of Poe. These potential keys to the narrative, though, are frustrated by how the narrative is structured and framed. For example, in 'Mrs Bathurst' Kipling uses multiple narrators, each of whom supplies part of the story surrounding the missing seaman, Vickery, and the woman he is haunted by, yet each narration is incomplete and framed by the other characters. There is no single presiding narrative voice and no final word to pass judgement upon the story that they each tell to the best of their abilities. As the character Pyecroft comments: 'I used to think seein' and hearin' was the only regulation aids to ascertainin' facts, but as we get older we get more accommodatin'' (Kipling 1987d: 277). The elisions that characterise these narratives connect the riddle story and the hoax to an emerging modernist aesthetic in which the emphasis falls not upon the object of the representation but upon its manner: its style and form. Conundrums are also marked by a sense of loss – missing objects, random details, shifting contexts – that disrupts the seemingly linear and causal narrative. At the root of many avant-garde fictions, for example Borges' detective pastiche 'Death and the Compass' (1942), there lies the trace element of the conundrum.

Each of these sub-genres, the riddle, the hoax and the conundrum, treats the apparently stable categories of truth and falsehood to increasing scepticism. In 'The Figure in the Carpet', readers reach the point of being unable to explain the story either as a riddle or a hoax. The truth, if there is one, appears to reside somewhere beyond the text, not within, as the characters are led to believe. Each story reveals the propensity of the form for mystery, play and pastiche. Yet, they also place a greater burden upon the reader to interpret the narrative while frustrating him/her in this responsibility. Although these sub-genres feed into the story-writing tradition that makes possible the self-reflexive and metafictional narratives of postmodernism, another important effect is taking place. Readers are increasingly made aware of the darkness that surrounds these narratives, a darkness to which they themselves are made responsible by the weight of interpretation being transferred from the author. In other words, an ethical imperative underlines these fictions (see also Chapter 15).

Further Reading

On the place of Hawthorne, Poe and James in nineteenth-century American fiction, see Martin Scofield (2006). The importance of Puritanism to the making of 'the American self' is explored by Sacvan Bercovitch (1975). On conundrums in short fiction, see also David Lodge's reading of 'Mrs Bathurst' in *After Bakhtin* (1990) and William Bonney's account of 'The Tale' in *Thorns and Arabesques* (1980).

3

Memory, Modernity and Orality

Riddles, hoaxes and conundrums pretend to be what they are not. This pretence not only characterises the enigmatic quality to be found in much short fiction but it also links the short story with its antecedent, the folktale. As the mystery deepens, so the narrative grows more layered and ambiguous. Nathaniel Hawthorne's 'Rappaccini's Daughter' (1844), for example, develops from an initial pastiche of Gothic romance into a moral quest. This tendency within short fiction for the narrative to become less transparent relates the form to the *morphological* quality of the folktale, which is to say, while there are fundamental characteristics to any genre, the rest of the narrative form operates in a flux. As Chapter 1 concluded, the folktale is mutable and open-ended. The enigma and dissimulation associated with the riddle and related forms extend this sense of mutability inherent to storytelling into print fiction.

'The Storyteller' (1936), by the German philosopher Walter Benjamin, is one of the most profound meditations upon storytelling and its relationship to social change. Benjamin's essay is inspired by the nineteenth-century Russian writer Nikolai Leskov, but it is effectively an elegy to a number of writers, among them J. P. Hebel, Rudyard Kipling and Edgar Allan Poe, whose work Benjamin feels 'most *resembles* the ancient oral forms' (Greaney 2002: 17). For Benjamin, the art of storytelling is dying out because the communicability of authentic experience is itself diminishing: 'a concomitant symptom of the secular productive forces of history, a concomitant that has quite gradually removed narrative from the realm of living speech and at the same time is making it possible to see a new beauty in what is vanishing' (Benjamin 1992: 86). According to Benjamin, the communication of wisdom learnt through experience could only be passed on from one generation to the next in closely knit communities.

Once families and rural societies are scattered by the forces of urbanisation and secularisation, the infrastructure upon which storytelling is dependent is displaced. The art of storytelling declines as individuals lose the ability of telling tales and as other forms of communication, most notably print media, take precedence. Benjamin is notably scathing of the short story: 'We have witnessed the evolution of the "short story", which has removed itself from oral tradition and no longer permits that slow piling one on top of the other of thin, transparent layers which constitutes the most appropriate picture of the way in which the perfect narrative is revealed through the layers of a variety of retellings' (Benjamin 1992: 92). Since Benjamin's account is poised between myth and history, it is difficult to deduce which types of short story he is criticising, but presumably he is thinking of the mass-produced fictions of writers such as O. Henry. For Benjamin, the key concept is *retelling*. Not only does the folktale offer wisdom and guidance, it proposes a chance to remember as opposed to the automatic offerings of mass culture.

Benjamin develops the importance of memory and experience in a further essay, 'On Some Motifs in Baudelaire' (1939). Here, Benjamin distinguishes between two kinds of experience: *Erfahrung*, in which the shock of events and impressions continues to reverberate, and *Erlebnis*, in which the rational mind screens itself against surprising or unsettling incidents by reordering them into a temporal sequence. Whereas the experience of *Erfahrung* continues to resonate, the experience of *Erlebnis* can only be consciously recalled. *Erlebnis* effectively diminishes the effect of *Erfahrung*, in which the spectator is left with an impoverished sense of his/her authentic experience (Benjamin 1992: 157–9). In this sense, the emphases upon retelling and remembrance to be found in the folktale are closer to the richer, more disturbing and less ordered experience of *Erfahrung*.

Benjamin's distinction is rooted in the notion of 'mnemonic art' proposed by the French poet Charles Baudelaire. In his essay 'The Painter of Modern Life' (1859), Baudelaire is concerned by how art can most appropriately represent modernity, which he defines as 'the ephemeral, the fugitive, the contingent, the half of art whose other half is the eternal and the immutable'. Baudelaire asserts that 'Every old master has had his own modernity' since 'each age has a deportment, a glance and a smile of its own'. He warns that 'this transitory, fugitive element, whose metamorphoses are so rapid, must on no account be despised or dispensed with', for if it is neglected, the artist will 'tumble into the abyss of an abstract and indeterminate beauty' (Baudelaire 1995: 12–13). Yet, since the object is moving so quickly, the artist must work from memory, a dilemma that Baudelaire describes as a duel:

> In this way a struggle is launched between the will to see all and forget nothing and the faculty of memory, which has formed the habit of a lively absorption of general colour and of silhouette, the arabesque of contour. An artist with a perfect sense of form but one accustomed to relying above all on his memory and his imagination will find himself at the mercy of a riot of details all clamouring for justice with the fury of a mob in love with absolute equality. (Baudelaire 1995: 16)

Baudelaire resolves this problem through his two-part method of mnemonic art: 'the first, an intense effort of memory that evokes and calls back to life . . . the second, a fire, an intoxication of the pencil or the brush, amounting almost to a frenzy. It is the fear of not going fast enough, of letting the phantom escape before the synthesis has been extracted and pinned down' (Baudelaire 1995: 17). In Benjamin's terms, Baudelaire attempts to recapture the experience of *Erfahrung*, the spirit of authenticity, before it fades and becomes the simple occurrence of *Erlebnis*.

The descriptions of art and memory offered by Baudelaire and Benjamin are pertinent for many short storywriters who view the form as a means of capturing the passing moment. V. S. Pritchett, for example, writes that the 'collapse of standards, conventions and values, which has so bewildered the impersonal novelist, has been the making of the story writer who can catch any piece of life as it flies and make his personal performance out of it' (in Current-García and Patrick 1974: 117). Nadine Gordimer has observed that human contact 'is more like the flash of fireflies, in and out . . . in darkness', and that 'Short-story writers see by the light of the flash; theirs is the art of the only thing one can be sure of – the present moment' (in May 1994: 264). Raymond Carver described his approach to writing short stories as 'Get in, get out. Don't linger. Go on' (in May 1994: 273). More recently, William Boyd has suggested an indirect relationship, in the era of digital media, between the short story and 'sound-bite culture' (Boyd 2006: 243–4). Yet, while writers have praised the short story for its air of immediacy, readers can regard this emphasis as a sign of superficiality. At the turn of the last century, G. K. Chesterton noted:

> Our modern attraction to short stories is not an accident of form; it is the sign of a real sense of fleetingness and fragility; it means that existence is only an illusion. A short story of to-day has the air of a dream; it has the irrevocable beauty of a falsehood . . . The moderns, in a word, describe life in short stories because they are possessed with the sentiment that life is an uncommonly short story, and perhaps not a true one. (Chesterton 1906: 69)

Similarly, the American critic and editor Bliss Perry considered that there was more of a solution 'to the great problems of human destiny in one book like "Vanity Fair" or "Adam Bede" than in all of Mr Kipling's two or three hundred short stories taken together'. Not only is the short story 'easy to write and easy to read', Perry also claims that it satisfies magazine readers' increasing 'incapacity for prolonged attention' (Perry 1920: 329–30). In contrast with this 'top-down' view of mass culture, surveys of British reading groups in 2001 found that readers were frustrated by the lack of character development in short stories, and by their tendency to close just as interest had been aroused (Taylor 2003: 10–11).

A further complication, which surrounds this question of immediacy versus insubstantiality, appears in academic criticism of the short story. Academics have tended to favour what Eileen Baldeshwiler has termed the 'lyrical' story over the 'epical'. The latter, 'the larger mass of narratives' according to Baldeshwiler, tend to be plot-driven, conclusive and realistic. The former, 'smaller group' tend to be character-based, inconclusive and symbolic (in May 1994: 231). Having made this distinction, Baldeshwiler glosses any further discussion of the epical mode, and concentrates instead upon writers such as Anton Chekhov, A. E. Coppard, Katherine Mansfield, Sherwood Anderson and Eudora Welty. The effect of academia on the development of the short story is discussed later, but suffice to say, Baldeshwiler marginalises the majority of short stories while demarcating the artistic claims of a few and, in particular, treating an associated element – the fleeting impression of emotional change – as an essential quality, a shibboleth of literary excellence.

The response of writers, who make an unmediated comparison between the brevity of the short story form and the fleetingness of modern life, and the reaction of critics, who either treat this impression as a lack of substance or a marker of cultural value, neglect the *dialectical* basis of the criticisms of both Baudelaire and Benjamin. Baudelaire's mnemonic art is not a willed activity: it is an attempt to capture the shock-impression before the memory fades altogether. The artwork is not incomplete because life is open-ended; it is incomplete because of the struggle between the artist's memory of the object and the physical exercise of its representation. Baudelaire's writing attests to the beauty of authentic experience as its memory vanishes, an effect that Benjamin attributes to the social and economic conditions of modernity. The capacity for the folktale to communicate diminishes as individuals, by the forces of capital and the organisation of urban life, are estranged from themselves and from each other. What is left, in the tales of Leskov, Kipling and Poe, is the afterglow of storytelling: the melancholic beauty of an art form as it disappears. The so-called lyricism of the short story is, on these terms, no more than romantic pathos because the rise of the short story is itself symptomatic of social change and the break-up of community. Despite the insistence of modernists such as Sherwood Anderson to use 'the common words of our daily speech' (in Current-García and Patrick 1974: 73), the short story has tended towards the representation of excluded or 'submerged population groups' (O'Connor 2004: 17), such as Anderson's own cast of psychological misfits in *Winesburg, Ohio* (1919). In this respect, the isolationism of the short story compounds the professional storywriter's own alienation from his/her audience: an estrangement effected by the economic forces of literary production.

Orality, though, is more than the sometimes mysterious conception of 'voice'. It describes how the inflections within tone and register, accent and idiom, are embedded within an underlying cultural and social context that predetermines spoken narration as mutable, open-ended, compromised, fragmented, stylistically shifting. The medieval texts of Boccaccio and Chaucer endure, in part, because of the mixing of tones, styles and registers: in effect, the writing echoes with the sound of its oral origins. Orality reveals spoken narrative to have always been impure and malleable. Joseph Conrad captures this distinction in 'The Partner' (1910) when the frame narrator, a professional writer, comments that 'for the story to be acceptable' it 'should have been transposed to somewhere in the South Seas':

> But it would have been too much trouble to cook it for the consumption of magazine readers. So here it is raw, so to speak – just as it was told to me – but unfortunately robbed of the striking effect of the narrator. (Conrad 1978: 116)

The question of authenticity is compounded by the absence of the speaker, a stevedore and amateur storyteller. Like Benjamin's lament for storytelling, Conrad's narrative revolves around a disappearing centre. Yet, the unedited quality of the narration, however much it might be a conceit, attests to the legacy of the storyteller. The vocal expressiveness of storytelling lingers but as a kind of spectre.

The ghostly presence of oral and folk culture has been especially important to postmodern writers. Donald Barthelme's 'The Glass Mountain' (1970), for example, links the transcendent beauty of the New York skyline with the enlightenment awarded to heroes of medieval quest narratives. As the hero scales the outside of the skyscraper, he leaves behind him the sidewalks 'full of dogshit' and his acquaintances swearing at him (Barthelme 1993: 179). Ahead of him lies 'a castle of pure gold' and 'a beautiful enchanted symbol' (Barthelme 1993: 180). Yet, Barthelme's protagonist is not a heroic knight and this destiny should not technically be his. An eagle swoops and carries him to his goal:

> 97. I approached the symbol, with its layers of meaning, but when I touched it, it changed into only a beautiful princess.
> 98. I threw the beautiful princess headfirst down the mountain to my acquaintances.
> 99. Who could be relied upon to deal with her.
> 100. Nor are eagles plausible, not at all, not for a moment. (Barthelme 1993: 182)

In casting down the Rapunzel-like figure, the narrator appears to be displacing the transcendent realm of myth for an acceptance of the mess and confusion associated with history. Yet, still 'the glass mountain' of the title is invested with 'layers of meaning'. Although the narrator is disappointed with the object of fairy tale desire, the need for something beyond the mundane remains: the myth-making appeal of narrative. Magical realists such as Gabriel García Marquez and contemporary fabulists, for instance China Miéville, draw upon a wealth of classical myth, fable and fairy tale. In many ways, the postmodern has defined itself by working upon the remains of pre-modern literature. This anachronistic process of reinvention describes, in its very operation, the crisis inherent to modernity that Benjamin diagnoses.

Nowhere is this approach more apparent than in Angela Carter's collection, *The Bloody Chamber* (1979). In the Afterword to her previous anthology, *Fireworks* (1974), Carter had distinguished between the tale and the short story by arguing that 'the tale does not log everyday experience, as the short story does; it interprets everyday experience through a system of imagery derived from subterranean areas behind everyday experience' (Carter 1995: 459). Unlike the greater realism of the short story, the tale is drawn to the unconscious and to subject-matter considered socially unacceptable. This distinction allows Carter to equate the tale with other non-literary forms such as the Gothic, ballads and pornography. By drawing upon the folktale as the basis for her fiction, Carter, who knew Benjamin's work, is referring to a culture that has all but disappeared. The folktale elements in Carter's fiction are the broken fragments of a vanishing culture, which are in turn refracted through one another and amalgamated with other literary and artistic texts. For example, 'The Bloody Chamber' refers primarily to Charles Perrault's 'Blue Beard' but it also alludes to 'Beauty and the Beast', 'Red Riding Hood' and 'Sleeping Beauty'. The story draws upon Greek mythology and biblical narrative as well as non-folk material: grand opera, painting (especially surrealism), photography and a mixed array of fictions by, among others, Daphne du Maurier, J. K. Huysmans, Sheridan Le Fanu, the Marquis de Sade and Bram Stoker. Carter's use of the folktale is not an act of conservation. Instead, it is more like a concatenation in which folktales resound through one another and are retold through other cultural sources. She not only emphasises the mutability and impurity of the folktale, as opposed to the polish of the professionally told short story, but she also scrutinises the values attached to folktales by treating them as readymade objects that can be redeployed and reinvented. As

Carter once remarked, her interest in folklore was 'because they *are* extraordinary lies designed to make people unfree' (Carter 1997: 38). By turning the fairy tale against itself, Carter reveals its ideological function, especially its use by men to instruct women, but by mixing the fairy tale with modern sources, Carter shows how this function persists in contemporary society. Like the refracted form of Carter's tales, in which texts are unconsciously displayed through one another, power and ideology surround her protagonists like an invisible web: 'I had played a game in which every move was governed by a destiny as oppressive and omnipotent as himself, since that destiny was himself, and I had lost' (Carter 1995: 137).

In contrast with postmodern approaches, orality continues to perform a vital role in immigrant and indigenous cultures. Unlike Benjamin's Eurocentric prognosis for the demise of storytelling, oral narrative remains a means for displaced peoples to reconnect with their submerged histories, and to comment upon their experience of emigration and exile. Grace Paley's 'A Conversation with My Father' (1974), besides offering a witty commentary on the writing process, contrasts the outlook of Paley's father, a Russian immigrant, with Paley herself, a confident and optimistic New Yorker. Paley's father wants 'a simple story . . . the kind Maupassant wrote, or Chekhov', populated with 'recognizable people'. Such a narrative is an anathema to Paley since it robs 'all hope' (Paley 1999: 237). Nevertheless, she attempts to please her father and offers a perverse fairy tale involving a neighbour and her son, a drug addict. Paley's father objects to the flatness of the description and persuades his daughter to try again. This time, Paley produces a more fanciful and extraordinary narrative that strains the believability of her characters, but which also makes the ending even more downbeat. Paley's father concedes that she 'can't tell a plain story', but says of the ending, 'You were right to put that down. The end' (Paley 1999: 241–2). Paley protests, insisting that the mother might be redeemed, but instead her father gets the last word: 'Tragedy! You too. When will you look it in the face?' (Paley 1999: 243). Paley, though, has the upper hand on her father by ending her narrative on a question since it leaves their dialogue open-ended. The unresolved tension hints at the possibility of hope as well as tragedy while also commenting upon the physical and emotional distance between father and daughter.

Generational disputes also underline Toni Cade Bambara's collection, *Gorilla, My Love* (1972). The stories were written between 1959 and 1971, and counterpoint the growth of the US Civil Rights Movement. Expressed in the urban dialect of her characters, Bambara's prose style is strong, rhythmical and sassy, creating a sense of pace as in the opening to 'The Lesson': 'Back in the days when everyone was old and stupid or young and foolish and me and Sugar were the only ones just right, this lady moved on our block with nappy hair and proper speech and no makeup' (Bambara 1984: 87). Bambara's speed and movement evoke the optimism of the period, the greater sense of freedom for African-Americans, which is also invoked by the struggles with authority of Bambara's teenage protagonist. In the lead story though, 'My Man Bovanne', this style neatly captures the frustrations of an older woman as she dances with a local handyman to the annoyance of her children, who she claims have been affected by Black Power 'till they can't be civil to ole folks' (Bambara 1984: 3). Although these stories are not overtly political, the characters are self-consciously the products of their environment, and they are aware of political events that are changing the relationships within their community. Bambara's style connects to an oral tradition within African-American culture that sets these changes into perspective, while at the same time dramatising their social effect.

In contrast, the title story of Leslie Marmon Silko's *Storyteller* (1981) attests to the power of storytelling within Native American culture, while lending credence to Benjamin's claim that 'death is the sanction of everything the storyteller can tell' (Benjamin 1992: 93). Silko's story effectively features two storytellers: the grandfather, and his repeated tale of a hunter pursuing a bear in the frozen wastes; and the granddaughter, who sleeps with the white oil drillers and claims to have murdered one of them by luring him onto the ice. Like her grandfather, as he approaches death, she refuses to change her story and willingly goes to her imprisonment: 'The story must be told as it is' (Silko 1981: 31). Storytelling becomes a form of protest insofar as the grandfather and the granddaughter choose the manner of their own annihilation.

Ana Menéndez's 'In Cuba I Was a German Shepherd' (2001) encapsulates many of the themes in this chapter. The title refers to a joke in which Juanito, a 'mangy dog' just off the boat from Cuba, attempts to seduce a rich American poodle that has nothing to do with him. Juanito responds: 'Here in America, I may be a short, insignificant mutt, but in Cuba I was a German Shepherd' (Menéndez 2001: 29). The joke describes the immigrant experience. To the onlooker, Juanito may be nothing but in his memory he remains a dog of status and worth. He has come to America in search of promise and opportunity but he remains attached to what he once was in Cuba. This self-division is felt also by Máximo, the joke's teller, who left Cuba in 1969 believing he would return after two or three years. Instead, he now spends his days in Domino Park, playing and reminiscing with acquaintances, while tourists gaze upon them like caged animals:

> Most of these men are Cuban and they're keeping alive the tradition of their homeland . . . You see, in Cuba, it was very common to retire to a game of dominos after a good meal. It was a way to bond and build community. Folks, you here are seeing a slice of the past. A simpler time of good friendships and unhurried days. (Menéndez 2001: 26)

Dominos and storytelling are transformed into a cultural spectacle, in which historical ties are forgotten and replaced by the rosy hue of nostalgia, the pathos for a culture that the tourists know nothing about, but in their mass consumption believe they do. The joke that Máximo tells is consumed along with the rest of the spectacle – storytelling has indeed become an art, that is to say, an object for contemplation – but Máximo's story describes the scars upon his own memory: his inability to forget Cuba, his wife and the man he once was. Memories haunt Máximo just as the residue of oral narratives – tales, jokes, anecdotes – haunt the exiled imagination.

Further Reading

On the relationship between oral and print culture, see Walter J. Ong (1982). Mary Louise Pratt considers the role of orality in 'The Short Story: The Long and the Short of It', reprinted by Charles E. May (1994). Roland Barthes' essay, 'The Grain of the Voice', in *Image Music Text* (1977) is suggestive for literature as well as music.

4

Poe, O. Henry and the Well-Made Story

In their respective essays, 'The Painter of Modern Life' (1859) and 'The Storyteller' (1936), Charles Baudelaire and Walter Benjamin praised the tales of Edgar Allan Poe. Yet, paradoxically, it was Poe who established the framework for the 'well-made' stories of commercial writers in the early twentieth century, such as O. Henry. The popular success of O. Henry's fiction, and the subsequent critical controversy, mark an important episode in both the development and the reception of the short story. O. Henry established a working model for the short story that has endured with magazines such as *The New Yorker*. Yet, the critical opposition to his success reveals underlying concerns, especially in the United States, surrounding the short story's cultural position, anxieties to do with taste, discernment and respectability.

Poe saw himself, primarily, as a poet in the Romantic tradition, especially in the fantasies of Samuel Taylor Coleridge, John Keats and Percy Bysshe Shelley. Frequently penniless, Poe wrote stories in order to support his family, his drinking and his ruling passion for poetry: a tactic that, to some extent, paid off with the publication of 'The Raven' in 1845. It was only after his death, in 1849, that Poe's stories gradually received acclaim; ten years earlier, his first collection, *Tales of the Grotesque and Arabesque*, had sold poorly. By contrast, no contemporary work of short story criticism would omit Poe's name since he is almost universally regarded as supplying the basis for the modern short story. In his day, Poe was a marginal figure, but arguably his distance from commercial and critical respectability allowed him to divine the future development of the short story.

Poe's self-image as an artist was contradictory. On the one hand, he saw himself as an aesthete, a poet and intellectual, but on the other hand, he regarded himself as a jobbing writer, who wrote tales of mystery and horror to suit the marketplace, and whose virulent essays were often an exercise in self-promotion. This sense of self-division not only suggests the psycho-biographical approach favoured by some of Poe's critics but also, more significantly, foretells the uneasy relationship between early modernists, such as Joseph Conrad and Henry James, and the mass market. Poe decided, retrospectively, that he had made an insight into the future direction for literature and the marketplace: 'I had perceived that the whole energetic, busy spirit of the age tended wholly to the Magazine literature – to the curt, the terse, the well-timed, and the readily diffused, in preference to the old forms of the verbose and ponderous & the inaccessible' (Poe 1948: 268). In the years before the American Civil War (1861–5), when the idea of a national literature was barely tenable, and when the novelist James Fenimore Cooper had argued that the American writer was hampered by a 'poverty of materials' (Cooper 1963: 108), Poe had concluded that the already vibrant periodical market was the source for artistic innovation.

The speeding-up of life underlines Poe's theory for short fiction. During the 1830s and 1840s, the first American railroads were laid, while new forms of communication, such as photography and telegraphy, were patented. The Frontier expanded as new trails were opened. In his scientific romances and detective stories, Poe is drawn to fresh discoveries, to the power of reasoning, and to tales of physical and psychological exploration. At the same time, Poe was physically and financially adrift before finally becoming resident in New York City in 1844. In this disordered context, Poe advised in his 1842 review of Nathaniel Hawthorne's *Twice-Told Tales* that for the tale-teller 'the unity of effect or impression is a point of the greatest importance'. Since, according to Poe, 'all high excitements are necessarily transient', formal unity is essential for literature to capture their 'deepest effects'. Without unity the impression will dissipate, but in a work which is too long, the unity will also be disrupted as 'worldly interests' intervene and 'modify, annul, or counteract . . . the impressions of the book'. Instead, Poe suggests that a tale should last 'from a half-hour to one or two hours in its perusal', to 'be read at one sitting' without expending 'the immense force' of the tale's artistic 'totality' (Poe 1965: 135). This unity should not only consist of brevity but also a 'preconceived effect': 'a certain unique or single *effect* to be wrought out' by concision in which 'there should be no word written, of which the tendency, direct or indirect, is not to the one pre-established design' (Poe 1965: 136). Although Poe takes his tales from transient desires, equivalent to Baudelaire's fugitive conception of modernity (see Chapter 3), he shapes these effects into an engineered and self-sufficient text. Poe's use of the tale is modern because of this mathematical precision. 'The Fall of the House of Usher' (1839), for example, starts with 'a sickening of the heart' (Poe 1998: 49), the melancholic prospect of the House itself, and concludes with the House collapsing upon itself as both building and occupants give way to the contagious melancholia, the effect perhaps of Roderick Usher's incestuous desires for his sister, Madeline, and of the moral decay signalled in the story's introduction. The completeness of the horror resounds long after the story's end.

Other nineteenth-century writers, such as Anton Chekhov and Guy de Maupassant, repeated Poe's strictures upon brevity and concision, while Robert Louis Stevenson echoed Poe's demand for there to be a predetermined design in writing a short story:

> The *dénouement* of a long story is nothing; it is just a 'full close', which you may approach and accompany as you please – it is a coda, not an essential member in the rhythm: but the body and end of a short story is bone of the bone and blood of the blood of the beginning. (Stevenson 1995: 155)

Poe's prescription for the tale received its greatest support from the American critic Brander Matthews, who popularised Poe's theory in England as 'symmetry of design' (Matthews 1901: 71). Symmetry, according to Matthews, delineated the 'Short-story' from 'the story which is merely short' (Matthews 1901: 25), such as the anecdote, sketch or fairy tale. Matthews' original article was published in the *Saturday Review* in 1884, and was a response to the debate on 'the art of fiction' between Henry James and the commercially minded editor Walter Besant. Whereas Besant and James confined themselves to discussions of the novel, Matthews sought to open the debate to include short fiction. Matthews' decision to capitalise and hyphenate the term 'Short-story' was two-fold: to elevate the form in relation to those 'more "important" tales known as Novels' (Matthews 1901: 13) and to indicate its artifice, the text as a made object: 'the Short-story is nothing if there is no story to tell' (Matthews 1901: 32). Matthews' critical intervention differs from Poe in two respects. First, he is seeking respectability for the short story by placing it on a par with the novel, whereas Poe acknowledged the origins of his writing in the melodramatic tales published by the British journal *Blackwood's*. Second, Matthews dispenses with any reference to the tale. The 'Short-story' is a thing in itself, to be judged upon its level of technique rather than its communication of folk wisdom: 'a *true* Short-story differs from the Novel chiefly in its *essential* unity of impression' (Matthews 1901: 15). Matthews effectively distances the short story from its popular and folk roots in order to present it as an object of aesthetic value equivalent to the novel. In effect, Matthews domesticates the form, casting it in a more harmonious style with a more mannered content.

As Dean Baldwin has observed, Matthews' dissemination of Poe's theory aided magazine editors as much as it did individual writers (Baldwin 1993: 31). Faced with the boom in short story writing at the end of the nineteenth century, Poe's theory gave editors both a model and a standard by which to judge the work of writers. It was in this period that Poe's criticism became a formula by which short stories could be written, a process that was encouraged by the profusion of creative writing handbooks that used the short story as a means with which to teach would-be writers how to write and sell their work. This type of story can be called 'well-made', a term first used in the nineteenth century to describe French drawing-room dramas that used the classical unities of time, character and plot, but which were mechanical in construction and devoid of feeling. As A. S. Byatt has noted of English short fiction from the early twentieth century, much of this writing 'is diligent, it is wrought, it is atmospheric, but it can be mildly admired and taken or left' (Byatt 1999: xvi). Looking back upon the 1890s, H. G. Wells lamented this over-rationalisation of the short story when instead he 'was peering into remote and mysterious worlds ruled by an order logical indeed but other than our common sanity' (Wells 1914: iv).

In the United States, similar criticisms were voiced by, among others, H. S. Canby and Herbert Ellsworth Cory. Canby argued that as short stories 'mount toward literature they seem to increase in artificiality and constraint; when they purport to interpret life they become machines . . . for the discharge of sensation, sentiment, or romance' (in Current-García and Patrick 1974: 51). The freedom of short stories to describe life faithfully is restricted, Canby suggests, by the conventions of the well-made story: 'a swift succession of climaxes rising precipitously to a giddy eminence' (in Current-García and Patrick 1974: 54). Cory goes one step further than Canby by arguing that the short story is a sign of 'our modern speed mania': it 'is the blood kinsman of the quick-lunch, the vaudeville and the joy-ride' (in Current-García and Patrick 1974: 63). The speeding-up of life that underlined Poe's review of Hawthorne is here taken as symptomatic of a social and cultural degeneration. Cory's reaction not only prefigures Edward O'Brien's critique of the short story as a standardised literary form that mirrors the uniformity of capitalist production (see Chapter 8) but also the response of postwar sociologists, such as Dwight Macdonald, to 'the spreading ooze of Mass Culture' (Macdonald 1998: 35).

Yet, despite these views, a brief survey of turn-of-the-century titles such as *The Strand* and *The Windsor* in Britain and *Harper's Monthly* in the United States reveals well-made stories jostling with sketches, anecdotes and picaresque tales that lack the compact design and intense effect advocated either by Poe or Matthews. Instead, the opinions of the comic writer Barry Pain appear to be just as accurate when he refers to magazine stories 'made like a flabby pudding from an aged recipe' (Pain 1916: 14). While there were certainly many formulaic well-made stories, their number has been exaggerated because of the presence of two highly successful writers (Rudyard Kipling in Britain, O. Henry in North America) and their band of imitators. Furthermore, the tendency to regard the popularity of the well-made story as a sign of cultural disease glosses the actual changes that were occurring within Anglo-American culture at the start of the last century: namely, the rise of 'middlebrow' culture (see below). Lastly, the well-made story not only covers plot-driven narratives but also artfully told stories of subtle impression: a nuance in emotion, a shift in perception and a use of delicate irony. In other words, the well-made story elides the distinction made by Eileen Baldeshwiler (discussed in Chapter 3) between 'epical' and 'lyrical' short stories. Some of the finest British practitioners of the well-made story during the twentieth century include Somerset Maugham, A. E. Coppard, H. E. Bates, V. S. Pritchett and Elizabeth Taylor. The range of their writing reveals the many different tones and styles covered by the term 'well-made'.

Yet, while these writers were aware of the effect that modernism had had upon literature, for example Maugham's debt to Conrad, they preferred to stay within the more familiar realms of plot and character. The writers of well-made stories were undeniably modern but they chose against the more disquieting possibilities in narrative form that the effects of modernity had opened up.

Then again, the well-made story was still a relatively recent invention. For most of the nineteenth century Poe's model went unrecognised, and even at the end of that period it took time to be popularised. While the short story continued to be undefined, not only was it formless (as many critics have argued) but also open to experimentation in a way that lacked the self-consciousness of modernist writers, who had to work against the strictures of the well-made story. The tales of Herman Melville are a case in point. While Melville is certainly a self-conscious writer, for example in his conceit of replaying the narrative of 'Benito Cereno' (1855), there is also naturalness to his writing, a temperamental inability either to tell a story straight or with Poe's compactness. The very looseness of his style runs counter to the needs of the periodical market and questions readers' expectations as to what constitutes a short fiction. The first half of the interlinked story 'The Paradise of Bachelors and the Tartarus of Maids' (1855) appears to be an inconsequential tale of London lawyers and their comfortable lifestyle, whereas the second half recounts a visit to a paper-mill in New England where the employees are all women. Taken together, the two halves lack the formal unity demanded by Poe, while a relatively unsophisticated reading would suggest that the hardship of the women is to be contrasted with the luxury of the men. Melville's technique, though, is more complex than that. The various parts of the factory are described in terms of female anatomy while the process of manufacturing foolscap is compared to childbirth: 'a scissory sound smote my ear, as of some cord being snapped; and down dropped an unfolded sheet of perfect foolscap, with my "Cupid" half faded out of it, and still moist and warm' (Melville 1997: 93). The women do not only serve the machinery, they are part of it: 'The girls did not so much seem accessory wheels to the general machinery as mere cogs to the wheels' (Melville 1997: 88). Not only are they objectified, their maidenhood is violated by the appropriation of their reproductive function to the mechanical process: 'I seemed to see, glued to the pallid incipience of the pulp, the yet more pallid faces of all the pallid girls I had eyed that heavy day' (Melville 1997: 95). Their exploitation is indirectly linked to the bachelor lawyers via the foolscap that is their main product, since the paper may in all probability be used within the legal offices of London's Temple Bar. In this way, the hedonistic lifestyles of the lawyers are implicated in an economic structure that necessitates the impoverishment of workers on another continent. The unseen unity of the two tales comments upon an oblique economic situation in which all its participants are implicated: as a writer, the narrator is also dependent upon the women's mistreatment. The exercise of writing is itself prone to the unseen network of economic processes.

The satires of Mark Twain also run counter to the doctrine of the well-made story. As Twain observes in his essay 'How to Tell a Story' (1895), 'The humorous story depends for its effect upon the *manner* of the telling . . . [It] may be spun out to great length, and may wander around as much as it pleases' (Twain 1993: 195). Twain links his own writing to two traditions, the yarn and the picaresque, both of which are oral in origin. As Twain demonstrates in the same essay, the pause is crucial to the comic effect of the story, and in that sense, all of his tales can be regarded as performances rather than as written texts. Nevertheless, as Twain's attention to the pause suggests, his tales are narrated with an eye for detail and precision: two key similarities with Poe's fiction. Within these strictures, however, tales such as 'A Visit to Niagara' (1869), 'The Facts Concerning the Recent Carnival of Crime in Connecticut' (1876) and 'The Stolen White Elephant' (1882) progress toward a farcical conclusion in which logic and proportion are thrown into confusion, and preconceptions of moral and social behaviour are cast into doubt. While Twain's absurd and ironic sense of humour prefigures twentieth-century humorists such as S. J. Perelman and Damon Runyan, the moral ambiguity of his tales looks forward to modernist innovators such as Ernest Hemingway and, even, Donald Barthelme. Beyond this large group of stories, though, Twain offers in 'A True Story Repeated Word for Word as I Heard It' (1874) a sincere monologue in the voice of an ex-slave. The title sounds the only ironic note. Was Twain told the story or did he overhear it, and if so, is the story accurately reported? Nevertheless, Twain's ear for regional dialect and cultural idiom gives the monologue its ring of authenticity.

A similar enterprise underlines Thomas Hardy's collection *Wessex Tales* (1888). In the tradition of folktale collectors, Hardy assembled family stories, eyewitness accounts and local legends to construct a picture of Dorset from the early part of the nineteenth century. Despite Lionel Stevenson's claim that Hardy 'achieved a more mature artistry than any of his Victorian predecessors' (Stevenson 1972: 268), these early stories have a more rough texture than his final collection, *Life's Little Ironies* (1894). Instead of small but powerful ironic effects, the *Wessex Tales* are characterised by sharp plot-twists and even sharper turns of fate, such as the apocalyptic events of 'The Withered Arm'. While this relative lack of sophistication may be partially explained by the Victorian taste for melodrama, it may also be understood by the tales' origins within oral narrative. Their escalating drama arises from the unpredictable shifts within folk narration and the effect of being retold, so that in some of the cases they have become mythology. Hardy the writer is equivalent to the narrator of 'The Melancholy Hussar' lingering for 'characteristic tales, dating from that picturesque time . . . in more or less fragmentary form to be caught by the attentive ear' (Hardy 1991: 39). The satisfaction of these tales lies in their lack of definition as well-made stories and in their capturing of an oral culture before that society disappears.

The well-made story, then, was not a part of the nineteenth century and while its streamlined form offered artistic and commercial advantages, its rationalisation of folk narrative and inhibition towards experimentation also presented disadvantages. It is not a surprise that the well-made story was criticised by academic figures such as H. S. Canby, but this complaint focused upon one writer in particular: O. Henry. Between 1904 and 1910, O. Henry published over two-hundred and fifty short stories, making him the most successful American storywriter of his day. His work was the epitome of the well-made story, in particular its use of the twist-ending, a form that had previously been associated with Maupassant's unrepresentative tale 'The Necklace' (1884). The twist, though, became an expected part of O. Henry's formula. Writing in 1923, the critic N. Bryllion Fagin attacked O. Henry's stories as 'sketchy, reportorial, superficial', arguing that the popularity of his fiction had arrested development of the American short story (in Current-García and Patrick 1974: 67). By contrast, the Russian formalist critic Boris Éjxenbaum contended that O. Henry had deliberately exposed the working mechanism of his narratives, so that 'the principle of approximation to the anecdote' is taken 'to the limit' (in May 1994: 87). This intellectualisation of O. Henry's method misrepresents the commercial incentive of his writing as much as Fagin overstates the haste in which the stories were written.

Instead, the success of O. Henry's fiction was symptomatic of the growth of middlebrow culture within Western societies since the end of the nineteenth century. 'Middlebrow' is a difficult term to describe – it was coined in 1906 – but a summary of O. Henry's most celebrated story, 'The Gift of the Magi' (1905), will help to illustrate. The story is set at Christmastime and centres upon a young, poor married couple. Della wants to buy Jim a present worthy of him so she sells her most valued possession: her hair. With the money, Della buys a platinum fob chain for Jim's gold watch, a family heirloom. That evening, Della confesses what she has done but is made to feel even guiltier when Jim presents her with a beautiful set of combs. Then Della gives Jim his present, only to discover that Jim has had to sell his watch to buy her gift. A short coda compares Della and Jim to the Magi for they had true wisdom, since they had discovered that their love resided not in possessions but for each other. As this description suggests, the story is deeply sentimental, and despite being set in New York, it has a Dickensian feel. Nonetheless, it does not have the sketchiness that Fagin asserts. Instead, there is a completeness about the story: a neatness in its tone and an efficiency in its construction. 'The Gift of the Magi' lacks the oddity of Melville's short fiction, the disproportion of Twain's tall tales or the roughness of Hardy's *Wessex Tales*, but instead it has smoothness and polish. It would not be unfair to say that O. Henry's fiction prefigures the neatly constructed and well-turned stories that are a feature of contemporary women's magazines. O. Henry's well-made stories are light without being banal, crafted without being difficult, accessible without being ineloquent. In short, they are middlebrow.

The real test of O. Henry's abilities was how to vary his stories within their narrow parameters. 'The Memento' (1908), for example, has a straightforward twist. Rosalie Ray had been a high-wire act on Broadway. At the end of each performance she would send a silk garter to the audience below. Rosalie retires and marries a reverend,

Arthur, whom she later discovers has had a previous affection for an 'ideal woman' who 'was far above' him (Henry 1995: 636). Arthur, though, has kept a memento and when Rosalie discovers it she finds, somewhat unsurprisingly, that it is one of the garters from her act. In contrast, 'Jeff Peters as a Personal Magnet' (1908) potentially tricks the reader by using a double-twist, in which Peters, the fake medicine man, is himself fooled and arrested, only for the arresting detective to be revealed as Peters' accomplice. The timing and the disguising of the twist demand genuine skill on O. Henry's part in order to be successful, especially at the rate at which he was producing his stories.

Despite the criticisms voiced of O. Henry in the period after his fame, the well-made story has remained part of the bedrock of the American short story. During the twentieth century it became most associated with *The New Yorker* (founded 1925), one of the bastions of short fiction in the United States. In the immediate postwar period the magazine promoted the work of writers such as John Cheever, J. D. Salinger and John Updike. During the 1950s and early 1960s they came to epitomise what has often been called 'the *New Yorker* story' or 'story of manners' pioneered in the 1930s by writers such as John O'Hara, whose own industriousness matched that of O. Henry. Highly crafted and accessibly told, the attention to living detail is given shape by the well-made structure, in particular the use of a leitmotif, a recurring image or symbol to express the characters' inner feelings. In Cheever's 'The Swimmer' (1964), the leitmotif is that of the various swimming pools into which the aging protagonist dives on his way home from a party. The swimming pool becomes a symbol for the illusion of lost youth and a dramatic image for the character's refusal to accept mortality even at the expense of his family. In Updike's 'Flight' (1962), the theme of escape acts as the story's leitmotif, drawing the narrative into a pattern that is harmonious and unified. For Allen Dow's mother, flight from poverty is symbolised by education. Through Allen's educational achievements, she will in effect escape the destiny of her own small-town existence. For Allen, though, flight means escaping his mother's hold over him by dating the reviled Molly Bingaman. Inevitably, their competing desires draw them into conflict, so that the theme of flight is finally cast as the irreparable tension between mother and son, between the generations' need to please both themselves and each other: 'In a husky voice that seemed to come across a great distance my mother said, with typical melodrama, "Good-bye, Allen'" (Updike 1987: 63). For a chronicler of contemporary American life, such as Updike, the well-made story not only acts as a model of technical efficiency but also as a means of communicating universal themes of generational and emotional change. Within the form's stylistic conservatism, this is no small achievement.

Further Reading

On the American periodical market and the use of creative writing handbooks, see Andrew Levy (1993). Recent studies of Poe's relationship to the mass market include Jonathan Elmer (1995) and Kevin J. Hayes (2000). A more theoretical response to Poe, as well as Melville, is offered by Douglas Tallack (1993). On Twain and O. Henry, see respectively Henry B. Wonham (1993) and Eugene Current-García (1967). Maupassant's influence on O. Henry and the American short story has been discussed by Richard Fusco (1994). On the history of *The New Yorker*, see Ben Yagoda (2000). For a general account of British well-made stories, see Walter Allen (1981). On the underlying theme of cultural taste, see Pierre Bourdieu (1984).

5

Economies of Scale:
The Short Story in England

J. G. Ballard has observed that 'short stories are the loose change in the treasury of fiction' (Ballard 2001: iv). The image of the short story as culturally marginal relates to its economic position. Though the American short story has survived within the periodical market since the early nineteenth century, its fortunes have fluctuated according to that market's strength. Today, the American short story depends upon a few established titles, such as *The Atlantic Monthly*, *Esquire*, *Harper's*, *The Kenyon Review* and *The New Yorker*, and a host of 'little magazines' associated with university departments. Since 1998, this effective cartel has been countered by Dave Eggers' journal, *McSweeney's*, which was launched as a home for both himself and his contemporaries. In Europe, the traditions of the essay, the speculative piece known as the *feuilleton*, and the independently produced pamphlet have encouraged a deep respect for short fiction, yet this reverence remains contingent upon market economics. Although magazine circulation has ensured an enduring role for the short story in Europe and the United States, it has also fostered the idea that the form is ephemeral. Magazine stories do not have the same physical or cultural status as fiction published in book-form. Even in the USA, where the short story is regarded as a national artwork, the question 'Where is the Great American Novel?' continues to be posed.

The state of short story publication in England offers an acute illustration of the form's cultural and economic marginality. Short story critics have often viewed English literature as dominated by the novel, and consequently have tended to diminish the achievements of English short storywriters. Taking the economic history of the English short story as a case study, though, highlights similar practices whereby the short story has, to a lesser extent, been marginalised in America and Europe. Furthermore, an account of the origins of the

English short story, its florescence at the end of the nineteenth century and its current struggle to survive puts into perspective the successes of English short storywriters in the face of adversity.

The Short Story in Eighteenth- and Nineteenth-Century England

The roots of short story publishing in England lie with satirical magazines such as *The Spectator*, founded in 1711 by Joseph Addison and Richard Steele. Unlike Steele's previous venture, *The Tatler* (1709), *The Spectator* consisted primarily of individual essays, each of which reflected and commented upon the changing political and social mores of the day with the aim of improving the conduct of its middle-ranking readership. Instead of adopting an opinionated or didactic tone, *The Spectator* used satire and irony to expose public vice and personal folly, often in the form of sketches with fictional characters. While *The Spectator* did not publish short stories as such, the self-sufficiency of the essay form, the contemporary content and ambiguous tone, and the use of allegory are elements that prefigure the short story. Allegorical tales appear in the midst of many eighteenth-century novels and periodicals, while the use of the essay as satire blurred the boundaries between fiction and non-fiction, most notoriously in Jonathan Swift's 'A Modest Proposal' (1729). Similar instances occur in Charles Dickens' *Sketches by Boz* (1836), most notably in 'A Visit to Newgate', which borders upon fact and fiction, and in Katherine Mansfield's 'The Journey to Bruges', a fictional sketch but published as a travel essay by *The New Age* in 1911.

As an offshoot of the essay, both Addison and Steele began to write oriental tales inspired by the recent translation of *The Thousand and One Nights*. During the course of the eighteenth century, many other writers wrote oriental tales, including, most notably, William Beckford and Samuel Johnson. Although the oriental tale rehearsed many of the elements of the *Nights*, including genies, princesses, sultans, magical objects and enchanted landscapes, it functioned as both moral allegory and exotic entertainment. In this respect, the oriental fable paralleled the social uses of the fairy tale while, at the same time, diverging from the trend towards realism in the English novel. Instead, oriental tales permitted the exploration 'of alternative possibilities, of fearless sexuality, and of a possibility of expression beyond the limitations of ordinary, day-to-day life' (Mack 1992: xvii). The oriental tale not only paved the way for the Gothic novel, for example Beckford's *Vathek* (1786), but also the use of the short story as a means of evading the constraints of literary realism and its basis in the agreed social norms of everyday society. It is no coincidence that later Gothic novels, such as Mary Shelley's *Frankenstein* (1818), Charles Maturin's *Melmoth the Wanderer* (1820) and Emily Brontë's *Wuthering Heights* (1847), as well as Victorian ghost writers like Elizabeth Gaskell and Sheridan Le Fanu, draw heavily upon the oral and folktale traditions.

Yet, as Wendell Harris has argued, the growth of the English short story was impeded by the pre-eminence of the realist novel, in particular its capacity to show the inter-relatedness between events, people, regions, classes and economics (Harris 1979: 16–21). Novels such as Charles Dickens' *Bleak House* (1853) and George Eliot's *Middlemarch* (1871) reproduced the new historical awareness of writers such as Thomas Carlyle and Thomas Macaulay, whose progressive view of social development was based upon the analysis of cause and effect. Since the short story was unable to sustain a similar panoramic view, it appeared to be a lesser form than the novel, both artistically and morally, and discouraged English writers from its use (except in the form of the ghost story: see Chapter 15). In France, by contrast, the distinction between *conte* and *nouvelle* was not as polarised.

Underpinning this aesthetic prejudice were legal, economic and technological factors. For the first half of the nineteenth century, the growth of the periodical market was constrained by the so-called 'taxes on knowledge' that were meant to curb the political influence of the press. Between 1853 and 1861, though, advertising duties, Stamp Duty and Paper Duty were repealed, with the result that many new newspapers and magazines were established, particularly in the provinces, while circulations increased. With new outlets to write for, writers were encouraged in 1842 by the extension of copyright law, so that an author's work was protected for forty-two years or seven years after his/her death. This amendment was further improved in 1891 with the establishment of an international copyright law, so that a British author's work could not be pirated in the United States, while American writers were protected for the first time. The profession of authorship increasingly looked like a viable career for many new writers from different social backgrounds.

There remained, though, a sharp divide between serious literature (for the upper and middle classes) and popular literature (for the working classes). With the possible exception of ventures such as Dickens' *Household Words* (1850–9), there was no English equivalent to American middle-range titles such as *Harper's Monthly*. Serious literature remained constrained until the 1890s by the dominance of the three-volume novel, the practice of serialisation and the moral censorship of the circulating libraries. The model for the 'three-decker' novel had been established with the phenomenal success of Sir Walter Scott's *Waverley* (1814) and had been maintained at an artificially inflated price by circulating libraries such as Mudie's and W. H. Smith. Since for many readers novels were expensive to buy, circulating libraries made fiction available through the use of an annual subscription fee. Consequently, they also wielded great influence over what their subscribers got to read. By the 1880s, writers such as Thomas Hardy and George Moore, whose work was morally ambiguous and sexually explicit, were in open conflict with the circulating libraries.

Journals, too, exerted considerable control as long as circulation rather than advertising remained the principal source of revenue. In the early part of the nineteenth century, periodicals such as *Blackwood's* (founded 1817) continued the eighteenth-century practice of disguising short fiction in the form of essays or sketches. Mid-Victorian journals tended to tolerate the inclusion of serialised novels until the launch of magazines either owned by publishing houses, such as *Macmillan's* (1858), or edited by novelists, such as Mary Braddon's *The Belgravia* (1866). The unfolding of events over a lengthy serialisation not only dramatised the historical dynamic of cause and effect, but to sustain interest it also fostered characteristic elements of Victorian fiction such as authorial omniscience, linear narrative, plot, realistic detail and character types. These tropes arguably ran counter to the short story form. Serialisation also allowed writers to edit their work as it appeared or for editors to impose cuts. By this method, serialisation enabled a moral code to be enforced. In contrast, when in 1891 the new art journal, *Black and White*, declared that it would only feature short stories, its decision was regarded as a novelty.

At the other end of the spectrum lay the world of 'penny dreadfuls', a pejorative term used by middle-class commentators to encapsulate cheap weekly magazines, such as *The London Journal* (1845–1912), melodramatic novels sold in weekly or monthly parts during the early Victorian period, serials in periodicals sold to a juvenile market from the 1860s onwards, and collected volumes of those serials. As with all such indiscriminate terms, it was used to demonise the literature and to create a sense of moral panic within middle-class society. Yet, 'the subtext of "dreadfuls" . . . appears primarily conservative, steadfastly maintaining orthodox beliefs through fidelity to the sentimental language of popular discourse' (Springhall 1998: 70). Instead, with little financial incentive for writers to experiment with form and content when they could be paid by the word for drawn-out serialisations, popular literature also remained resistant to the development of the short story.

After the 1870s, though, a combination of factors changed the literary culture. The expanding periodical market was aided by technological improvements. By mid-century, the introduction of rotary presses had enabled more efficient typesetting, while the use of machine-made paper led to a seven-fold increase in production between 1800 and 1860. The look of newspapers was enhanced by good-quality illustrations, and by 1882, the reproduction of photographs. In the last two decades of the nineteenth century forty-eight new journals appeared, and by 1910 there were 155 quarterlies in London and 797 monthlies (Richardson 2005: xlv). Each of these outlets demanded fresh material, while the diversification of their readership resulted in a demand for greater candour, for fictions that represented the lives and concerns of their readers. Not only did the moral reticence of the circulating libraries begin to look antiquated, they also encountered increased competition from the growth of public libraries, which did not demand subscription fees, and a price-cutting war between publishers that reduced the price of single-volume reprints. During the 1880s, popular writers such as H. Rider Haggard began to write directly for the single-volume market, while entrepreneurial publishers such as John Lane refused to support outmoded business practices. Faced with high storage costs and budget restraints, the circulating libraries could no longer finance the three-volume novel which effectively collapsed after 1894.

The 1890s saw a profusion of popular literary genres, the emergence of highly professional writers (the equivalents to O. Henry in America) and the proliferation of the short story. As H. G. Wells commented, 'short stories broke out everywhere' (Wells 1914: v). Wells, like Arthur Conan Doyle and Rudyard Kipling, benefited from appearing in *The Strand Magazine* (founded 1891). *The Strand* quickly became the archetypal model for the middlebrow English journal with its mix of romantic short fictions, human-interest stories, celebrity interviews and attractive presentation. The success of *The Strand* allowed its editor, George Newnes, to reward his contributors handsomely and to establish a stable of writers. Since short stories were in demand, writers were especially well-paid. Joseph Conrad, for example, was paid £40 for 'Karain: A Memory' (1897) by *Blackwood's*, a huge sum considering that the average yearly earnings for an adult male was £56 (Conrad 1997: viii). Commercial success brought with it, though, a new degree of self-consciousness. Whereas mid-Victorian writers, such as Dickens and Anthony Trollope, had thought little about the aesthetics of short fiction, late Victorians, such as Hardy and Robert Louis Stevenson, gave careful attention to the making of the short story. In the cases of Conrad and Henry James, this attentiveness was derived from French and Russian influences.

Despite the extraordinarily high earnings that could be achieved, the boom in short story publication masks some important facts. First, because the short story was tied to the periodical market, its fortunes could diminish as the market contracted; a point that underlies Wells' preface to *The Country of the Blind* (1914). Second, the vast sums accorded to short stories were based upon magazine sales. Single author collections were another matter, as Stevenson makes clear:

> They say republished stories do not sell. Well, that is why I am in a hurry to get this out. The public must be educated to buy mine or I shall never make a cent. (quoted Keating 1989: 463)

Despite his association with popular romantic fiction, Stevenson's attitude towards his audience marks a growing divide between the literary writer and the mass-reading public. For writers such as Conrad, short stories were a way of keeping their careers afloat; Conrad's debts were only cleared with the unexpected success of his novel, *Chance*

(1913). At the lower end of the market, for writers employed on cheap magazines, the production of short stories could be more like working on a treadmill.

The English Short Story Today

Despite the anecdotal evidence of studies such as Q. D. Leavis' *Fiction and the Reading Public* (1932), no statistical analysis of the British short story was carried out until 2002, when the market research groups Book Marketing Limited and Jenny Brown Associates were commissioned by Arts Council England and the Scottish Arts Council. Their findings underpinned the Save Our Short Story campaign, which had been launched in Newcastle upon Tyne by writers, editors, publishers and academics.

In the first phase of the research, it was discovered that, in 2002, 53.5 per cent of anthologies and short story collections were published by independent publishers compared to 39.5 per cent from mainstream publishers. Furthermore, this was a steadily growing trend over the previous three years. While the number of anthologies had increased, single author collections published by mainstream publishers had declined from 215 in 2000 to 135 in 2002. By contrast, the number of collections from independent publishers had risen from 203 in 2000 to 287 in 2002. The implications were that writers were likely to receive smaller advances, less publicity and less high street distribution. The most commonly cited reasons for buying short fiction – that it was seen in the bookstore or that its price was discounted – meant that if the collections weren't visible, their sales were low. Yet, despite over half of all short story books being published by independents, nearly all of the hundred best-selling titles were from mainstream publishers. Most were also written by novelists, including the top-selling titles, *The Veteran* by Frederick Forsyth (116,310 copies) and Catherine Cookson's *The Simple Soul and Other Stories* (48,555 copies). These books were also the most frequently borrowed titles from public libraries. Other authors in the top ten included Jeffrey Archer, Stephen King and J. R. R. Tolkien, as well as the cult celebrity, Howard Marks. The peak periods for buying short stories were in the lead-up to Christmas and during the summer holidays. In line with general adult fiction, 57 per cent of purchases were by consumers aged over 45 and 60 per cent of purchases were by women. Short story collections tended to be bought on impulse, often as a gift or as summertime reading, where the consumer recognised the author's name.

Of two-hundred adults interviewed, slightly over half of all light and medium readers said that they occasionally read short story books. Two-thirds of those who did not said that this was due more to accident than design, but half of this number acknowledged that they read short stories in magazines: 82 per cent of women compared to 35 per cent of men. They also admitted, though, that they tended to read the stories because they were there, were happier to read one story rather than several, and that magazine stories tended to be easier and aimed at the core audience. When prompted, one in four respondents thought that short stories were harder to read than longer stories, while fewer than one in ten thought they were easier. Lastly, while more than half of light and medium readers said that lack of time prevented them from reading more, only 15 per cent thought that short stories would be a possible solution. In other words, the brevity of short stories was not in itself a selling point.

The second phase of research, carried out between July and November 2003, explored the commissioning, publishing and selling of short stories. Agents and publishers both agreed that artistic quality was the most significant factor in accepting new fiction, but mainstream publishers admitted that it was difficult to launch a debut writer with a short story collection. Consequently, they were more likely to buy a collection on the understanding that there would be a novel, while it was more likely for an independent press to accept a short story collection from a first-time writer. Smaller publishers tended to experience greater comparative success with a collection, but like mainstream presses, the advances paid to writers were much lower than for novels. Agents and publishers tended to discourage writers from writing short stories, since the success of a collection depended upon the reputation of the writer, but that a themed collection was easier to sell than one that was not interlinked. Increasingly, publishers tended to market a themed collection as if it were a novel, for example Bloomsbury's decision in 2006 to promote George Saunders' novella, *The Brief and Frightening Reign of Phil*, as a novel despite more than half of the book's contents being devoted to a short story collection, *In Persuasion Nation*.

The lack of faith displayed in the idea of a short story collection was felt also by booksellers, who considered that the marketing was often poor. Promotions, such as three books for the price of two, could result in improved sales with readers taking a chance on the third. Since most collections are bought on impulse, shelving was a decisive factor, with collections included alongside other sale items and general fiction stock rather than kept separate. The packaging of collections and anthologies was another factor, including a strong design, a definite identity and the inclusion of well-known writers. Marketing short stories on their substance rather than their brevity was considered to be the better strategy.

Both pieces of research concluded that, contrary to the belief of publishers and academics, readers were generally well-disposed to the short story, and that selling the form to them as a shorter or lighter read was a negative tactic. What was absent, and which arguably has been absent since the late nineteenth century, was a culture of reading and appreciating short stories. Among the conclusions that were drawn was the need to develop a reading culture by working with schools, libraries, readers' groups and booksellers. To do this required the establishment of an organisation equivalent to the Poetry Society and the formation of an infrastructure for short story writing, for instance, by the English and Scottish art councils prioritising their support to independent presses, magazines and literary festivals with a commitment to the short story. (In 2004, the short story festival, Small Wonder, was launched in East Sussex.)

The unanimous recommendation, though, was the foundation of a literary prize devoted to the short story with an accompanying anthology marking the best in contemporary short fiction. American models, such as the O. Henry Memorial Prize and the *Best American Short Stories* series, were used in both cases. In autumn 2005, the National Short Story Prize was co-launched by BBC Radio and the magazine *Prospect*, and awarded in June 2006. The winning entry was James Lasdun's 'An Anxious Man'. Ironically, Lasdun has lived for several years in upstate New York. His story features an all-American cast and an American setting; it is beautifully well-crafted with an elegant turn of irony worthy of *The New Yorker* or, indeed, *The Paris Review* where it was first published. Very little about the story singles it out as distinctly British, let alone English. Despite the attention raised by the Save Our Short Story campaign, and the excellent work of independent presses such as Comma and Maia, it seems that even at the start of a new century the English short story is in the shadow of its American cousin.

Further Reading

On eighteenth-century English short fiction, see Benjamin Boyce (1968). For further discussion of the oriental tale, see Ros Ballaster (2005). Studies of the Victorian short story include Dean Baldwin (1993), Wendell V. Harris (1979) and Harold Orel (1986). On the changes in late-Victorian publishing, see Peter Keating (1989). The merits of serialisation are discussed by Linda K. Hughes and Michael Lund (1991). On the contemporary short story, see Debbie Taylor (2003) and the full report, 'The Short Story in the UK', by Jenny Brown Associates and Book Marketing Limited (2004).

6

Brought to Book:
The Anthology and Its Uses

One of the recurring impressions from the preceding chapter was that while readers were content to read individual short stories, they were less inclined to read several. Single-author collections tend to sell or to be borrowed from public libraries if the writer's name is already familiar, usually if s/he is a popular novelist. This gap has been partially filled by the use of anthologies, which present in book-form the work of various writers, conferring upon them the visual and cultural presence that the ephemeral form of a magazine or newspaper lacks. Anthologies are, therefore, one of the gateways that readers have into the history and sub-genres of the short story. Yet, the role of the anthology is fraught with problems. Edited collections presuppose issues surrounding the selection of writers and texts, the extent to which anthologies set the agenda for the making of literary canons, and the degree to which anthologies publicise the work of individual writers, or groups of writers, within the marketplace. Then, there is also an aesthetic concern: the extent to which reading several short stories together violates Poe's contention that a short story is to be read as a single and self-sufficient unit. (The degree to which a themed collection extends formal unity across the whole work, such as a cycle or sequence, is the subject of a later chapter.) This chapter explores the various uses made of the anthology – artistic, entertaining, instructive – before concluding with a trio of case studies: *Mirrorshades* (1986) edited by Bruce Sterling, *Disco Biscuits* (1997) edited by Sarah Champion, and *All Hail the New Puritans* (2000) edited by Nicholas Blincoe and Matt Thorne.

Prehistory of the Anthology

The modern anthology has its roots in the annual gift-books which were published during the nineteenth century. Before then, shorter

fiction occasionally appeared in random publications, such as miscel-
lanies and chapbooks, but these titles were not devoted exclusively to
fiction and made no stipulations upon the length of the texts. From the
second quarter of the nineteenth century, elegant publications such as
The Keepsake (1828–57) in Britain and *Godey's Lady's Book* (1830–98)
in the United States published original fiction on the basis that it
was no more than ten-thousand words. The success of the annuals
depended upon their 'appearance, an impressive list of contributors,
a variety (or at least multiplicity) of offerings, and the eschewal of anything which anybody might find offensive' (Harris 1979: 24). The gift-
books were, consequently, an important outlet for the development
of the short story, but while they featured writers such as Harrison
Ainsworth, Mary Russell Mitford and Walter Scott (in Britain) and
Nathaniel Hawthorne, Edgar Allan Poe and Harriet Beecher Stowe (in
the USA), much of what they published were sentimental tales of love
and heroism. Despite the restriction upon length, the gift-books did
little to enhance the aesthetics of short fiction. Many of the contributions tended to be sketches or remnants from longer works.

What the gift-books did introduce, however, was the idea of an
edited anthology, in which tales were included according to criteria
other than a miscellaneous arrangement. While they were morally and
artistically conservative, the gift-books lent their fictions a recognisable
identity and a niche within the marketplace. Moreover, the influence
of annuals in America can be seen in the cultural tastes of periodicals,
such as *Harper's*, which began publishing in the second half of the
century. The subsequent boom in short story publication further
encouraged the use of anthologies as compendiums of recently published fiction. Anthologies became a means of highlighting the best in
short fiction, of marking the current state of the art in the fast-moving
traffic of magazine publication, and of informing the reader's own
appreciation. Whereas stories published in newspapers and periodicals were disposable, anthologies leant them a degree of permanence.
Today, this illusion (or 'aura' as it might be termed) is defined by the
type of anthology in which the stories appear: the publisher and the
choice of editor, the selection of material, the intended uses and readership. At the same time, anthologies that publish new writing do so
with clear commercial and aesthetic aims; to play upon current trends
in publishing or to reinvigorate the tradition of the short story.

The Anthology as Popular Entertainment

Just as the vast majority of short stories are written for the women's magazine market, so the majority of anthologies are published for the purpose of entertainment. Appealing to the target audience is, therefore, a crucial factor for the anthology's commercial success, although this is not a guarantee of the anthology's artistic quality. Erotic fiction, for instance, far outsells literary anthologies. Following the recent successes of Philip Pullman, J. K. Rowling and the film adaptations of J. R. R. Tolkien, fantasy has also proved a popular genre, with Bloomsbury publishing their annual series of *Magic* anthologies. These collections have an additional 'feel-good' factor since part of their profits goes to charity. A similar volume, *Girls' Night In* (2000), not only traded upon the popularity of so-called 'chick-lit', following the success of Helen Fielding's character, Bridget Jones, but also gave its profits to the international charity, War Child. *Speaking with the Angel* (2000) had similar motivations but its success was also due to the status of its editor, the popular novelist, Nick Hornby. The involvement of a celebrity – not necessarily a writer – can also be a hook with which to sell the anthology, but in these cases both the quality and the overall identity of the anthology can be disappointing and shapeless. Anthologies can be sold to particular audiences who might not usually be heavy readers, for example sports fans, or to consumers of particular genres, such as horror, science fiction and fantasy, who tend to be both voracious and knowledgeable readers.

The success, then, of a commercial anthology is not necessarily a straightforward process. Yet, this achievement occurs against the backdrop of a small literary market, especially in Britain where there is, as yet, no long-running annual literary anthology. *All Hail the New Puritans*, for example, sold twenty-thousand copies but only after an extensive media campaign, while many other 'literary collections barely pay their way' (Taylor 2003: 10). Due to the invisibility of literary anthologies, commercial collections not only dominate the marketplace but also make it potentially difficult for readers to access literary short fiction. Yet, literary anthologies have also used the marketing techniques associated with their popular counterparts. Dermot Bolger's *Finbar's Hotel* (1997), for instance, featured named writers such as Roddy Doyle and Colm Tóibín, but its central conceit of seven writers writing stories set within the same building looked too much like a publishing gimmick, while also playing up to the image of the Irishman (and woman) as a teller of tall tales. Nevertheless, it spawned a sequel, while the cultivation of a devoted fan base has also proved an important factor behind the anthologies distributed by the publishing imprint McSweeney's. In other words, literary and popular anthologies are not necessarily antithetical but occupy the same cultural space with both of them seeking to cultivate the tastes of their readers. Consequently, we need to look further at how the literary anthology has been used as an instrument of culture.

The Cultural Function of the Literary Anthology

Literary anthologies are inextricable from the traditions – hidden or otherwise – that they address. Their composition is necessarily linked to the so-called *canons* of English literature, meaning both the landmarks of prose fiction and the mental maps by which readers make sense of literary history. Although these critical issues go beyond the short story per se, the genre's history is inter-related with the traditions that underwrite modern fiction.

One very clear example of the way in which the literary anthology is concerned with the making of canons is the use of critical readers by students at college and university. Titles such as Ann Charters' *The Story and Its Writer* (1983) and Dean Baldwin's *The Riverside Anthology of Short Fiction* (1998) not only aim to guide students through the history of the short story but also literary criticism and the study of fiction. By being set on college and university syllabuses, anthologies with a pedagogic or instructional basis assume great importance in establishing the canon of short fiction. Furthermore, by reflecting developments in critical thought elsewhere in literature and the humanities, they contribute to the formation of canons across the whole discipline. While attempting to be inclusive and representative in both their selection and their approach, anthologies like these set the terms by which not only short fiction but also imaginative prose are taught and understood. Their tendency is to cultivate an ideal reader trained in specialised reading skills, which is in sharp contrast to the more typical reader of short stories: a light, usually female, reader of magazine fiction.

In the United States, though, the making of a literary culture that accommodates the short story has not only operated within the confines of academia. In 1915, Edward O'Brien founded the long-running series of anthologies, *Best American Short Stories*. O'Brien was the most trenchant critic of the commercial and sentimental short stories that followed in the wake of O. Henry. He regarded the short story as part of the national culture, and consequently demanded the promotion of higher literary standards. To this extent, O'Brien was reflecting the views of early modernists such as Sherwood Anderson, and in its publication of new, innovative writers such as Ernest Hemingway, the *Best American Short Stories* helped to further the claims of literary modernism in America. Following O'Brien's death in 1941, Martha Foley continued his critical legacy while also including provocative new figures such as Donald Barthelme and Leslie Marmon Silko. Since 1978, the series has been published annually with guest editors, usually leading short story writers such as Richard Ford, Lorrie Moore and Tobias Wolff. Although the guest editors have paid respect to the traditions of the series, and have sought to present a cross-section of the contemporary American short story, they have also displayed their own tastes, and in so doing, have widened the content of the series.

Despite its espousal of an objective literary standard, the *Best American Short Stories* has always mediated the likes and dislikes of its editors. Although academic and upmarket anthologies can shape the canon of what is read, they nevertheless describe subjective tastes and distinctions. The most revealing aspect of an anthology can be the light that the selection of stories sheds upon the editor. The female protagonists featured in Angela Carter's *Wayward Girls and Wicked Women* (1986) offer insight into her own fiction: 'They are prepared to plot and scheme; to snatch; to battle; to burrow away from within, in order to get their hands on that little bit extra' (Carter 1986: xii). The sentiments of her observation tell the reader more about Carter's worldview than the chosen stories, in which the women 'at least contrive to evade the victim's role by the judicious use of their wits' (Carter 1986: xi), while as in Carter's fiction, the selected writers invert the stereotypes used by men against women. Carter's selection reveals both her interest in the by-ways of literature – 'New Woman' writers such as George Egerton and Vernon Lee, avant-gardists such as Djuna Barnes and Leonora Carrington – and her political affiliations in the inclusion of oppressed writers, such as the South African author Bessie Head. Despite the personal idiosyncrasies of the selection, Carter's anthology exemplifies the feminist project of publishing houses, such as Virago, to reclaim the work of neglected women writers. At the same time, the choice of Carter as editor, a writer well-known for her controversial and unorthodox views, offers a hook for potential readers absent in a more academic re-visionary exercise, such as Bronte Adams' and Trudi Tate's *That Kind of Woman* (1991). Both texts, though, oppose the condescension of previous anthologists.

With the advent of historical movements such as modern feminism, Gay Liberation and post-colonialism, literary anthologies have served a dual function in recording the impact that these phenomena have had upon the literary canon and by furthering this effect. Anthologies such as *The Penguin Book of Lesbian Short Stories* (1993) recover the literary history of sexual minorities, while collections such as *The Picador Book of the New Gothic* (1991) document the extent to which critically neglected genres have been reclaimed by contemporary writers, thereby reshaping the canon in order to explore renewed concerns surrounding social and sexual identity. It is also noticeable in these examples how the publisher inserts its own name into the title to both legitimate the process of reclamation and to secure some kudos for itself. Mainstream presses have realised the added benefits of being associated with a pioneering work: the extent to which a literary anthology cannot only record a cultural moment but also contribute to its success. One such instance is the collection *African Short Stories*, edited by Chinua Achebe and Lyn Innes, which was published in 1985, just as postcolonial writing began to have a considerable impact upon university syllabuses. Arranged into four sections, offering stories from around the continent, *African Short Stories* established itself as one of the most important introductory texts to postcolonial fiction from Africa and exerted great influence upon how African writing was viewed and taught. As a sign of its influence, a companion volume, *The Heinemann Book of Contemporary African Short Stories*, was published in 1992. The series of anthologies published by Oxford University Press from the mid-1980s, which offered academic cred- ibility to popular genres such as Gothic and science fiction as well as surveys to national literatures, such as Australia and Ireland, served a similar purpose.

An area in which the anthology has had an especially formative role is feminist science fiction. Whereas general fiction is largely consumed by women, science fiction has traditionally been read by a young, male audience, while the overwhelming majority of the writers have been men. Despite the inclusion in mainstream literature of Hermione Lee's avowedly feminist anthology *The Secret Self* (1985), collections such as Patricia Craig's *The Oxford Book of Modern Women's Stories* (1994) and Susan Hill's *The Penguin Book of Contemporary Stories by Women* (1995) lack a feminist bias. Since they are general fiction anthologies, they do not need to take a political stance in order to attract a female audience. In the case of a sexually hidebound genre like science fiction, anthologies such as Pamela Sargent's *Women of Wonder* (1974) and *Despatches from the Frontiers of the Female Mind* (1985), edited by Jen Green and Sarah Lefanu, openly declare their political commitment by drawing inspiration from the Women's Movement and reacting against the male domination of the genre. Besides the inherent quality of the writing, these collections are exciting to read because of the cultural dynamic between academic thought, political activism and popular fiction. These texts blur the boundaries between commercial and literary anthologies in ways that are artistically and (potentially) socially transformative.

Mainstream publishers, though, have recognised the anthology's capacity for documenting and fashioning an artistic or cultural water-shed. In 2003, Hamish Hamilton (part of the Penguin Group) pub-lished *The Burned Children of America*, which had originally appeared in Italy in 2001, edited by Marco Cassini and Martina Testa. The anthology features many of the writers associated with Dave Eggers' quarterly *McSweeney's*, including Eggers himself, Arthur Bradford, Jonathan Safran Foer, A. M. Homes, Rick Moody and George Saunders. The title is derived from David Foster Wallace's featured story, 'Incarnations of Burned Children' (2000), but is applied to the collection to suggest that it is recording a new literary generation, one that is defined by being scarred. Cassini and Testa are evidently devo-tees of this fiction – the motivations, though, of the English publisher are less clear. Bound in a red, white and blue cover, the main title lettering fractured, and a burnt match in the lower right-hand corner, the collection melodramatically reasserts its claim to documenting the current literature and state of the nation. The title, though, has been amended: it is now *Zadie Smith introduces The Burned Children of America*. Although Cassini and Testa receive acknowledgement both in Smith's introduction and a publisher's note, it is now Smith, a young and currently fashionable British novelist, who is the reader's principal guide. Smith's name acts as the bait with which to attract the British audience, while her prominent inclusion establishes her as an authoritative figure. Smith regards the collection's underlying theme as sadness, and while she makes no direct reference, her comment that 'the frequency of mass-death apocalyptic fantasy in recent American short stories can't be an accident' locates this trauma within the events of 11 September 2001 (in Cassini and Testa 2003: xv). Except that most of the collected stories predate the attacks upon the World Trade Center and the Pentagon, in some cases by several years. Although the anthology offers an excellent selection of young American writers, many of them relatively unknown by a British readership, the packaging and Smith's introduction play upon recent political events in order to give the collection an unnecessary contemporary resonance. In effect, the publisher is using the literary anthology's ability to document a cultural moment in order to increase sales: a response that not only sits awkwardly with Smith's anti-corporate sentiments but also some of the featured writers, among them Eggers and Saunders.

Aesthetics and the Anthology: Three Case-Studies

The Burned Children of America claims to represent a new generation of writers. In this final section I shall look at three anthologies that make a similar claim. The earliest, *Mirrorshades*, is a compilation of science fiction known as 'cyberpunk'. By contrast, *Disco Biscuits* and *All Hail the New Puritans* feature newly written stories. The former celebrates the tenth anniversary of so-called 'rave' music since its inception in Britain in 1987; the latter is co-edited by one of *Disco Biscuits'* authors, Nicholas Blincoe, and commissioned work according to a set of pre-established rules. All three anthologies are bound in time by their preoccupation with technology and lifestyle, especially changing patterns of work and leisure. Despite their claims to innovation, particularly the mixing of high literary standards with contemporary pop culture, they embody many of the uses that have typified the anthology.

Mirrorshades (1986) was largely responsible for introducing the work of contemporary American science fiction writers to a British mainstream audience. In his editorial preface, Bruce Sterling struggles with the term 'cyberpunk', arguing that 'labels never quite fit the individual', but concludes that they are 'a valid source of insight – as well as great fun' (Sterling 1986: vii). Yet, while on the one hand Sterling romanticises the cyberpunk writer as an outlaw, 'crazed and possibly dangerous' (Sterling 1986: ix), on the other hand he is keen to place the writing within the history of the genre. Consequently, Sterling has a conservative regard for cyberpunk that leads to him valuing the use of labels despite his initial protest. Contrary to Sterling's depiction of the cyberpunk as a maverick figure, he knows that it makes greater commercial sense to market writers as a group rather than as loners. The collective identity gives the individuals a presence that they would otherwise lack, resulting in higher critical and commercial recognition. Although writers such as William Gibson and John Shirley were in close contact before the collection, the anthology has ensured that these authors have been read together. Of their number, only Gibson has transcended the confines of the group identity, and even then, the description of cyberpunk has remained tied to his fiction.

Mirrorshades encourages the writers to be viewed as a coterie and their work as a watershed moment within the history of science fiction. By anthologising previously published work, *Mirrorshades* documents what has already been achieved while at the same time seeking to push the artistic revolution forwards. The writers are not only regarded as special in themselves but as also reshaping the history of the genre, for example in synthesising the rival traditions of 'hard', technology-based science fiction and 'soft', socially concerned science fiction. Although Sterling delights in the image of the cyberpunk writer as outlaw, he (and, in Pat Cadigan's case, she) is portrayed as saving the genre from internal division.

This notion of reintegration is encapsulated in the vocabulary of 'hard-wiring' that cyberpunk draws from information technology. Although presented as a decisive moment within the genre, the fiction is also cast as a conjunction between literature and a scientific culture that is 'surging into culture at large' at the expense of 'traditional institutions' (Sterling 1986: x). Cyberpunk is, allegedly, the literary equivalent to the global pop culture that fuses the imagery of video and digital technology with an anarchic ethos that transgresses national borders. Just as the flow of capital is unstoppable so, too, is the flood of information. Sterling suggests that cyberpunk gives a literary form to this new situation. The recurring motifs of the writing are the use of computer-generated realities, lone hackers versus global corporations, mass advertising, inner-city deprivation, technologically modified bodies, paranoia and conspiracy theories. Yet, unlike feminist interventions such as Sargent's *Women of Wonder* that acknowledge the long and often neglected history of women's writing, Sterling's aim in linking literary innovation to cultural revolution is to reinforce the radicalism of the group identity. Put another way: *Women of Wonder* honours the history of lone female voices, united by their common subjection as women, while *Mirrorshades* disrupts and redefines literary history by forging a new collective identity for its writers. It is notable that, within this redefinition of the past, Sterling omits any mention of experimental women writers such as Joanna Russ. Furthermore, his decision to preface each story recalls the editorial practice of one of the most canonical figures of American science fiction, Isaac Asimov.

The technological *noir* of cyberpunk entered British culture just as the 'rave' scene began to emerge from its underground origins into the commercial mainstream. Rave music complemented the counter-cultural ethos of cyberpunk through its use of unofficial venues and informal methods of publicity, the anonymity of DJs and the technology of digital sampling, anti-materialist values, and the mind-altering effects of the drug Ecstasy. 'DJNA' by the science fiction writer Jeff Noon, published in Sarah Champion's *Disco Biscuits* (1997), exemplifies this cross-over by describing a future Manchester in which dancing is proscribed and DJs have been replaced by an automaton, Jesus Boom, playing approved sounds. The story extrapolates a future scenario from the Criminal Justice Act of 1994 in order to satirise the moral panic that underlined the legislation.

Champion's anthology commemorates ten years of dance music, in which the movement went 'from illegal raves and anarchic warehouse parties to corporate clubbing' (Champion 1997: xiii). The political regulation and subsequent commercialisation of the scene lends an elegiac quality to the collection. As Champion suggests, a true history of the music involves 'personal stories of messiness, absurdity and excess – best captured in fiction' (Champion 1997:

xvi). Champion also claims that this history, involving drugs, sex and criminals, is already the stuff of fiction, 'the elements of a bestselling story' (Champion 1997: xiv). She notes furthermore the use of public readings alongside DJ sets, for example by Irvine Welsh, whose work appears in the collection and is synonymous with the scene due to his cult novel *Trainspotting* (1993). Besides conventional book-store distribution, *Disco Biscuits* was also sold at raves. The publisher targeted young and light fiction readers with a volume that mirrored their lifestyles, and at the same time sought additional kudos by distributing the anthology in an unconventional style similar to rave culture. In effect, though, *Disco Biscuits* merely added to the already growing commodification of the scene that the writers tend to lament but to which they resign themselves. Despite Champion's equation of fiction and history, the writing is surprisingly unoriginal, and with the exception of Mike Benson's stream-of-consciousness text, 'Room Full of Angels', fails to capture the social experience. There are some interesting moments, for example in Steve Aylett's 'Repeater' when the sound of a police raid is sampled as it occurs, but these are rarely developed. In the case of *Disco Biscuits*, it is almost as if the idea of commemoration, allied to the publisher's intentions, had stifled the writers' imaginations.

Two of the writers, Nicholas Blincoe and Alex Garland, subsequently appeared in *All Hail the New Puritans* (2000), edited by Blincoe with Matt Thorne. Whereas *Disco Biscuits* observed a general theme, *All Hail the New Puritans* commissioned writing on the basis of ten rules, the inspiration for which appears to have been the Dogme95 manifesto associated with Danish film-makers such as Lars von Trier. The rules written by Blincoe and Thorne argued for narrative-based forms, a shunning of poetic devices, open-endedness, no rhetoric, linearity, pure grammar, realistic details, contemporary settings, ethical awareness and artistic integrity. The manifesto, then, overtly demonstrates how anthologies attempt to bind individual short stories to an overall purpose and identity. In their introduction, Blincoe and Thorne added their own comments to each rule and christened the writers 'New Puritans', a phrase taken from the alternative rock band The Fall. Although the writers had broadly agreed with the manifesto, they did not necessarily approve the additional comments or the label.

Despite the apparent novelty of the manifesto, prescriptive rules have often been used in literature, for example in the verse forms that govern poetry. More recently, the writers who formed the international grouping known as OuLiPo used rules in order to constrict their writing, forcing them to extend their imaginations, as in Georges Perec's achievement of completing his novel, *La disparition* (1969), without use of the letter 'e'. Consequently, there is nothing new in Blincoe and Thorne proposing a set of prescriptions, some of which may be generally agreed upon by most writers, while their insistence on simplification mirrors the trend in American short fiction towards minimalism, following the lead of writers such as Raymond Carver. Although suspicious of postmodern experimentation, Blincoe and Thorne are nonetheless informed by postmodernism, for instance Blincoe's satirical story on marketing, 'Short Guide to Game Theory'. Despite the prescriptive manifesto, the anthology has greater stylistic range than *Disco Biscuits*, because though the rules are ultimately arbitrary, there is no overwhelming theme or concept. Writers appeared to have followed some of the rules, while also circumventing others, for example Scarlett Thomas' use in 'Mind Control' of the Christian symbol of the fish despite the ban on poetic licence. On the other hand, writers who tended to follow the rules more closely may have finally found them too restrictive, for example Toby Litt's subsequent turn to a more subjective style in his novel *Ghost Story* (2005).

Despite the 'call to arms' advocated in the introduction (Blincoe and Thorne 2001: xvii), *All Hail the New Puritans* is no more consistent as an anthology than any other. Like other anthologies discussed in this chapter, it is an exercise in publicity and canon-formation. Without the collective identity, the lesser-known writers in the anthology may have struggled for recognition. In the longer term, the label may be more of a hindrance than a help. It also fails to define the commissioned stories, because some of them may have used some of the rules and not others. Anthologies lend readers a map of past and present short fiction, but these maps, while sometimes claiming to be comprehensive and path-finding, are inconclusive and incomplete. Although they offer readers a way into the history of the short story, anthologies disproportionately affect the way that history is received and understood. This effect has to be countered by exploring the often unorthodox routes through which short stories have been produced, distributed and consumed.

Further Reading

On the role of canons in literary criticism, see Patricia Waugh's essay in her reader *Literary Theory and Criticism* (2006). On the influence of Edward O'Brien, see Jacquelyn Spangler (2001). Upon cyberpunk and its problematic relationship to women's science fiction, see Jenny Wolmark (1993). For the Dogme95 manifesto, see Lars von Trier and Thomas Vinterberg, 'The Vow of Chastity' (1995).

7

Between the Lines: Dissidence and the Short Story

In 1935, the left-leaning writer and critic James T. Farrell reviewed recent changes in the American short story. Farrell argued that the reaction against the plot-driven stories of O. Henry had led to character-based writing that assessed 'the cost of American capitalist democracy in terms of human destinies and human suffering'. The greater social range of these stories drew their readers into 'the bottom of the so-called American melting pot' (Farrell 1948: 113). Yet, despite this new-found awareness, Farrell found the attempts at political criticism to be forced, 'glued on . . . to the ending as a slogan or revolutionary direction sign'. Alternatively, the content was often so generalised that the stories left no 'flashes of insight' but were 'exhausted as soon as they [were] read' (Farrell 1948: 114). Instead, by referring to writers such as Erskine Caldwell and Langston Hughes, Farrell argued that political radicals needed to use the tendencies of the short story toward implication and obliqueness on which to base their social criticisms.

Farrell's account is significant because it illustrates one of the perennial questions that surround the short story, the extent to which a self-reflexive narrative mode can successfully address wider social issues, and offers a way of surmounting this conundrum. Yet, Farrell's critique is also a product of its time (the middle years of the Great Depression) and of an ideological view of the author, one associated with American novelists such as John Dos Passos and Richard Wright, in which the writer declares a political stance to their work. Farrell would have far less to recommend about an experimental writer such as Samuel Beckett, whose fractured and disjointed texts question so many of the certainties surrounding human identity.

An alternative approach to thinking about the role of dissidence in literature is offered by the Marxist critic Terry Eagleton in his book *Criticism and Ideology* (1976). Eagleton regards the literary text as the result of cultural modes of production that emerge as part of the economic base, the 'unity of certain forces and social relations of material production' (Eagleton 1978: 45), which include relationships between personal, artistic and social ideology. The text is constituted within a complex interaction of economic and ideological pressures. Eagleton illustrates the matrix of influences through reference to the 'privileged status of the "three-decker" (three-volume) novel within the aesthetic ideology of Victorian England' (Eagleton 1978: 52). This status was achieved through the financial power of the circulating libraries such as Mudie's and W. H. Smith, which in turn shaped the structures of literary production (the economic existence of the writer) and consumption (the expectations and habits of the reader). Not only did the libraries exert a moral influence on what was written and read but they also reproduced the ideological values of Victorian society. Within this tension, writers such as the Brontës and Thomas Hardy were caught between fulfilling their own personal and artistic beliefs and the needs of the productive process.

Yet as Eagleton suggests, this power relationship is also subject to historical change. Although never pure or immune from the dominant modes of economic and cultural production, new and emergent literary modes of production offer possible points of resistance. The decision of mid-Victorian writers, such as Elizabeth Gaskell, to occasionally abandon the novel in favour of genres such as the ghost story implies their incapacity to express themselves within the more circumspect form of the novel. Merely electing to write in a less dominant form, such as the short story, sets writers against the norm, for instance the following comment by Ian Jack, then editor of *Granta*, on choosing the 'best young British novelists of 2003': 'we would also consider shorter fiction, the story and novella, as allowable evidence of a writer's intent in the novel's direction, despite the fact that two writers on previous lists – Helen Simpson and Adam Mars-Jones – had dented this faith by sticking firmly to the short-story form' (Jack 2003: 11). How did they dare to be so impudent?

In the late Victorian period, 'little magazines' enabled writers to circumvent the influence of the circulating libraries (only to fall foul, in the case of *The Savoy*, of the booksellers). Using Eagleton's model as a way of looking at the short story in terms of dissidence, this chapter will focus upon alternate methods of production and distribution, including little magazines and small presses, writers writing in code or through underground networks, and lastly, what theorists have termed a 'legitimation crisis' between mainstream and avant-garde culture.

Little Magazines and Small Presses

Despite notable precursors, such as the Pre-Raphaelite journal *The Germ* (1850), and in the United States the Transcendentalist journal *The Dial* (1840–4), little magazines did not flourish until the end of the Victorian era when 'the relentless fragmentation and categorisation of fiction' (Keating 1989: 340) encouraged the growth of specialised readerships and niche publications. As Chapter 5 described, British short storywriters benefited from the multiplication of newspapers and periodicals during the 1880s and 1890s (a parallel movement occurred also in the USA). Yet, while magazines such as *The Strand* appealed to a conventional middle-class audience, the splintering of the marketplace created opportunities for less orthodox titles.

Little magazines are characterised first by their fugitive quality, and second by their passionate (if irreverent) commitment to a way of conceptualising art and society. They are driven less by commercial desires (although commercial relations ultimately determine their continued existence) than by an overarching belief. Although a high-minded journal such as T. S. Eliot's *The Criterion* (1922–39) also fits this description, its aristocratic patronage and cultural ambitions run counter to the more enthusiastic and experimental little magazines, such as Wyndham Lewis' *Blast* (1914) or Margaret Anderson's *The Little Review* (1914–29). Little magazines were 'often an analogue or extension of the manifesto formula' by 'functioning as the logical obverse to the solemn, serious, debating Great Review' (Bradbury and McFarlane 1976: 203). They acted as sites of dissidence by championing ideas and writings that might not be published else-where, for example *The English Review* edited by Ford Madox Ford during 1908–9, *The Egoist*, relaunched in 1914, and the sole short story title, *Story* (1931–48), founded by Whit Burnett and Martha Foley.

The prototypical little magazine was *The Yellow Book* (1894–7), which was published by John Lane in order to capitalise upon the public controversy surrounding Decadent writers such as Oscar Wilde. Although *The Yellow Book* quickly became the most influential little magazine of its time, its notoriety was due less to its Decadent associations (Wilde never appeared, assistant editor Aubrey Beardsley was dismissed after one year) than to Lane's acumen for publicity. A handsome and expensive hardback, *The Yellow Book*'s most likely readership was 'a middle-class reader who is mildly daring' and ready to pay for 'a product that looks as if it is worth much more' (Bishop 1996: 291). Yet, while *The Yellow Book* may not have been what it claimed to be, it still published important work, especially short fiction. The lack of a coherent identity might even have been an advantage since the editor, Henry Harland, was able to persuade Henry James to contribute three stories, including his satires on the literary marketplace 'The Death of the Lion' (1894) and 'The Next Time' (1895). Harland was also able to include Decadents, such as Ernest Dowson, alongside arch-conservatives, such as John Buchan. Other regular contributors included Hubert Crackanthorpe, whose pessimistic tales captured much of the ennui associated with the Decadent movement, and feminist writers such as Victoria Cross, George Egerton and Vernon Lee. All of them benefited from the lack of a prescribed word length, which allowed James, on the one hand, to extend his writing, and Crackanthorpe and Egerton, on the other hand, to experiment with brevity and states of mind.

The fugitive appearance of the little magazine – its defence of innovation and its existence in spite of looming closure – also suggests a correlation with at least one version of the modern short story: the tendency towards impressionism that can be seen in Dowson's 'The Dying of Francis Donne' (*Savoy* 1896) or Egerton's 'A Lost Masterpiece' (*Yellow Book* 1894). Yet, not all stories published in little magazines tended in this direction: Rebecca West's 'Indissoluble Matrimony' (*Blast* 1914), for example, shares the editor's impatience with the impressionist ethos of Ford's *English Review*. In other words, a straight line cannot be drawn from the proto-impressionism of the 1890s to the development of the modernist short story. Instead, little magazines granted writers a degree of frankness not afforded elsewhere. For instance, Katherine Mansfield's 'Bains Turcs' (*The Blue Review* 1913) is more open about lesbian identity than her better known but symbolic tale 'Bliss' (1918).

In tandem with the little magazine was the number of small, privately owned presses during the early twentieth century. Small presses granted the authors greater artistic control over their work while also developing networks between writers, for instance the publication of Mansfield's 'Prelude' (1918) by Leonard and Virginia Woolf's Hogarth Press. Woolf also published herself, including 'Kew Gardens' (1919), while in 1920, Mansfield published her story 'Je ne parle pas français' through her husband's Heron Press. When the story was later reprinted in book-form, the publisher, Constable, censored the text. Whereas *The Yellow Book* had sought to appeal to as wide an audience as possible, many of the little magazines and small-press publications that appeared during the modernist period were designed for a coterie of readers. Although this route might characterise modernism as an exclusive affair, for the writers it was an *inclusive* strategy, since it guaranteed them the imaginative freedom with which to communicate themselves to an informed and responsive readership. For writers such as D. H. Lawrence and Virginia Woolf, intent upon revolutionising the traditional novel, the short story (aided and abetted by the little magazine and the small press) was an important medium in which to experiment.

Writing in Code

Although American critics, such as Martha Foley and Edward O'Brien, attacked what they saw as the marginalisation of the short story, its very lack of status has appealed to writers at odds with the dominant values of their society: women writers, colonial subjects, sexual minorities. For writers from the so-called developing nations of Latin America, such as Jorge Luis Borges and Gabriel García Marquez, the flights of fancy permissible within the short story have been a way of skirting the economic deprivation and political oppression of military regimes. The marginality of the short story has been an aid, not a hindrance, to artistic expression, as can be witnessed by the Czech writer Franz Kafka and the Russian writer Isaac Babel.

Little of Kafka's writing was published in his lifetime. Poems, short stories and other fragments appeared either in little magazines or slim volumes with small print runs. His work, though, was admired by friends and acquaintances. Kafka's self-estrangement arose as much from historical and cultural circumstances as psychological factors.

Linguistically, Kafka belongs to German literature insofar as he wrote in German and his early influences were German. Historically, Kafka wrote during the growth of European modernism when national borders were increasingly transgressed by cultural movements from other countries. Geographically, Kafka was born into central Europe and the multi-ethnic Habsburg Empire. Kafka's alienation embodies the experience of a Jew torn between assimilation and cultural separatism, compelled to choose the precarious position of aligning himself to a foreign language.

'A Report to an Academy' was published in *Der Jude* [*The Jew*] in 1917. The story is ostensibly a lecture given by an ape to a learned society describing its intellectual development. The ape recounts its capture and its struggle for freedom by learning the language of its captors. Its first act is to renounce all knowledge of its former life: 'I had to stop being an ape' (Kafka 2005: 253). Then, it begins to imitate the physical actions of the sailors, including a drunkard, whom the ape sees as a teacher: 'sometimes indeed he would hold his burning pipe against my fur . . . but then he would himself extinguish it with his own kind, enormous hand' (Kafka 2005: 257). The ape accepts these abuses as part of the learning process: 'one learns when one has to; one learns when one needs a way out; one learns at all costs.' As the ape's fame spreads, and it acquires greater skill, it employs its own language tutors, learning 'from them all at once by dint of leaping from one room to the other.' The ape, though, is modest about its achievements. It has reached 'the cultural level of an average European', enjoys a contented, middle-class lifestyle, and pleasures itself with 'a half-trained little chimpanzee' (Kafka 2005: 258–9). The estranging device of the ape, allied to the formal setting of the lecture, create an effective allegory with which to satirise the politics of cultural assimilation.

Kafka's near-contemporary, Isaac Babel, was discriminated not only by his Jewish identity but also by his regional birth in the coastal city of Odessa. As Babel writes, 'Turgenev poeticized the dewy morning, the calm night' while 'with Dostoyevsky you feel . . . the mysterious and heavy fog of Petersburg', but eventually Russian readers will 'be drawn to the south, to the sea, to the sun!' (Babel 2002: 77–9). Babel's greatest success was the war cycle *Red Cavalry* (1926), but stories such as 'First Love' and 'The Story of My Dovecote' (both 1925) already indicated a retreat from public affairs into the personal. His adherence to the aesthetics of storytelling, summarised in 'Guy de Maupassant' (1932) as 'No iron spike can pierce a human heart as icily as a period in the right place' (Babel 2002: 681), contrasted with the socialist realism approved by the Soviet regime. Babel's stylistic precision counterpoints the naturalism and moral ambiguity of his content: the lovers in 'Guy de Maupassant', for instance, consummate their adulterous affair as they translate Maupassant's story 'The Confession'. Such writing was officially regarded as decadent, while Babel was also accused of deliberately withholding his work from publication. Eventually, Babel was executed in January 1940. Despite rehabilitation in 1954, his fiction remained censored in the Soviet Union until 1990.

The persecution of writers such as Babel, Osip Mandelstam and Boris Pasternak led Soviet authors to pursue other means of publication, most notably the method known as *samizdat*, underground magazines and newssheets that could be cheaply reproduced and circulated among a close network of fellow readers. Samizdat was not only practised throughout the Soviet Empire but also during the apartheid regime in South Africa and the military dictatorships of Latin America, and continues to exist in the Middle East. The underground presses associated with the Anglo–American counter-culture of the late 1960s took samizdat as their model. The ephemeral yet self-contained short story was an ideal component within contemporary little magazines such as Emma Tennant's *Bananas* (founded 1975).

As part of its covert message, samizdat fiction not only drew upon fantastical elements in the work of experimentalists such as Kafka but also popular sub-genres such as science fiction. The potential dissidence of popular fiction is the subject of a later chapter, but it is relevant to mention here the case of Abram Tertz, the pseudonym of Andrei Sinyavsky, who was controversially tried and imprisoned by the Soviet authorities in 1966. Sinyavsky was indicted on the basis of three works, including his critical study of socialist realism and his science fiction novel *The Makepeace Experiment*. His short stories, including 'Pkhentz' (1963), were also cited during the trial. Sinyavsky criticised socialist realism because the writing lacked the scepticism of nineteenth-century Russian literature, and that without self-doubt the goal of a truly enlightened, classless society could not be achieved. Sinyavsky pinned his faith on 'a phantasmagoric art, with hypotheses instead of a Purpose . . . in which the grotesque will replace realistic descriptions of ordinary life' and 'teach us how to be truthful with the aid of the absurd and the fantastic' (Tertz 1960: 94–5). Sinyavsky's own fiction draws upon a tradition of Russian fantasy that includes the fairy tales of Alexander Afanas'ev, the short stories of Nikolai Gogol and the banned novels of Mikhail Bulgakov.

'Pkhentz' is narrated by a hunchback whose social unease and sexual anxiety seem, initially, to arise from his disability and an unspecified psychological trauma. He is obsessed with another hunchback whom he spies upon at the local laundry. Finally, they encounter one another:

> 'Cut it out,' I said quietly. 'I recognized you at first sight. You and I come from the same place. We're relatives, so to speak. PKHENTZ! PKHENTZ!' I whispered, to remind him of a name sacred to us both. (Tertz 1987: 230)

At first, the narrator explains the other's ignorance by having 'entered too fully into his part, gone native, become human', only to realise that 'he was a normal human, the most normal of humans' (Tertz 1987: 231–2). For the narrator believes himself to be an alien from another planet, who has been compelled to take the form of a hunchback as 'fancy dress', 'a bit better-looking than the rest of them here, though they are monsters too' (Tertz 1987: 225). The narrator's true identity is never revealed. Instead, his profound alienation from both himself and those around him, allied to the themes of surveillance and self-inspection, amount to a powerful allegory about the fracturing of identity under a totalitarian regime.

Legitimation Crisis, or Postmodern Dissidence?

The artistic effect that little magazines, small presses and underground publications have had upon contemporary culture can be seen in the response of mainstream journals. As the innovation and experimentation characteristic of the avant-garde came to be seen as historically significant during the course of the twentieth century, so the traditional art institutions, whether they be galleries, museums, concert halls or journals, had either to accommodate their products or appear old-fashioned. At the same time, the avant-garde had enjoyed comparative freedom by displaying its work through unconventional means – the little magazine, the installation, the happening – and had defined itself against the accepted art-work of the institutions. Not only might these artefacts be difficult to include on moral grounds, but a loss of integrity might also be incurred by both parties. Nevertheless, without some accommodation of the avant-garde, the institution might gradually lose its authority, while the artist could lose greater acceptance, status and commercial value. This dilemma has been described as a *legitimation crisis*, since both artist and art institution vie with one another to legitimate the viability of their work, and it is often seen as underlining the elements of postmodern culture.

In fact, this dilemma had also been prevalent during the modernist period. Fledgling little magazines, such as *The Yellow Book* and *The English Review*, needed to include major cultural figures, such as Henry James, to lend them status within the literary marketplace. Equally, commercial titles gained valuable cultural kudos by featuring the work of non-commercial but serious writers such as Joseph Conrad. Consequently, despite their mainstream publication, stories such as 'Il Conde' (1908), in which a mysterious incident, the meaning of which is unknown to the teller, is told to an unwitting frame-narrator, are among Conrad's most enigmatic fictions. Other writers took advantage of this market relationship. F. Scott Fitzgerald, for example, established a niche for himself as the guide to an era that he himself named in *Tales from the Jazz Age* (1922). However, the multiplication of new media during the twentieth century (cinema, radio, television, video, digital) has further fragmented the availability and accessibility of culture within the marketplace, and placed additional pressure upon the traditional art organisations to justify their continued authority. In other words, the legitimation crisis has arguably deepened throughout this period.

A pertinent example in terms of the short story is that of Donald Barthelme, who became a regular contributor to *The New Yorker* following 'L'Lapse' (1963). Barthelme, who had been a lecturer at the University of Houston and editor of the little magazine *Forum*, had recently become managing editor of *Location*, the art and literary journal published by Thomas B. Hess and Harold Rosenberg, art critic with *The New Yorker*. *Location* was itself a product of the close interaction between literature and the visual arts in New York at this time, which included Barthelme's friend, the experimental poet Kenneth Koch. Barthelme was himself part of a literary generation that included innovative writers such as John Barth, Joseph Heller and Thomas Pynchon. *The New Yorker*, by contrast, was still identified with the well-made stories of writers such as J. D. Salinger and John Updike. Despite its high reputation, *The New Yorker* could only maintain its authority within a competitive marketplace by including examples of the new avant-garde. Due to Rosenberg's connection with the journal, Barthelme's mix of collage, allusion and pastiche found an amenable venue at *The New Yorker*. For Barthelme, the appeal of *The New Yorker* meant association with a venerable literary tradition and the opportunity of reaching a large audience. Initially, though, Barthelme's fiction was greeted with incredulity and derision by several of *The New Yorker*'s readers, but the magazine offered Barthelme a regular contract because the controversy had helped to recast *The New Yorker* as an innovative journal, thereby re-emphasising its leading status. To some extent, then, Barthelme's iconography as an independent and free-thinking artist was co-opted by the magazine to serve its own needs for legitimation.

In Britain, legitimation is mediated by the lack of an economic infra-structure for short story magazines. The leading title, *Granta*, survives on institutional and overseas sales; its content tends to be conserva-tive in the style of Raymond Carver. The comparatively innovative journal *Ambit* sells less than three-thousand copies and is dependent upon financial support from the Arts Council. The success, then, of Ra Page's *Comma* is a notable exception. Starting in 1998, *Comma* was distributed as a free supplement within the pages of the Manchester review *City Life*, where Page was deputy editor. Increased sales led to *The City Life Book of Manchester Stories* (1999), which sold a rea-sonable three and a half-thousand copies, and the formation in 2002 of Comma Press, a non-profit publishing collective that publishes annual anthologies of new fiction, short story collections and themed series. Unlike *Granta*, Comma is drawn towards formal innovation, a symptom of both its regional identity and unconventional history of distribution.

Comma has also made use of the Internet to promote its works. On the one hand, digital technology offers fresh opportunity for lit-erary dissidence by forging a community of writers and readers. On the other hand, it represents a further phase within the legitimation crisis. *McSweeney's Internet Tendency*, for example, is a humorous website that emerged from *Timothy McSweeney's Quarterly Concern* launched by Dave Eggers in 1998. Association with the Internet lends McSweeney's a samizdat-like quality. In an era of corporate ownership, resemblance to an underground press is a valuable commodity, lending Eggers' various outlets the allure of authenticity. In practice, though, it acts as a vital marketing tool drawing attention to Eggers and his chosen writers, who are now often branded as a recognisable literary generation (as in the anthology *The Burned Children of America*, 2003). The extent to which McSweeney's represents the latest avant-garde within American fiction must be set against Eggers' willingness to use the look of samizdat in order to publicise his product. And, as the lesson of computer hackers who debugged William Gibson's 1992 text 'Agrippa: A Book of the Dead' (originally sold on CD-Rom with an in-built virus that corrupted the text at its conclusion) suggests, readers still want to be able to consume the whole package.

This desire also underscores so-called 'hypertext' fictions, such as Michael Joyce's 'Afternoon' (1987), which was composed on a software program that allowed readers to interact with the text. Despite claims that hypertext has rendered the printed book obsolete, by offering greater interaction and multiplicity within the reading experience, the strategies associated with hypertext remain grounded in the rhetoric of modernism. As Jay David Bolter has written, seemingly unconscious of the New Critical echo, '"Afternoon" is about the problem of its own reading' (Bolter 1991: 127). The language of academia has, arguably, proved one of the most effective restraints upon the dissidence of the short story.

Further Reading

The Little Magazine (1946), edited by Frederick Hoffman et al., is an indispensable guide. Little magazines and small presses are also discussed by Katharine Lyon Mix (1960), Ian Fletcher (1979) and Gillian Hanscombe and Virginia Smyers (1987). The relationship between 'genre and gender' is explored by Mary Eagleton (1989). For details of the Sinyavsky trial, see Erika Gottlieb (2001). On the underlying theme of the writer's responsibility, see Theodor Adorno's critique of Jean-Paul Sartre, 'Commitment', in *Notes on Literature, vol. 2* (1992). For a discussion of legitimation and the avant-garde, see Peter Bürger (1984). For a defence of hypertext, see Michael Joyce (1995).

8

Enclosed Readings: The Short Story and the Academy

Dave Eggers has observed that 'there are probably over a hundred high-quality literary journals' in the United States and that 'just about every state in the union has its own journal' (Eggers 2004: vii). Despite this optimistic view, many of these journals are based in and around university campuses. There are notable exceptions, such as the long-established *Paris Review* and the more recent little magazine *Fence*, but among the titles that Eggers cites, *Grand Street* has ceased publication while *StoryQuarterly* is published through the online journal *Narrative*. The durability of magazines such as *Callaloo* often relies upon some form of academic infrastructure. Mary Rohrberger has argued that by teaching short stories on creative writing programmes, 'the university was not only hiring writers and producing writers skilled in the form but also training readers. In this way, the academy created a reading public knowledgeable in how to read a short story' (in Fallon et al. 2001: 1). Yet, Charles May has contended that 'the short story is largely scorned by agents, editors, readers, and scholars' because of the way in which it exposes 'the inauthenticity of everyday life' and discomforts 'the inadequacy of our categories of perception' (in Winther et al. 2004: 14, 24). Putting aside the validity of May's argument for one moment, there is clearly a discrepancy between his position and that of Rohrberger. May, as he has frequently done, emphasises the cultural marginalisation of the form. Rohrberger, by contrast, suggests that a reading culture has been created, initially within the university, in which the short story can be understood and appreciated. Between their respective positions lies a debate concerning the role of the academy and, as explored in the previous chapter, the legitimation of culture. This academic dispute has a practical consequence because, as Eggers continues, despite 'all that was being published, there were literary forms that were strangely under-represented' (Eggers 2004: viii). In other words, the ways in which the university has shaped the understanding of the short story directly affect what gets published and read.

Returning to May's proposition, his explanation for why the short story is underappreciated rests upon the difficulty of the form: its enigmatic quality and resistance to closure. Yet, May has already made a judgement about the form. His thesis applies to lyrical short stories written within a post-Chekhovian mode such as James Joyce and Katherine Mansfield; it does not apply to all the popular sub-genres and commercial magazines where most short stories actually appear. In other words, he makes a very clear distinction about a form that is allegedly so ambiguous that it disturbs readers from reading it at all. I want to suggest here that May makes an equation between the literary and interpretative difficulty, that the one is understood in terms of the other. Ease of communication, by contrast, through the use of accessible language or generic conventions is implicitly regarded as non-literary. Although May contends that short stories are rarely read, his implicit thinking about the short story cuts not only himself but also other academic readers off from the major areas in which the short story is read and consumed. By effectively fetishising interpretation as a struggle with the text, academic criticism not only appropriates certain kinds of short story but also promulgates an exclusive form of reading practice. Instead, as Chapter 5 indicated, most potential readers of the short story do not necessarily regard the form as more difficult than any other kind of literature and are open-minded towards it depending upon how it is presented to them.

How did this divide between academic and non-academic readers of the short story emerge? In this chapter, my comments will primarily focus upon the United States, since the short story has played such a major role within the development of American literary criticism. Yet, with the recent formation of the North West Short Story Network, an organisation supported by several north-western British universities, the discussion is not exclusive to the USA alone. The analysis will examine how the concept of a national literature became intermeshed with the rise of New Criticism, cultural politics in the postwar period and the growth of creative writing as another form of professional discourse.

There has been a long and enduring tendency for American writers to regard the short story as part of their national literature.

Bret Harte, for example, equated the rise of the short story with the expansion of the United States following the 1848 Gold Rush, since the latter created 'a condition of romantic and dramatic possibilities . . . unrivalled in history' (in Current-García and Patrick 1974: 31). Nearly a century later, Joyce Carol Oates wrote that American short fiction was tied to the pioneer spirit: 'For ours is the nation, so rare in human history, of self-determination: a theoretical experiment in newness, exploration, discovery' (Oates 1992: 12). Oates' chauvinistic use of 'ours' effectively excludes non-American readers of the short story with damaging consequences, since her anthology is a set text-book for short story courses outside of the United States. In contrast, Robert Coover writes that 'the only thing truly American about the short story is the American effort to possess it, to colonize it and add a new state to the union' (in Lounsberry et al. 1998: 135). This tendency for monopolising the short story, as well as academic criticism upon the form, suggests an underlying insecurity within American literary culture, the lack of foundational materials as noted by James Fenimore Cooper in Chapter 4. The need to assert a distinct American literary heritage became especially important during the twentieth century as a symptom of political change.

The annual series of anthologies devoted to the *Best American Short Stories*, which Edward O'Brien launched in 1915, not only sought to distinguish between literary and commercial short fiction but also contributed to the building of an American literary culture in which the short story was a standard-bearer. In 1923, the same year as Fred Lewis Pattee published his historical survey *The Development of the American Short Story*, O'Brien published his own account, *The Advance of the American Short Story*. Both books mediate the rhetoric of Progressivism that had been dominant in the United States throughout the period 1890–1920. Intellectually, Progressivism was a middle-class, Protestant movement that sought to widen democracy and reform social welfare through an attack upon centralised business interests, for example in Edward Bellamy's novel *Looking Backward* (1887). While on the one hand, Progressivism was idealistic and forward-looking, on the other hand, it was nostalgic and echoed a utopian vision of America that could be found within the nation's Puritan origins. Consequently, both O'Brien and Pattee return their readers to the start of the nineteenth century (Washington Irving is their key starting-point) and then recount a history of the short story that emphasises its progressive and democratic qualities: its appeal to community, region and dialect. As O'Brien says of his own study, 'a history of our literary achievement in the past hundred years, as measured by the American short story, may make . . . the path of future progress easier to trace' (O'Brien 1931: 19).

Both O'Brien and Pattee share their dislike of commercial short fiction. Pattee isolates the pernicious influence of O. Henry, writing that 'he worked without truth, without moral consciousness, and without a philosophy of life' (Pattee 1975: 364). But Pattee also suggests that O. Henry was himself the product of 'the new journalistic tendency' in short fiction and 'its grosser tendencies'. Like critics before him, such as H. S. Canby and Herbert Ellsworth Cory (see Chapter 4), Pattee associates this new emphasis upon the mechanical and external features of the story with the emerging mass culture of city crowds, tabloid newspapers and cinema:

> The colors are vivid and startlingly splashed, the humor is broad, the characters stand out like caricatures. Everything is keyed for the Main Street multitude whose reading centers in *The Saturday Evening Post* and whose ideals of art are satisfied by the moving pictures. The primary object is entertainment, gross entertainment – laughter, sensation, the exhilaration of success won through difficulties, eternal newness, adventure, the thrill of movement, always movement. (Pattee 1975: 369)

O'Brien develops Pattee's complaint into a full-scale critique of mass culture in which the formulaic, commercial short story is one instrument within the increasing mechanisation of everyday life:

> This soulless machine is hypnotizing the masses, and reducing the imagination by which they might evolve into a higher plane of civilization to a least common denominator of sluggish indifference. When this sluggish indifference, which is being educed by the daily press and the motion-picture and the automobile, as well as by the short story and the mechanical play and the jazz band, has sunk into the fens of utter spiritual indifference and apish imitation of the herd, the conquest of the machine will be complete, and the slave and the master will have changed places. (O'Brien 1931: 6)

O'Brien's aim, then, was to reclaim certain kinds of short fiction, especially the work of Sherwood Anderson, which counteracted this alleged 'indifference'. He was joined in this mission by the judges of the first O. Henry Memorial Prize in 1919, among them Blanche Colton Williams, who 'sought originality, excellence in organization of plot incidents, skill in characterization, power in moving emotions' (quoted in Pattee 1975: 372). Considering that for many readers O. Henry represented the harbinger of the mechanical short story, an amazing reassessment was taking place. A group of writers and critics, agitated by what they saw as the encroachment of a vulgar, unthinking and homogeneous mass culture, was seeking to retrieve the short story and relocate it as part of an older, more vibrant national tradition. While on the one hand, this project was symptomatic of a resurgent cultural nationalism during the years of 'Splendid Isolation', when the United States' official foreign policy was to sever its political ties to Europe, on the other hand, it paralleled the modernist aims of American journals such as *The Dial* (1920–9), and in Britain T. S. Eliot's *The Criterion* (1922–39), as well as the academic criticism of F. R. Leavis. Cleansed of its commercial connotations, the short story became a perfect vehicle for the American equivalents to Leavis and I. A. Richards, the so-called 'New Critics'.

The origins of New Criticism (the phrase comes from a book of the same name by John Crowe Ransom) lie in Nashville, Tennessee. A group of students at Vanderbilt University, among them Ransom, Allen Tate and Robert Penn Warren, founded a poetry magazine, *The Fugitive*, in 1922. They were inspired by the objective and neoclassical ideals of modernist poetry, and in particular by the ethos of literary tradition and personal detachment that underwrote Eliot's provocative text *The Waste Land* (also 1922). As the sons of Southern families that had suffered following the defeat of the American Civil War (1861–5), the *Fugitive* writers saw in the rhetoric of modernism, such as order, hardness and clarity, a means for distancing themselves from the chaos of history and for placing it into perspective. In their prose and poetry, and above all in their criticism, the *Fugitive* writers placed artistic unity at the heart of composition. While on the one hand, they realised that personal experience acted as a catalyst for writing, on the other hand, the very act of writing transformed that initial experience and made it something other: art. For the New

Critics, the most successful art-work was the one that strove for the most perfect formal unity at the expense of authorial intention or social context. In language that could not be presented in any other form, the successful literary writer expressed the paradox and ambiguity of human existence in a style that was technically refined.

With another graduate of Vanderbilt, Cleanth Brooks, Warren wrote two influential studies, *Understanding Poetry* (1938) and its successor *Understanding Fiction* (1943). In fact, the latter does not focus upon fiction per se. It focuses instead upon the short story, which is regarded as a distillation of all narrative fiction (generic and historical contexts are put to one side). In accordance with the methodology of New Criticism, successful short stories are ones that most effectively balance and integrate elements such as location, atmosphere, character, point of view, conflict and resolution. The widespread acceptance of Edgar Allan Poe's review of Nathaniel Hawthorne had already given Brooks and Warren a model of the short story to work from, and they acknowledge their debt to Poe by emphasising the importance of concision, design and single effect. A key aspect to *Understanding Fiction* is the way that it is written as a practical guide for the teaching of university students. The objective tone and analytical approach, despite lacking any real or quasi-scientific basis, casts the book as a serious and up-market version of the creative writing handbooks that had already been popular since the turn of the century. The book's assumed air of authority helped to legitimate both the study and the practical writing of short stories as part of university syllabuses. Yet, it also glossed the writers' ideological beliefs: their commitment to a moral humanism in which order is restored at the expense of internal disagreement. The teaching and writing of short stories, in the light of New Critical values, effectively became a means of manufacturing consensus.

Instead, the rise of New Criticism is inseparable from the years leading up to World War Two. The economic effects of the Great Depression, allied to the implementation of the New Deal, altered how Americans regarded themselves and their country. The burgeoning sense at the start of the 1920s of a literary tradition and a national culture found new emphasis in a period of social hardship and democratic change. In 1941, the Harvard academic F. O. Matthiessen published *American Renaissance: Art and Expression in the Age of Emerson and Whitman*. As Matthiessen claims in his preface, the nineteenth

century was the period in which America affirmed 'its rightful heritage in the whole expanse of art and culture' (Matthiessen 1941: vii).
Later critics have attempted to expand Matthiessen's limited canon of
writers by including figures such as Emily Dickinson without discarding the basic template. Yet, as Donald Pease has suggested in his re-
reading of Matthiessen's account of *Moby Dick* (1851), the concept of
an 'American renaissance' was the product of political conflicts during
the 1930s and early 1940s, in which Ishmael (representing democracy)
opposed Ahab (the authoritarian figure) (Pease 1985: 113–55). In
other words, an American nation in touch with its cultural past was all
the stronger to fight for liberty and promote freedom.

In the wake of Matthiessen's work, the pioneering figures of
American Studies, such as R. W. B. Lewis, Leo Marx and Henry Nash
Smith, published a series of texts that tended to mythologise early
American history through the use of archetypes such as the 'American
Adam', the 'machine in the garden' and the 'virgin land'. By obscur-
ing the very history these studies were meant to be exposing, the
writers could still uphold the utopian vision of the Founding Fathers
and place the American nation outside of history, associating it with
nature. In the era of the Cold War, this strategy had the effect of natu-
ralising American ideology as pure and wholesome while the Soviet
Union, by contrast, remained ideological, unnatural, evil. Academic
study of the short story, which had for some time been dehistoricised
by the influence of New Criticism, was also prone to this process.
William Peden's *The American Short Story* was originally published in
1964 with the sub-title *Front-Line in the National Defense of Literature*
(it was later republished in the period of détente with the blander title
Continuity and Change, 1940–1975). Peden immediately announces
that the short story 'is the only major literary form of essentially
American origin and the only one in which American writers have
from the beginning tended to excel' (Peden 1975: 1). He continues by
arguing that the American short story 'has always been characterized
by individuality, freedom and variety' (Peden 1975: 4). This move
allows Peden to incorporate such potentially troubling writers as John
Barth and Donald Barthelme: their awkwardness is seen as a sign of
their true, independent American selves.

Peden is also tolerant in his attitude towards the magazine market:
another instance in which a potential site of conflict is defused and

absorbed within a predetermined consensus. Yet, at the same time as Peden, sociologists such as Dwight Macdonald and David Riesman were questioning the very basis of consensus as the product of a repressive society that encouraged social uniformity and stifled dissent through the spread of mass culture. Writing in 1953, Macdonald observed that mass culture had 'developed new media of its own, into which the serious artist rarely ventures: radio, the movies, comic books, detective stories, science fiction, television' (Macdonald 1998: 22). At a stroke, Macdonald not only inserted a division between serious and popular culture, echoing O'Brien's critique from the 1920s, but he also dismissed two of the most innovative sub-genres of the short story, detective fiction and science fiction. Yet, Macdonald was also severe on literary short fiction:

> The '*New Yorker* short story' is a definite genre . . . which the editors have established by years of patient, skilful selection the same way a gardener develops a new kind of rose. They have, indeed, done their work all too well: would-be contributors now deluge them with lifeless imitations, and they have begun to beg writers not to follow the formula *quite* so closely. (Macdonald 1998: 28)

As the botanical metaphor suggests, an evolutionary principle underlines Macdonald's critique, in which only the fittest culture will survive, and in which he fears a 'spreading ooze' will 'engulf everything' (Macdonald 1998: 27). The failure of mass culture theorists to differentiate within their chosen subject helped to reinforce the use of canonical literatures as part of a manufactured consensus, one aspect of which was the New Critical appropriation of the short story.

Despite the political changes that affected British and American society after 1960, including the so-called 'theory wars' that raged through the Humanities during the 1970s and '80s, short story criticism has changed relatively little. Returning to the earlier quotation from Charles May, where he argues that the short story is neglected by readers because of the way in which it reveals the inauthenticity of experience and the unreliability of perception, in point of fact, these questions have been central to literary theory for the last thirty years. The overadherence of short story criticism to New Critical or formalist principles has denied it the possibilities of a poststructural critique (see Clark and Royle 2004). Instead, the emerging tendency within American short story criticism has been the application of cognitive psychology to, what Susan Lohafer has termed, 'storyness' (in May 1994: 301–11). In the mid-1980s, Lohafer's *Coming to Terms with the Short Story* (1983) and John Gerlach's *Toward the End* (1985) paid careful attention to how the reader's imminent expectation of closure affected how the short story was read as a narrative form. As Gerlach noted, 'we can sense, can feel narrative structure in the short story with an intensity the novel rarely permits' (Gerlach 1985: 161). This intense awareness of narrative is what discourse analysis of the short story attempts to understand.

Despite Lohafer's claim of 'subversive results' (in Lohafer and Clary 1989: 274), insofar as discourse analysis unsettles overprofessionalised academic reading, and that the method has placed short story criticism 'in the vanguard' of literary theory, I think the opposite is true. In attempting to distinguish discourse analysis from earlier forms of structuralism, Lohafer argues that 'what was the new was the attempt . . . to locate the source of these grammars experimentally' (in Lohafer and Clary 1989: 211). In actual fact, both I. A. Richards in *Practical Criticism* (1929) and, before him, the aesthete Vernon Lee had used quasi-scientific experiments to test readers' responses to literary texts. What was happening, instead, was an updated form of close reading that used the language of discourse analysis, though not even that was essential: 'We may not need the technical language, but we can use the standpoint.' In turning to discourse analysis, a deeper issue was involved, since 'this kind of study offers a middle ground between an elite aesthetics and a respect for readership in a broad sense' (in Lohafer and Clary 1989: 271). In the movement away from the poetics of literary criticism towards an empirical form of data analysis, American short story theory was attempting to justify itself as part of an academy increasingly under attack from central government and widely seen as divorced from the rest of society. The rise of cognitive psychology within short story criticism, in which the equally 'technical language' of aesthetics is displaced for a quantifiable and mathematically recognised product, has to be seen within the context of universities seeking to legitimate their relevancy to contemporary society.

Furthermore, the supposed objectivity of discourse analysis merely reinforces the dehistoricised accounts of the short story already offered by New Criticism. Such narrow formalism can help conceal reactionary ideological positions, for example when John Gerlach suggests that 'by demonstrating the effect closure has had on the American short story, I hope to improve our understanding of stories of any country in any period' (Gerlach 1985: 6). The universalising claim of this statement mystifies the short story, since it proposes that not only can all short stories be reduced to the effects of closure but that readers can also be reduced to one essential reading subject without consideration of historical, cultural or geographical differences. (This is also the inherent risk within the statistical researches of discourse analysis.) Such a claim can also help to justify the continued chauvinism of earlier critics such as Peden. For example, in *The Short Story: The Reality of Artifice* (1995) Charles May offered a series of synopses of individual writers, only three of whom – Anton Chekhov, James Joyce and Jorge Luis Borges – were born outside the United States. Although American short story criticism has been attentive to its own ethnic minorities, it has been slow to appreciate the work of postcolonial writers from around the world, while contemporary European writers have scarcely been recognised. (Examples might include from France, Assia Djebar, Michel Tournier and Boris Vian; from Germany, Jurek Becker, Heinrich Böll, Judith Hermann, Ingo Schulze and Christa Wolf; from Italy, Italo Calvino, Dacia Maraini and Antonio Tabucchi; and from Russia, Yuri Buida and Victor Pelevin.)

A couple of cures to this deadlock present themselves. One, following the precepts of New Historicism, would be to historicise and demystify the short story. The other comes in the form in which the short story is most popularly experienced as part of the university syllabus: creative writing. Too often, creative writing programmes are used as a way of drawing students into university, of making the literary 'accessible', and thereby establishing the continued social relevance of the academy. For similar reasons, the short story is often a key component of creative writing courses, with the result that even very recent guides to writing short stories reiterate Poe's prescriptions on the form (see Burroway 2003: 47–8). Yet, the ideal of creative writing, as opposed to its institutional practice, suggests a more radical future for literary studies by reconnecting the activity of critique with its original sense of a critical rewriting of the text: not merely a commentary but a direct challenge and alteration of the words on the page. Creative writing introduces notions of play – parody, pastiche, inversion, subversion – that intervene within and expose the mechanics of the text. These ideas of play grow implicitly from a conflict model of communication as opposed to the enclosed, consensual readings that this chapter has explored. In this respect, creative play-making with the short story reveals the form not to be the hermetically sealed device idealised by New Criticism, but rather, the contradictory and episodic form understood by modernist writers, such as Ernest Hemingway and Katherine Mansfield, to whom I now turn.

Further Reading

Andrew Levy debates the short story as a national art form in *The Culture and Commerce of the American Short Story* (1993). On the history of Progressivism, see J. A. Thompson (1979). The relationship between modernism and New Criticism is recounted by A. Walton Litz et al. (2000). For a critique of the foundational narratives in American Studies, see Robert Clark (1984). The best guide to writing short stories, due to its engagement with both theory and practice, is by Ailsa Cox (2005). My views on play and creative writing have been influenced by the work of Rob Pope, see for example *Creativity* (2005). On the underlying theme of the university and the nation-state, see Bill Readings, *The University in Ruins* (1996).

9

Modernism and the Short Story

In his pre-Marxist study, *The Theory of the Novel* (1920), Georg Lukács wrote that 'the short story is the most purely artistic form':

> It sees absurdity in all its undisguised and unadorned nakedness, and the exorcising power of this view, without fear or hope, gives it the consecration of form; meaninglessness as *meaninglessness* becomes form; it becomes eternal because it is affirmed, transcended and redeemed by form. (Lukács 1971: 51–2)

Though Lukács would become one of modernism's most trenchant critics, here he diagnoses one of its chief underlying qualities: the need to grasp the meaninglessness of existence through a heightened, self-conscious use of artistic form. As discussed in Chapter 3, the poet Charles Baudelaire had defined modernity as 'the ephemeral, the fugitive, the contingent, the half of art whose other half is the eternal and the immutable' (Baudelaire 1995: 12). If modernity was insubstantial, devoid of lasting content and evacuated of meaning, then how to reconnect the 'torn halves' (Adorno and Benjamin 1999: 130) of art and culture? One solution, as Baudelaire suggests, was a type of 'mnemonic art' that grasped the essential outlines of the object as it faded from view. In itself, this method would not only entail a new approach to writing but also the adoption of new forms, one of which was the short story. The emergence of modernism towards the end of the nineteenth century does not so much constitute a resolution of this question as a dramatisation of its fundamental tensions.

Flaubert and Early Modernism

In 1857, both Baudelaire and Gustave Flaubert published their landmark texts, respectively *The Flowers of Evil* and *Madame Bovary*. The novel was Flaubert's first successful attempt to write 'a book about nothing, a book dependent on nothing external, which would be held together by the strength of its style'. For Flaubert, there were 'no noble subjects or ignoble subjects; from the standpoint of pure Art . . . there is no such thing as subject, style in itself being an absolute manner of seeing things' (Flaubert 1954: 131). Almost as influential were Flaubert's *Three Tales* (1877).

The opening story, 'A Simple Heart', is the most famous of the trio. It recounts the life of a housemaid, Félicité, her adoration for her mistress, her unsophisticated devotion to duty and to faith, and her beloved parrot that Félicité identifies with the Holy Ghost. The loss of both her health and those close to her is contrasted with the mounting debris in Félicité's bedroom: 'a mixture of religious knick-knacks and other miscellaneous bits and pieces', a cross 'between a chapel and a bazaar' (Flaubert 2005: 34). On the surface, there is nothing profound to this story: it appears as simple as Félicité herself. Yet, at the moment of her death, Félicité imagines 'she saw a huge parrot hovering above her head as the heavens parted to receive her' (Flaubert 2005: 40). This apparition is profoundly ironic since it suggests that we should now accept Félicité's unworldly identification of the bird with divinity as, in fact, other-worldly and imbued with metaphysical insight (Culler 1985: 210–11). Yet, this reinterpretation of Félicité's history as ultimately meaningful is contradicted by the plainness and simplicity in which the narrative is told, and in particular, by the positioning of Félicité herself as an object within the discourse. She has been abused, is uneducated, makes a literal connection between words and objects, and with her increasing deafness, becomes 'enclosed in an ever-diminishing world of her own' (Flaubert 2005: 31). The absence of Félicité as an autonomous, speaking subject means that the reader is compelled to interpret her story for her with all the inherent risks that that implies for misunderstanding. While the narrative circles Félicité as a kind of void, the reader is persuaded to retrace its trajectory: the ways in which the story has been designed to be read rather than what it necessarily signifies.

Flaubert's influence was felt directly by his protégé, Guy de Maupassant, whose novels and short stories were translated into English during the 1880s. Henry James once described Maupassant as 'a lion in the path' (James 1987: 237), yet it was Flaubert who exerted greater influence over James and his associates, such as Joseph Conrad, Stephen Crane and Ford Madox Ford. Flaubert's attention to the activity, rather than the object, of representation fed into conundrums such as James' 'The Figure in the Carpet' (1896). Yet, Flaubert's approach was more than an intellectual exercise; it could also engender moving narratives such as Conrad's 'Amy Foster' (1901). In a characteristic strategy, the story is told by an internal narrator, Dr Kennedy, to an anonymous frame-narrator. Kennedy is described as being able to make 'people talk to him freely' and of possessing 'inexhaustible patience in listening to their tales.' Yet, he is also said to have an 'unappeasable curiosity which believes that there is a particle of general truth in every mystery' (Conrad 1997: 96). Although Kennedy has the ability to translate the inarticulate speech of common people into the language of the storyteller (Carabine 1992: 192), he is motivated by an optimistic belief in the presence of truth. By comparing Amy's love for the Polish castaway Yanko to 'a Greek tragedy' (Conrad 1997: 96), Kennedy tends to intellectualise his material:

> There are other tragedies, less scandalous and of a subtler poignancy, arising from irreconcilable differences and from that fear of the Incomprehensible that hangs over all our heads – over all our heads. (Conrad 1997: 97)

The shift in register from a factual account of Amy's family towards a metaphysical and encompassing vision, redolent of similar passages in *Heart of Darkness* (1899), describe Kennedy's need to find some 'general truth' within the enigma of Amy's love for Yanko. Although Kennedy is sympathetic to Yanko's plight, 'a lost stranger, helpless, incomprehensible' (Conrad 1997: 100), he seeks to englobe Yanko's story within an existential discourse, 'the supreme disaster of loneliness and despair' (Conrad 1997: 119), that says more about Kennedy's decision to voluntarily resign himself to a rural practice after years as a naval surgeon and colonial explorer. Instead, Kennedy's inability to see Yanko's death not as the result of despair or isolation but as the ironic result of Amy's fright and abandonment of Yanko, while he is feverish and delirious, makes Yanko's tragic story all the more pathetic. For despite Kennedy being the sole character with the imaginative ability to empathise with Yanko's condition, he can only see the void into which Yanko's body returns. The unobtrusive, and therefore compliant, frame-narrator acquiesces in Kennedy's judgement, which transfers the questions raised by the narrative to the reader.

Conrad's sophisticated use of narrative framing, so that the story is mediated by one or more narrators who are usually unreliable, produced celebrated examples such as his tale of doppelgangers, 'The Secret Sharer' (1910). More particularly, it only allowed readers a partial or selective viewpoint as conferred by the narrator(s). This strategy has immediate resonance with the theory of literary impressionism propounded by Conrad's friend and occasional collaborator, Ford Madox Ford. Ford wrote that Flaubert had decided 'that the author must be impersonal, must, like a creating deity, stand neither for nor against any of his characters, must project and never report and must, above all, forever keep himself out of his books. He must write his books as if he were rendering the impressions of a person present at a scene [who] does not see everything and is above all not able to remember immensely long passages of dialogue' (Ford 1964: 60). In overturning the Victorian convention of the omniscient narrator, Ford was arguably getting closer to the authenticity of subjective experience by concentrating upon only what is seen, known or felt by his protagonists, such as the unreliable narrator of Ford's best-known novel, *The Good Soldier* (1915).

The theory of impressionism was especially conducive to the short story, for instance in this vivid passage from Stephen Crane's 'The Open Boat' (1897):

> Gray-faced and bowed forward, they mechanically, turn by turn, plied the leaden oars. The form of the lighthouse had vanished from the southern horizon, but finally a pale star appeared, just lifting from the sea. The streaked saffron in the west passed before the all-merging darkness, and the sea to the east was black. The land had vanished, and was expressed only by the low and drear thunder of the surf. (Crane 1993: 68)

Crane describes only what his characters experience, thereby removing his readers from a position of assumed comfort and placing them in the position of his protagonists. Impressionism was an important step within the development of modernism by remaking literary traditions in relation to new and emerging reading cultures (Gasiorek 2001:

3–27). In his pivotal role as editor of *The English Review* (1908–9), Ford was well-placed to influence a generation of writers, some of whom, most notably Wyndham Lewis, would overturn the principles of impressionism. For the short story, though, impressionism has had a lasting effect. By suggesting a possible link between literature and the visual arts, impressionism introduced into the language of short story criticism a series of visual metaphors that, as in the work of Eileen Baldeshwiler and Suzanne Ferguson, became equated with poetic moments of illumination (see May 1994: 218–41). In contrast, the selective and ambiguous viewpoints of stories such as Conrad's 'The Tale' (1917) obscure rather than clarify the reader's perspective in ways that prefigure developments in European intellectual thought (March-Russell 2006: 267–82).

In a parallel movement to the innovations of Conrad, Crane and Ford, Rudyard Kipling assembled what might be called a popular modernism. Like Crane, and later Ernest Hemingway, Kipling began as a journalist and his beliefs in 'Higher Editing' (Kipling 1937: 207–8) were influenced as much by his journalistic training as his reading of Maupassant. Like Ford, Kipling believed in the paring and selection of details so that, as in his early Indian tales, his writing is spare and evocative. Later, as Kipling became concerned with the design of individual stories and the overall shape of his collections, his writing became as dense as anything achieved by the early modernists while working within popular modes such as the invasion story ('Mary Postgate', 1915) or the supernatural tale ('The Wish House', 1924). 'Dayspring Mishandled' (1928) reworks another mode familiar to Kipling's readers: the revenge tale. Manallace's attempt, however, to discredit his literary rival, Castorley, by forging an undiscovered Chaucerian text is riddled with ironies, not the least of which is that the story is narrated by an anonymous 'I' who becomes Manallace's accomplice. Whereas, at first, the reader is encouraged to support Manallace's scheme, by the end of the story the reader is asked to support Manallace again, this time in his attempt to *preserve* Castorley's reputation against the machinations of his widow. The shifting network of alliances means that the reader's own allegiance is uncertain, a point underlined by the fact that Castorley's apparent slight against the woman that both he and Manallace had desired is never fully disclosed.

Chekhov and the Beginnings of High Modernism

The first English translations of Anton Chekhov during the 1910s are often seen as a key moment within the development of the modernist short story (Shaw 1983: 121–31). However, James Joyce had already composed the stories that make up *Dubliners* (1914) between 1904 and 1907, while Katherine Mansfield's early story 'The Tiredness of Rosabel' (1908) is already redolent of her later style. Instead of being regarded as a direct influence, Chekhov's example can be seen as affirming the directions in which modernist writers were taking short fiction while also bolstering the confidence of innovators such as Mansfield and Virginia Woolf.

While Flaubert had emphasised authorial detachment and stylistic precision, Chekhov revolutionised the short story by stripping away plot to its bare minimum. Even in the narrative of 'A Simple Heart', there is a sense of roundedness, although that effect might itself be an illusion. To take as an example Chekhov's most famous story, 'The Lady with the Little Dog' (1899), the opening plunges the reader into the midst of gossip: 'People were saying that someone new had appeared on the seafront' (Chekhov 2004: 167). Despite this dramatic beginning, the reader gradually makes the acquaintance of the mysterious stranger, Anna, through her seduction by the male protagonist, Dmitry. In so doing, the reader also learns about Dmitry and that, despite his ungallant attitude towards women, he is both ensnared by a loveless marriage and, ultimately, his unexpected affection for Anna. At one point, Dmitry's wife tells him that he is not suited to 'the role of the romantic' (Chekhov 2004: 176), and indeed, one of the questions raised by the story is the idea of romance. In what could be seen as a conventional romantic gesture, Dmitry returns to Yalta to see Anna once more, but he has no notion of what he is doing, and when they do meet, further complications arise. They begin an illicit affair that calls into doubt Dmitry's own assumptions about his public and private lives: 'And he judged others to be like himself, not believing what he saw, and always supposing that each person's real and most interesting life took place beneath a shroud of secrecy, as if under the veil of night' (Chekhov 2004: 181). At last, it is only when Dmitry catches sight of his own reflection, sees the waste and decay of his own life compared with the warmth and beauty of Anna although 'probably already on the point of fading and wilting' like himself (Chekhov 2004: 182), that he openly commits himself to her. Neither character is a conventional romantic hero; instead, they are two ordinary, middle-aged people, bound together in circumstances not of their own making, yet which makes their personal drama all the more poignant. In a perfectly judged ending, Chekhov quits his protagonists, believing that 'a new, wonderful life would begin', but that 'the end was still a long way off and that the most complex and difficult part was only just beginning' (Chekhov 2004: 183). This opening-out at the very end prefigures the enigmatic conclusions of modernist fiction.

Despite the de-emphasis upon plot, the overriding sense in Chekhov's story is that a turning-point has been reached although, as with the ending to 'A Simple Heart', this feeling might be an illusion. Critics, following the innovations of Joyce, tend to refer to such moments as *epiphanies*. In the surviving fragments of his unpublished novel, *Stephen Hero* (1904–6), Joyce's protagonist, Stephen Daedalus, describes an epiphany as 'a sudden spiritual manifestation', in which the viewer sees the underlying 'integrity', the 'wholeness, symmetry and radiance', within any chance occurrence (Joyce 1991: 216–17). The terms that Stephen uses are strikingly similar to those used by Edgar Allan Poe to describe the tales of Nathaniel Hawthorne, while the visual metaphor is also comparable to the language of literary impressionism. Consequently, epiphany as a turning-point or single effect that illuminates the sub-text of a short story has become a standard critical tool within short story criticism. Its usage, though, obscures the fact that epiphany pre-dates Joyce, for instance in William Wordsworth's allusion to 'spots in time' in *The Prelude* (Wordsworth 1995: 478, 479), and that Stephen is Joyce's ironic alter-ego, not his mouthpiece. Joyce's use of the epiphany should instead be seen as part of the emerging critical discourse between the neo-classical ideals of high modernism and the Romantic virtues of authentic and subjective expression. Following T. E. Hulme's essay 'Romanticism and Classicism' (1911), poets such as Richard Aldington, T. S. Eliot and Ezra Pound argued for a dry, hard and objective literary style in contrast with the intense feeling of Romanticism. Joyce's deployment of the epiphany, as opposed to Stephen's theorising, works to undercut Romantic sentiment.

'Eveline', for example, focuses upon the mixed emotions of its central character as she prepares to elope with Frank, a sailor. She dreams of a respectable, married life in Argentina, but her desires are expressed in romantic cliché:

> Escape! She must escape! Frank would save her. He would give her life, perhaps love, too. But she wanted to live. Why should she be unhappy? She had a right to happiness. Frank would take her in his arms, fold her in his arms. He would save her. (Joyce 2000: 28)

The ellipsis that follows in the text severs Eveline's moment of self-revelation from the final part of the narrative when she decides not to follow Frank onto the boat. In one sense, the ending confirms *Dubliners'* overall theme of paralysis at the expense of epiphany. In another sense, though, the ending is revealing for the reader, though not for Eveline, insofar as the absence of romantic closure implies that the text should be read again. Frank's heroic status is established in contrast with Eveline's fearsome father. Yet, Frank tells her 'tales of distant countries' and 'of the terrible Patagonians' (Joyce 2000: 27), stories that suggest that his claim of wealth is also a fabrication. In contrast, Eveline remembers genuine times when her father was generous and kind-hearted. In other words, the ending also acts as an epiphany, but one that undercuts illumination, and instead encourages us to re-read the story, to perceive the darkness that surrounds Eveline and obscures our understanding of her narrative. The reader re-enters the 'abyss of ambiguities' (James 1987: 500).

Katherine Mansfield achieves a similar effect in her story 'Bliss' (1918). Preparing for her party, Bertha Young experiences a childlike 'feeling of bliss – absolute bliss! – as though you'd suddenly swallowed a bright piece of that late afternoon and it burned in your bosom' (Mansfield 1984: 305). Later, as she and Pearl Fulton stand in the 'unearthly light' of the moon, gazing 'at the slender, flowering' pear tree and 'understanding each other perfectly', Bertha senses a 'blissful treasure that burned in their bosoms and dropped, in silver flowers, from their hair and hands' (Mansfield 1984: 312–13). But when Bertha realises that Pearl is having an affair with her husband, she turns to her pear tree to find it 'as lovely as ever and as full of flower and as still' (Mansfield 1984: 315). The story's conclusion suggests that the previous epiphany of Bertha and Pearl in the moonlight, including Bertha's tentative recognition of her same-sex desire for Pearl, is a delusion produced by Bertha's naïve and immature understanding of bliss. Yet, the narrative's intricate use of repeated symbols, phrases and mirror images undercuts this reading. Instead, this symbolic network is mediated through Bertha's own consciousness: she assigns meanings to objects and events that are otherwise arbitrary. To attribute a meaning to the silent pear tree, which is both 'as lovely as' Pearl and as unloving, is to replicate Bertha's own naïvety as a reader. Instead, the apocalyptic conclusion to the story not only calls epiphany into doubt but also the meaning of bliss. Whereas Bertha has previously associated bliss with romantic notions of love, joy and happiness, genuine bliss arises from the pain of revelation and insight. Far from undermining bliss itself, the story undercuts romantic conceptions, including the identification of epiphany with spiritual transcendence. Like Joyce's 'Eveline', the narrative structure of 'Bliss' is anti-transcendent: it returns both Bertha and her readers to the ambiguity of human relations.

Mansfield's own sense of personal identity was criss-crossed by her status as a colonial subject, her rejection of orthodox Christianity and middle-class childhood, her bisexuality and her uneasy friendships within the English avant-garde. Her fractured sense of self meant that she distrusted the 'stream of consciousness' techniques associated with writers such as Dorothy Richardson and Virginia Woolf. Richardson's 'The Garden' (1924), for example, describes a young child's experience of the natural world, except that the child has no clear sense of herself:

> There was no one there. The sound of feet and no one there. The gravel stopped making its noise when she stood still. When the last foot came down all the flowers stood still. (Richardson 1989: 21)

The disassociation between cause and effect is further complicated by the child's inability to organise her memories, so that past and present events converge to create a feeling of simultaneity. Similarly, in Woolf's 'The Mark on the Wall' (1917) the mysterious object becomes a co-ordinate for a random series of associations on the narrator's part, 'for of course there is not one reflection but an almost infinite number' (Woolf 2003: 79).

In contrast, Mansfield saw this interplay between subject and object as dissolving not only the self but also the social relations through which the self is constituted. There is something prematurely utopian about the position adopted by Richardson and Woolf. For example, in Mansfield's 'At the Bay' (1922), 'the relief' felt by the Burnell family occurs only when the father has gone to work: 'Their very voices were changed . . . they sounded warm and loving and as if they shared a secret' (Mansfield 1984: 446). This liberating space, though, is under-cut by the gender relations determined by the patriarchal order even when the man is absent: Linda, the mother, is terrified of having more children, Beryl, the eldest daughter, dreams of romance, Kezia and the other children adopt stereotypical roles in their games, while only Linda's mother, Mrs Fairfield, seems at ease now that she is freed from the prospect of childbirth. The family is also beset by two other men: Harry Kember, a married man who attempts to seduce Beryl, and Jonathan Trout, to whom Linda is attracted, but who is maudlin and melancholic. Consequently, while on the one hand Mansfield fears losing the self as a centre, on the other hand, she is aware that the self is already the product of external social and ideological forces. The self, then, becomes a site of conflict in Mansfield's fiction between forces that would subjugate the individual, for example the psychological repression that scars 'The Daughters of the Late Colonel' (1921), and half-expressed desires that might release the individual, for instance in 'Bliss' or 'The Escape' (1920). Yet, running through Mansfield's oeuvre, from early satires such as 'The Modern Soul' (1911) to 'Miss Brill' (1920), is the belief that the self may also be an illusion that deludes and incarcerates the individual. As one of Mansfield's most perceptive critics has written, she is 'at times, one of the toughest and darkest of the modernists' (Fullbrook 1986: 19).

In this respect, there is a surprising correspondence between Mansfield's fiction and that of Wyndham Lewis, who wavered between an almost sculptural sense of the self and a feeling that the self was non-existent (Ayers 1992). This internal debate was waged publicly in his attacks upon impressionism and the aesthetics of Bloomsbury as exercises in extreme subjectivity. Contrary to modern-ists such as Ford and Woolf, Lewis sought an art-form that was hard, objective and external, in which the individual subject was viewed with unsparing detachment. The stories that comprise *The Wild Body* (1927) were written and revised at various times from 1909 onwards until their final publication. Consequently, they offer an insight into

Lewis' developing aesthetic, in particular the role of humour. In his accompanying essay, 'The Meaning of the Wild Body', Lewis inverts the distinction between subject and object by arguing that 'all men are necessarily comic: for they are all *things*, or physical bodies, behaving as *persons*' (Lewis 2004: 158). Lewis regards conventional human behaviour as no more than a habit in which the participants, that is to say, you and I, act out the part of being human. Lewis' hero, the 'soldier of humour' known as Ker-Orr, realises this distinction and uses laughter and mischief as means of triumphing over those who still believe that they are anything but automata. Laughter, as Lewis intimates, reconnects the mind and body otherwise estranged by the activity of pretending to be human (Lewis 2004: 152–4). As an example of Lewis' technique, here Ker-Orr describes his sometime mentor, Bestre:

> His tongue stuck out, his lips eructated with the incredible indecorum that appears to be the monopoly of liquids, his brown arms were for the moment genitals, snakes in one massive twist beneath his mamillary slabs, gently riding on a pancreatic swell, each hair on his oil-bearing skin contributing its message of porcine affront. (Lewis 2004: 77)

What appeared in the 1920s to be a dead-end in terms of literary style, a symptom of Lewis' self-exile from the rest of modernism, would influence postmodernists such as Will Self and Iain Sinclair who similarly twist and contort language and perspective.

Gertrude Stein and American Modernism

If Wyndham Lewis, partially by design, appears to be a maverick figure within the history of the modernist short story, then it is another apparent misfit, Gertrude Stein, who was most influential in the exchange between European and American models of literary modernism. Stein's work is discussed more fully in a later chapter but, suffice to say, her avant-garde salon in Montparnasse Avenue became a focal-point for American émigrés to Paris, such as Sherwood Anderson, F. Scott Fitzgerald and Ernest Hemingway. In her first published work, *Three Lives* (1909), Stein drew upon the inspiration of Post-Impressionist artists such as Paul Cézanne and Henri Matisse.

The opening story, 'The Good Anna', freely rewrites Flaubert's 'A Simple Heart', but whereas Flaubert's narrative still obeys causality, Stein's story is composed in blocks akin to Post-Impressionist techniques that disrupt linear progression:

> Lindheims was Anna's favorite store, for there they had bargain days, when flour and sugar were sold for a quarter of a cent less for a pound, and there the heads of the departments were all her friends and always managed to give her the bargain prices, even on other days.
>
> Anna led an arduous and troubled life.
>
> Anna managed the whole little house for Miss Mathilda. It was a funny little house, one of a whole row of all the same kind that made a close pile like a row of dominoes that a child knocks over. (Stein 1990: 3)

The beginning of Stein's project to disassociate cause from effect, word from object, inspired Sherwood Anderson: 'words used by the tale-teller were as the colors used by the painter' (in Current-García and Patrick 1974: 72). Although Stein moved increasingly towards abstraction, Anderson saw in her technique the means of rendering an authentic American idiom at the expense of literary contrivance. This authentic voice can be heard in the opening to 'I Want to Know Why' (1918):

> We got up at four in the morning, that first day in the east. On the evening before we had climbed off a freight train at the edge of town, and with the true instinct of Kentucky boys had found our way across town and to the race track and the stables at once. Then we knew we were all right. (Anderson 1998: 8)

The simplicity of Anderson's style alongside the complexity of his themes, implying the many-sidedness of even the plainest of lives, appealed directly to Ernest Hemingway. His experiences of working as an ambulance driver in World War One deeply affected Hemingway as he suggests in his novel *A Farewell to Arms* (1929):

> I was always embarrassed by the words sacred, glorious, and sacrifice and the expression in vain . . . I had seen nothing sacred, and the things that were glorious had no glory and the sacrifices were like the stockyards at Chicago if nothing was done with the meat except to bury it. There were many words

that you could not stand to hear and finally only the names of places had dignity. Certain numbers were the same way and certain dates and these with the names of the places were all you could say and have them mean anything. (Hemingway 2005: 165)

Hemingway's external method, then, is quite different from another war veteran such as Wyndham Lewis. Whereas Lewis' technique exposes the absurdity of human pretence, Hemingway's shunning of metaphor and simile in favour of adjectives and concrete nouns is a way of sustaining human courage in the face of untold emotional distress. As Hemingway notes, 'the dignity of movement of an iceberg is due to only one-eighth of it being above water' (Hemingway 1932: 183). Despite the frequent and understandable accusations of male chauvinism, Hemingway's lean style is at its best when communicating inexpressible hurt.

A fine example of this effect is 'Hills Like White Elephants' (1927). An anonymous man and woman sit in a bar at a Spanish railway station. Their dialogue is emotionally unaffected ('he said', 'she said'), is circular and contradictory, the hills 'look like white elephants' and then they don't (Hemingway 1993: 262–3). The man mentions an operation, so 'awfully simple' that it's 'not really an operation at all' (Hemingway 1993: 263). He repeats that it will 'let the air in' (a euphemism or an actual technique?), she plays with a bead curtain (is she Catholic? do the beads stand in place of a rosary?). He insists that 'if you don't want to you don't have to' (Hemingway 1993: 264), she responds she will do it if it will make him happy. The man attempts to encourage her: 'we can have everything . . . we can have the whole world.' She replies that 'it isn't ours any more' (an allusion to the biblical Fall?). He refers to a 'they' who 'haven't taken it away', and says 'I don't want anybody but you' (reassurance? statement? threat?) (Hemingway 1993: 265). At last she breaks, 'Would you please please please please please please please stop talking?' (Hemingway 1993: 266), the sheer repetition emphasising the constant pain in being forced to talk about something that otherwise is so damaging that it cannot be expressed. Critics have speculated that this 'something' is an abortion but the text offers no conclusive evidence. Instead, what can be deduced is that the text throws up possible ways in which it can be read while, at the same time, the fragile dialogue teeters upon collapsing into a meaningless void, the '*nada*' or nothingness that serves as the keynote to the later story, 'A Clean, Well-Lighted Place' (1933).

Hemingway's sense of nullity is felt also by William Faulkner, for instance in 'That Evening Sun' (1931), one of several stories featuring the Compson family from his novel *The Sound and the Fury* (1929). Here, Quentin Compson narrates an episode from his childhood when their Negro cook, Nancy, sought refuge from her violent husband, the ironically named Jesus. Although Mr Compson is sympathetic, he insists that Nancy should return. Secretly, she convinces the children to go with her, but when she is no longer able to amuse them, she pleads with them:

> 'Listen. Tell him. Tell him we going to have fun. Tell him I take good care of yawl until in the morning. Tell him to let me come home with yawl and sleep on the floor. Tell him I won't need no pallet. We'll have fun. You member last time how we had so much fun?'
>
> 'I didn't have fun,' Jason said. 'You hurt me. You put smoke in my eyes. I'm going to tell.' (Faulkner 1985: 306)

Nancy's desperation is matched by the children's incomprehension at her plight, a product of the racism that underwrites the community and which is already affecting the children's, especially Jason's, perception of their servants. While in one sense, the spare and anecdotal structure of the story recalls the tall tales of the Southern oral tradition, such as Mark Twain, in another sense, the episodic and sketch-like quality emphasises that linear narrative is impossible where racism pollutes and contaminates communication between, and within, the races. Yet, in focusing upon the articulation of a national idiom, American modernists, like their British counterparts, explored new methods in which the unknowability of existence could be given artistic form.

Further Reading

There are several guides to modernism: see, for example, Michael Levenson (1984), Peter Nicholls (1995) and Randall Stevenson (1998). On the relationship between impressionism and modernism, see James Nagel (1980) and Jesse Matz (2001). Studies of the modernist short story include Clare Hanson (1985) and Dominic Head (1992). For individual writers, see Daphna Erdinast-Vulcan on Joseph Conrad (1999), Sandra Kemp (1988) and Jan Montefiore (2007) on Rudyard Kipling, and Kate Fullbrook (1986) and Sydney Janet Kaplan (1991) on Katherine Mansfield. On Joyce, see the special *Dubliners* issue of the *James Joyce Quarterly* (1991). For Mansfield's own views of Dorothy Richardson and Virginia Woolf, see her *Critical Writings* (1987). Martin Scofield (2006) gives an overview of several American modernists.

10

The Short Story Cycle

As the previous chapter argued, modernist writers were drawn to the meaninglessness of contemporary existence in order to give it a tentative significance in the form of art. This response meant that the strategies of linear narrative and authorial omniscience, key components to Victorian novels such as George Eliot's *Middlemarch* (1871), were discarded for forms that were partial, open-ended and fleeting. For, as Virginia Woolf wrote in her essay 'Modern Novels' (1919):

> Is it not possible that the accent falls a little differently, that the moment of importance came before or after, that, if one were free and could set down what one chose, there would be no plot, little probability, and a vague general confusion in which the clear-cut features of the tragic, the comic, the passionate, and the lyrical were dissolved beyond the possibility of separate recognition? (Woolf 1988: 33)

Yet, modernist writers stopped short of absolute dissolution, an aesthetic of scattering and fragmentation associated with the avant-garde (see Chapter 17). Following in the wake of precise stylists such as Gustave Flaubert and Anton Chekhov, modernists such as James Joyce and Ernest Hemingway sought methods of capturing the many points of view that constitute an objective reality without either dissolving the text altogether or subsuming these multiple perspectives within the homogenising tendency of the realist novel. Instead, they found a solution in the use of interlinked short stories, described variously by critics as a 'cycle', 'sequence' or 'composite novel'. Since the high-point of modernism, the form has proved remarkably popular, considering the low sales of short story books, while blurring the boundary between what constitutes a short story collection and a novel.

Taxonomy of the Short Story Cycle

The word 'taxonomy' describes a system of classification. The history of short story criticism has largely been concerned with questions of taxonomy, in particular the essential features that define the short story. Until now I have avoided this issue, agreeing with reader-response critics such as Hans Robert Jauss that literary forms evolve in relation to our constantly shifting 'horizons of expectation'. The taxonomic debate that surrounds the short story cycle, though, cannot be ignored.

The term 'short story cycle' was popularised by Forrest Ingram at the start of the 1970s and given greater currency, in the late 1980s, by Susan Garland Mann. Between them, Ingram and Mann defined the short story cycle as either a pre-conceived set of related tales, such as Joyce's *Dubliners* (1914), a series of tales that expands in order to elaborate a theme discovered in the course of the writing, for example William Faulkner's *The Unvanquished* (1938), or separate tales that are reassembled so as to form a recognisable pattern, for instance John Updike's *Olinger Stories* (1964). The stories may be unified through the use of a recurring character, such as Rocío Esquibel in Denise Chávez's *The Last of the Menu Girls* (1986), a location or community, for instance in Sherwood Anderson's *Winesburg, Ohio* (1919), or a dominant motif such as the theme of motherhood that recurs in Helen Simpson's *Hey Yeah Right, Get a Life* (2000). The tendency in both Ingram and Mann is to emphasise formal unity within the short story cycle, an extension of the New Critical principle that the short story constitutes a closed and self-sufficient unit.

In contrast, critics such as Robert Luscher and J. Gerald Kennedy have argued that the cycle should instead be regarded as a sequence, in which themes and motifs progressively develop, so that while the stories can be read both individually and as part of a whole, the act of reading becomes the accumulated perception of successive orderings and repeated patterns. This accumulative process underlines Luscher's ideal of what he describes as 'an open book'. Here, the reader is invited 'to construct a network of associations that binds the stories together and lends them cumulative thematic impact' (in Lohafer and Clary 1989: 149). Despite the suggestion of openness, however, the emphasis upon sequential reading restricts the degree of open-endedness that critics have claimed. Instead of emphasising the non-linearity of texts such as Hemingway's *In Our Time* (1925), the idea of the short story sequence glosses these aspects of reading in order to preserve the sequence as a whole.

More recently, Maggie Dunn and Ann Morris have proposed the notion of a 'composite novel' in which an extended narrative is composed not only from shorter prose sections but also other genres such as poetry and drama. Jean Toomer's *Cane* (1923) and Leslie Marmon Silko's *Storyteller* (1981) might be regarded as examples of this hybrid form. Yet, a brief comparison between *Cane* and another collage-based text, William Carlos Williams' *Spring and All* (also 1923), suggests the limitations of this idea. Originally, Williams' text was published with fictional vignettes separating his poems. Yet, for most readers, *Spring and All* is regarded as a poetry collection while *Cane*, despite featuring poems in-between the prose, is typically regarded as a book of short stories. In other words, whatever intentions there might have been behind their composition, their classification is dependent upon the uses to which they are put by their readers. The idea of the composite novel tends to gloss the extent to which subjective interpretation plays in how these texts are perceived and understood.

Instead, the emergence of the composite novel, in which the short story cycle plays only one part, can be diagnosed as a symptom of the modernist legacy, in particular the episodic structures of novels such as D. H. Lawrence's *Women in Love* (1921) and Virginia Woolf's *To the Lighthouse* (1927). The increasing tendency towards episodism in the contemporary novel is apparent in texts such as Ali Smith's *Hotel World* (2001), Adam Thorpe's *Ulverton* (1992) and David Mitchell's *Ghostwritten* (1999), the last subtitled as 'A Novel in Nine Parts'. Increasingly, the boundaries between the novel and the short story cycle are dissolved, so that the question becomes not what defines the short story cycle but what defines the novel? Although postmodern novels such as Mark Z. Danielewski's *House of Leaves* (2001), with its blend of text and image, appear to be innovative and contemporary, in another sense the experimental novel is returning to the typographical play of eighteenth-century novels such as Samuel Richardson's *Clarissa* (1747–8) or Laurence Sterne's *Tristram Shandy* (1759–67). In other words, the concept of the composite novel cannot adequately redefine the short story cycle since it is itself symptomatic of far wider tendencies within modern fiction.

Critical definitions also gloss the extent to which publishers exert a taxonomic influence by promoting short story cycles, such as Sandra Cisneros' *The House on Mango Street* and Louise Erdrich's *Love Medicine* (both 1984), as if they were novels. Instead, a more pragmatic approach to the question of the short story cycle is required, as indicated by Cisneros' own comments on her method of composition:

> I wanted to write a series of stories that you could open up at any point. You didn't have to know anything before or after and you would understand each story like a little pearl, or you could look at the whole thing like a necklace. (quoted in Kelley 1997: 74)

Cisneros' repeated emphasis upon 'you', the reader, transfers responsibility from the act of interpretation to the activity of reading: discernment through readerly pleasure. Consequently, another approach to the short story cycle might be through the enjoyment of reading and, before that, of listening to how stories are told.

1001: A Textual Odyssey

The historical roots of the short story cycle lie within the oral tradition and, in particular, medieval novellas such as Boccaccio's *Decameron* or Chaucer's *The Canterbury Tales*. The effectiveness of these texts is largely dependent upon the framing of their narratives. For example, Chaucer's 'The Clerk's Tale', which also appears in Boccaccio, tells the story of Griselda, whose patience is tested by her aristocratic husband. The story is complicated, though, by the fact that the Clerk's narration is framed by the prologue told by Chaucer's anonymous narrator, which in turn is framed by its relationship to the other tales in the collection that, ultimately, are framed by the 'General Prologue', in which the characters are first introduced and the purpose of the pilgrimage described. Consequently, the meaning(s) of 'The Clerk's Tale' are understandable only in relation to its position within the open-ended, or dialogic, structure of the whole. The importance of narrative framing, then, is integral not only to the medieval novella but also the short story cycle.

This tendency is repeatedly seen in *The Thousand and One Nights*. Dating back some three-thousand years, the tales were popularised in

Western Europe at the start of the eighteenth century. Besides their atmospheric content, the narrative design of the tales was also influential. Following his wife's execution for infidelity, King Shahriyar takes an innocent bride every night before putting her to death at sunrise. Shahrazad volunteers to marry the King in order to stop the killings. Her plan is to ask permission to see her sister, Dunyazad, one last time and to tell her a story. By the power of her storytelling, Shahrazad charms the King so that she may be reprieved for one more night. Eventually, after a thousand and one nights, she rehabilitates the King, but to achieve this result Shahrazad's tales must be rich, dense and multi-layered. Frequently, as in 'The Tale of the Hunchback', which becomes so complicated that the starting-point is almost lost, there are tales within tales within tales. The cessation of death is effectively exchanged for the pleasure of storytelling, for life in all of its forms, registers and nuances. As the collective title indicates, a thousand symbolising infinity plus one, the novella veers not only towards plurality but also excess. One of the central lessons, then, that *The Thousand and One Nights* teaches for an understanding of the short story cycle is that a cyclical narrative does not necessarily produce an enclosed structure, but rather, an open and concentric design in which multiple narratives circle one another. Like a circular argument, the short story cycle can be contradictory and paradoxical rather than formal and closed.

Modernity and the Short Story Cycle

The narrative framework of the short story cycle is historically embedded in the oral tradition, in the mutability of storytelling and in the social structures that supported folk culture. As Walter Benjamin observed (in Chapter 3), the disintegration of those structures under the impact of economic modernity, and the growth of a professional print culture, meant that the communication of folk wisdom became weaker. Yet, whereas Benjamin contrasts the brevity of the short story with the richness of the traditionally spun folktale, both the construction and the incentive that lie behind the short story cycle – the desire to produce a work in which the sum of the parts is greater than that of the whole – reconnect as residual elements of oral culture. The emergence of the short story cycle during the nineteenth century, as the minor counterpart of the novel, is implicated in the social changes caused by the effect of modernity upon traditional ways of life.

The most influential of the early short story cycles was Ivan Turgenev's *Sketches from a Hunter's Album* (1852). Here, Turgenev records the lives of the Russian peasantry as observed by his interested, dispassionate, aristocratic huntsman. Representative of Turgenev's technique is the story 'Bezhin Lea', which begins with a richly evocative account of the Russian countryside. So successful at his game, and so distracted by the surrounding beauty, the huntsman stays out late and loses his way home. He is forced to spend the night, sitting around a camp fire, with a group of peasant boys as they guard their horses. The huntsman lies 'down apart from them', 'from time to time look[ing] in their direction' (Turgenev 1967: 57), while he overhears their conversation of ghost stories, folktales and rural customs. Turgenev, therefore, dramatises the way in which folktale collectors, such as Giambattista Basile and Giovan Straparola, had traditionally garnered their tales through chance encounters with the lower orders. Yet, unlike the peasant boys, the huntsman is an educated man and he retells their dialogue with a professionalism that emphasises the disparity between his own learning and the vanishing way of life that he describes. On a last, poignant note, the huntsman records that one of the boys died later that year. His death is not only symbolic of a disappearing peasant culture but also of the shortness of life: a grim yet true realism that counters the nostalgia of the huntsman's introduction into which we might all lose ourselves.

Turgenev's balance of symbolism and realism influenced a number of writers following his translation in the 1880s, among them the Irish author George Moore. Moore had made his reputation through naturalistic novels, such as *Esther Waters* (1894), but he adopted a more symbolic style for his short story cycle *The Untilled Field* (1903). Previous to Moore, the most faithful treatment of the Irish rural poor had been offered by William Carleton in two series, *Traits and Stories of the Irish Peasantry*, published in the early 1830s. A product himself of the Irish working classes, Carleton had drawn upon his own experiences in order to present an unromantic portrait of rural Ireland. The decimation of the Irish peasantry following the Great Famine of 1845–9 resulted in its surviving members being treated either as nostalgic or humorous remnants, for example in Edith Somerville and

Martin Ross' *Some Experiences of an Irish RM* (1899). As an expatriate member of the 'Celtic Revival', the exercise in cultural nationalism of organisations such as the Gaelic League, Moore sought to revive a distinct Irish identity by focusing upon the lives of rural communities. Unlike Carleton, though, Moore assumed some of the dispassion associated with Turgenev in order to set his characters into historical context. *The Untilled Field*, then, is important not only as a work of literary nationalism but also in its political use of the short story cycle. It appropriates the address of nineteenth-century novelists, such as Charles Dickens, Leo Tolstoy and Emile Zola, towards the state of their respective nations while, at the same time, declining to resolve that address into a single continuous narrative. Nevertheless, Moore's anti-clericalism unsettles the dispassionate tone while his vision of Ireland remains late Victorian: strangely depopulated and melancholic, anti-urban and anti-modern.

Moore had no direct influence upon James Joyce. Three of the stories that became *Dubliners* (1914) had already been drafted before Joyce read *The Untilled Field*. Yet, Moore's text could be said to be an influence by embodying what Joyce sought to oppose in the writing of *Dubliners*. As Joyce saw it, Moore's nationalism represented part of the paralysis that acts as the central motif of *Dubliners* by seeking to purify Irish culture and reclaim a mythical origin. Nationalist politics, according to Joyce, actually held Ireland back by refusing to see the past as an invention. Instead, they contributed to the political limbo of Ireland caught between the past and the future, the rural and the urban, the Catholic Church and the British Empire. *Dubliners* contrasts with *The Untilled Field* not only through its lack of political commitment but also through its concentration upon individual lives set against the backdrop of the city. While, on the one hand, the short story cycle has been used successfully to create a sense of regional identity, on the other hand, it has been an effective tool in describing the modern city where social ties are looser, kinship systems less structured and personal identity more alienated (see Chapters 12 and 13).

As if to offset the sense of fragmentation in *Dubliners*, the final story, 'The Dead', is the longest in the collection and draws together the central themes of the text. Gabriel Conroy, an educated middle-class man who regards himself as cultured, is to speak at a New Year's Eve party held by his sister-in-law. He frets over the wording of his speech, fusses over his appearance, and worries about his standing within the family. Gabriel disregards his wife, Gretta, until 'in a dark part of the hall' he sees 'a woman . . . standing near the top of the first flight, in the shadow also.' He slowly realises that it is his wife and that she is listening silently to a far-off tune. Shrouded in darkness, Gabriel is faced with an ethical decision, to see Gretta as he has not seen her before, but instead Gabriel treats the moment as an aesthetic experience:

> He asked himself what is a woman standing on the stairs in the shadow, listening to distant music, a symbol of. If he were a painter he would paint her in that attitude. Her blue felt hat would show off the bronze of her hair against the darkness and the dark panels of her skirt would show off the light ones. *Distant Music* he would call the picture if he were a painter. (Joyce 2000: 165)

Subsequently, Gabriel learns that the tune was sung by a boy who was in love with Gretta, and who died a week after she left Galway for Dublin. As Gretta sleeps, and as snow falls outside, Gabriel experiences a feeling of revelation: 'Generous tears filled Gabriel's eyes. He had never felt like that himself towards any woman but he knew that such a feeling must be love' (Joyce 2000: 176). Yet, how can the reader be so sure? Gretta has previously called Gabriel 'generous' (Joyce 2000: 171), but on the basis of very little evidence, since the story's point of view is focused around Gabriel. Generous can also mean copious and Gabriel has, if nothing else, an expansive view of himself. Even as he lies in bed, considering the proximity of life to death, Gabriel is thinking of himself: the words that he will 'cast about in his mind for' and find 'only lame and useless' (Joyce 2000: 175). His supposed transcendence re-enacts the paralysis and delusion that entrap all of Joyce's characters while the responsibility to the dead, symbolised by the falling snow, continues to weigh upon the living.

Among the texts indebted to *Dubliners* was Sherwood Anderson's *Winesburg, Ohio* (1919). Most of the stories are seen from the point of view of George Willard, a young journalist, who is unwittingly told tales by members of the community. In some of the stories, though, George is also a participant, so that he is not a dispassionate observer like Turgenev's narrator. The stories that feature George seem to amount to a *bildungsroman*, or educational novel, in which George learns about the world around him and finds his place within it. George, though, is remarkably inattentive and he rarely understands either the stories he has been told or the situations in which he finds himself. His incomprehension transfers the responsibility of interpretation to the reader, but this displacement also means that the reader is less likely to sympathise with George. The *bildungsroman* element is also weakened by the narrative gaps that emerge between stories: the necessary links between cause and effect are missing, while in some of the stories, such as 'Godliness', George is himself absent.

Instead, *Winesburg, Ohio* is less a unified work that comes together in the development of George than a fractured text that describes the historical discontinuities within American progress. Anderson supplies an additional framework to George's narrative through a preface, 'The Book of the Grotesque', an unpublished memoir of an old writer featuring all the grotesques he has known, the people who built their lives around a truth, and in doing so, 'embraced . . . a falsehood' (Anderson 1976: 24). An anonymous 'I', though, disturbs the authority of the preface: the old writer may himself be a grotesque. In that sense, he complements the characters that constitute Winesburg, Ohio, a neglected backwater in the wave of expansion from East to West during the nineteenth century. Instead, like Wing Biddlebaum in the opening story, 'Hands', they lead isolated lives haunted by years of social and sexual repression. Just as Joyce undercuts Gabriel Conroy's final attempt at transcendence, so Anderson undercuts any account that reads *Winesburg, Ohio* as a unified narrative. George's departure seems, at best, a provisional ending as the text dissolves into the historical mess of lived experience.

History and Trauma: War in the Short Story Cycle

Among the American writers inspired by Anderson was Ernest Hemingway. His debut, *In Our Time* (1925), was Hemingway's first attempt to come to terms with his war experience. The collection is composed, first, from a series of stories that feature Hemingway's alter-ego, Nick Adams; second, a set of vignettes that Hemingway had published in Paris in 1924 and which he incorporated as chapter breaks between the stories; and last, an array of stories, all of which, apart from 'Cat in the Rain', Hemingway had previously published. Hemingway added 'The End of Something', 'The Three Day Blow' and 'The Battler' to the opening sequence of stories so as to establish Nick's *bildungsroman*. As in *Winesburg, Ohio*, this narrative element is rendered discontinuous by the chapter breaks, the first five of which are narrated by an anonymous first-person, while the sixth switches to third-person in order to describe Nick's shooting. Thereafter, beginning with the sixth piece, 'A Very Short Story', the *bildungsroman* is submerged within the collection until Nick returns in the twelfth story, 'Cross-Country Snow'. Hemingway's inclusion of the last and longest story, 'Big Two-Hearted River', with its symbolism of emotional redemption through physical contest, seems to confer a unity upon the text. Yet, just as Joyce undercuts the epiphany of 'The Dead', so 'Big Two-Hearted River' is queried by the final, enigmatic vignette, 'L'Envoi'. To focus upon the Nick Adams stories loses sight not only of their relationship to the whole but also their displacement. Like *Winesburg, Ohio*, the closure to *In Our Time* is tentative and open-ended.

An alternative approach is to think of *In Our Time* as a collage in which narrative fragments are juxtaposed with one another, and ideas are forced into expression through the collision of elements, but are not necessarily resolved. The scarring and suturing of the text act as analogies to physical mutilation. One of the many casualties of war, as Paul Fussell shows in *The Great War and Modern Memory* (1975), is the linear narrative: the ability to tell a story straight is irredeemably affected by the stop-start procedure of trench warfare, in which intense bursts of violence are contrasted with long periods of boredom. World War One had a profound effect upon the development of modernism, but in *In Our Time* it emerges most graphically in the textual arrangement, whereby narrative elements are suspended in relation to one another just as the wounded mind and body never quite heal.

This irresolution determines not only war-related stories, such as 'Soldier's Home', but also tales of flawed romance, such as 'Mr and Mrs Elliot'. Marriage, the traditional resolution of romantic narrative, is used here as the starting-point, while the inability of Cornelia to conceive is rendered in a stylistic echo of Gertrude Stein's aesthetic of repetition. The barrenness of the marriage is contrasted with Hubert's

ability to write 'very long poems very rapidly.' A virgin until marry-
ing Cornelia, fifteen years his senior, Hubert prides himself on his
purity, 'the same purity of mind and body that he expected of her'
(Hemingway 1993: 153). Through a metaphorical association with
his writing, Hubert's sexual incompetence is shown to be rooted in
his puritanical attitude towards Cornelia: 'He was very severe about
mistakes and would make her re-do an entire page if there was one
mistake' (Hemingway 1993: 155). Cornelia begs Hubert for her
(unnamed) girl friend to join them at a château in Touraine. She
not only becomes Hubert's typist but replaces him as Cornelia's
bed-partner. Hubert lives separately, writing 'a great deal of poetry
during the night', and appearing 'in the morning . . . very exhausted.'
Cornelia and her friend, meanwhile, share 'many a good cry together'
(Hemingway 1993: 156). The story's final sentence acts as a tableau,
in which the use of co-ordination, so that no part of the sentence is
more significant than any other part, establishes their *ménage a trois*.
Without mentioning the War, the story is still related to the wartime
themes that pervade the collection, in particular the renegotiation of
gender roles. The symbolism of Hubert's emasculation is contrasted
with the poetic figure of the matador that appears in the later vignettes,
and with Nick's personal recovery through his sporting contest with
the natural world.

Isaac Babel's *Red Cavalry* (1926) also achieves a similar collage
effect through its varied use of literary registers. Babel worked as a
correspondent during the disastrous Soviet–Polish War (1920–1).
Without directly criticising the military leadership, Babel offered an
unromantic view of army life that sided with the common soldier and
countered the unalloyed heroism of state propaganda. The extreme
brevity of the stories means that they act as a cluster of oddly positioned fragments, in which their totality is further dissolved by their
presentation in the form of diary entries, letters and reports. Like
Hemingway, Babel invents for himself an alter-ego, Kiril Lyutov, who
acts as both an observer and, through his pro-Russian sentiments, as
a shield for Babel. Unlike Hemingway, though, Babel narrates stories
from the point of view of other characters, such as the murderous
Balmashov, who shoots an unarmed woman in the story 'Salt': 'And I
took the loyal rifle from the wall and wiped that blot off the face of the
working land and the republic' (Babel 2002: 276). This disquieting use

of first-person and multiple narrators, alongside vivid descriptions of military fighting, creates a moral chaos in which no history of violence can be properly accounted for.

Among contemporary writers, Tim O'Brien is notable for his attempt to rethink the meaning of history in relation to warfare. In novels, memoirs and short stories, he has returned repeatedly to the subject of the Vietnam War, the conflict in which he himself served. In 'How to Tell a True War Story', republished as part of *The Things They Carried* (1990), the narrator observes that 'you can tell a true war story if you just keep on telling it' (O'Brien 1991: 80), and indeed, this story retells the same event from different angles in different styles. O'Brien extends this principle throughout his collection, so that the same emotional and physical territory is retraced by narratives that overlap and counterpoint one another, while characters recur from story to story. The historical event of Vietnam forces narrative into being – it is a story that has to be told – but no single narrative can encompass its meaning. As in Babel, the authenticity of reportage dissolves, for as the character Mitchell Sanders observes:

> For the common soldier, at least, war has the feel – the spiritual texture – of a great ghostly fog, thick and permanent. There is no clarity. Everything swirls. The old rules are no longer binding, the old truths no longer true. (O'Brien 1991: 78)

Even this passage is not necessarily to be taken as authentic, since Sanders' observation is retold by the older version of O'Brien's fictional self. Evidence of a violent event is no longer to be trusted, since 'there is always that surreal seemingness, which makes the story seem untrue, but which in fact represents the hard and exact truth as it *seemed*' (O'Brien 1991: 70). It would instead appear that in order to retell the historical effect that war has upon individuals, history has to abandon any claim to authenticity and reclaim the mutability of storytelling as a shared experience: 'You can tell a true war story by the way it never seems to end' (O'Brien 1991: 73). For, ultimately, 'a true war story is never about war': 'It's about love and memory. It's about sisters. It's about sisters who never write back and people who never listen' (O'Brien 1991: 80).

History and Memory: Ethnicity in the Short Story Cycle

The American short story cycle has flourished alongside a contemporary awareness of ethnic identity. Important precursors within the African–American tradition include not only Jean Toomer but also Richard Wright and Paule Marshall. More recent examples from various ethnic traditions include Denise Chávez, Maxine Hong Kingston and Gloria Naylor. The high proportion of female practitioners is significant. Women writers, such as Sarah Orne Jewett in *The Country of the Pointed Firs* (1896) and Jean Rhys in *The Left Bank* (1927), have often turned to the short story cycle where the looser, more episodic structure entails a difference in point(s) of view from the traditional novel. For the purpose of this summary, I shall limit myself to four texts: Julia Alvarez's *How the García Girls Lost Their Accents* (1991), Sandra Cisneros' *The House on Mango Street*, Louise Erdrich's *Love Medicine* (both 1984) and Amy Tan's *The Joy Luck Club* (1989).

All four texts play with notions of chronology. Cisneros recounts the maturation of her protagonist, Esperanza Cordero, in forty-four vignettes, so that causal links are either broken or misplaced. Erdrich's family saga of the Kashpaws and the Lamartines begins in 1981, retreats to 1934, and then proceeds by leaps and bounds to 1984. Tan tells her story of mothers and daughters in four sections, each section consisting of a further four stories told alternately by either one of the parents or one of their children. Alvarez follows Yolanda García back to the Dominican Republic by reversing the chronology, so that she starts in 1989 and finishes in 1956. These experiments in chronology describe the experiences of migration and colonisation whereby the individual's sense of personal and collective history is subject to the dominant discourse of the coloniser, in each of these instances white, Anglo-Saxon, Protestant America. The break with chronology does not so much suggest liberation as alienation: the impossibility for the individual to reclaim his/her authentic history without the contaminating influence of the oppressor.

Each of these texts describes history in terms of family networks. Although Tim O'Brien is also concerned with the authenticity of historical narrative, his fictional self remembers comrades, such as Rat Kiley and Mitchell Sanders, whom he knew during a brief but intense period. By contrast, the four ethnic writers more closely resemble William Faulkner, who recounted the decline of the American South through the disintegration of the family in texts that frequently blur the boundary between novel and short story cycle. Yet, they are also indebted to their own oral traditions: *Love Medicine* draws upon the structure of Native American folktales while *The Joy Luck Club* utilises Chinese mythology. Consequently, literary and folk traditions are intertwined, a hybrid form that inscribes the contamination of authentic history while also complementing the mutability that runs through the network of family relations. For these female writers, the family with its in-built ties and attractions becomes a more apt metaphor for the vagaries of historical experience than the intense, but also alienating, environment of *The Things They Carried*.

While other short storywriters, notably Susan Minot, have explored the conflicts that exist within the family, these four writers set these tensions within the contingency of historical change. The family is regarded simultaneously as both a defence and as insecure to outside influence. Poverty, racism and loss underwrite the family in each of the texts. These factors drive Esperanza to seek a wealthier life away from Mango Street while Yolanda and Jing-Mei Woo, in *The Joy Luck Club*, seek reconciliation by revisiting their motherlands. Yet, in becoming the storyteller of *The House on Mango Street*, Esperanza only goes 'away to come back' (Cisneros 1991: 110). Each text circles in upon itself, enacting a melancholic recall, which in *Love Medicine* is given an overriding ethical imperative by the historical mistreatment of the Native American peoples. A new sense of personal identity is forged through the retracing of memory and its associations, a fresh awareness that discards the purity and authenticity of the self for something both more unstable and more inclusive at the same time. Consequently, the non-linearity that characterises each text also complements this sense of the self as both a social and historical process. It is this belief that gives each text its ultimate feeling of optimism despite the underlying pain and hardship.

Terminus: The Atrocity Exhibition

Of contemporary short story cycles, J. G. Ballard's *The Atrocity Exhibition* (1970) is perhaps the most circular of all. Assembled from pieces that were originally published in underground magazines such as *New Worlds* during the late 1960s, the text defies orthodox criteria of readability and comprehension. The plot concerns a psychiatrist, known in different stories by a different name each beginning with the letter 'T', who has suffered a nervous breakdown. His mental collapse seems to stem from the meaninglessness of the consumer society, in which traumatic events such as the assassination of John F. Kennedy become commodities within the ceaseless flow of media and information. Recognising himself as a relay within this system, 'T' seeks to negate its insignificance by restaging historical events in ways that are both analogous and meaningful to him. 'T' designs a series of scenarios, most of which end in the virtual death of another character, Karen Novotny. Since the woman is posited as the site of meaning, and since her significance can only be brought to book within a narrative account that always ends in her death, the text cannot progress by accumulating meaning. Instead, this serial killing of the same person merely accretes significances that are neither resolved nor countered, but shadow the excess of media-based data. Rather than successfully exploding the meaninglessness that surrounds him, the activities of 'T' ensnare him ever further, so that by the later episodes, he has practically disappeared from the text by dissolving into it.

The repetitiveness of the text is predicated upon 'T'' s reversal of the chronograms of Étienne-Jules Marey. During the 1880s, Marey had devised a system of time-lapse photography so that he could record the exact motion of moving objects. 'T', by contrast, treats objects 'as if they were already chronograms and extract[s] the element of time' (Ballard 1993: 5). Without the existence of duration, objects reside simultaneously within the same space-time: 'The concrete landscape of underpass and overpass mediated a more real presence, the geometry of a neural interval, the identity latent within his own musculature' (Ballard 1993: 14). Human beings become geometrical arrangements in an extension of Wyndham Lewis' claim in *The Wild Body* (1927): 'The young woman was a geometric equation, the demonstration model of a landscape' (Ballard 1993: 40). Ballard's bizarre use of simile, 'overhead wires like some forgotten algebra of the sky', and his elision of incompatible linguistic registers, 'neuronic icons on the spinal highway' (Ballard 1993: 47), equates his writing with surrealist practice. As in the paintings of Salvador Dali, the inner and outer worlds of the psyche become fused and intertwined. Yet, Ballard's division of his stories into sub-sections that become a narrative in themselves also recalls the methods of Cubism, in particular collage, while his fascination with the iconography of the mass media explicitly references Pop Artists such as Andy Warhol. In other words, a number of distinct avant-garde techniques are harnessed, including the random and repetitive methods of Dada that ultimately dissolve and negate the text. The many permutations of the twentieth-century avant-garde are not only rehearsed but also absorbed by *The Atrocity Exhibition*.

The lack of an external reference-point, in itself a problem of taxonomy, underlines the enigma posed by Ballard's text. Simultaneously a work of science fiction and the avant-garde, written when both high and low art came into contact with another set of discourses, namely the consumer society and its mirror image, the counter-culture, *The Atrocity Exhibition* embodies the problematic inherent to this engagement. The text cannot adequately be defined as either science fiction or avant-garde, modernist or postmodern, critical or reflective. Instead, it calls into question the categories by which fiction is routinely read, and in that respect *The Atrocity Exhibition* is a useful test-case by which to reassess short story criticism. In particular, it explodes the taxonomic dispute with which I began this chapter. While unlike nearly all of the short story cycles I have discussed, with the exception of Hemingway who is pastiched in 'Tolerances of the Human Face', *The Atrocity Exhibition* takes the inexhaustibility of the short story cycle, prefigured by *The Thousand and One Nights*, to new levels of paradox. Not the least of which is the protagonist's violent dualism of sex and death, meaning and non-meaning, which finally results in his own self-dissolution. If nothing else, *The Atrocity Exhibition* performs a disturbing assault upon the integrity of character to which I shall now turn.

Further Reading

On the critical debate surrounding the short story cycle, see Forrest L. Ingram (1971), Susan Garland Mann (1989), J. Gerald Kennedy (1995), Maggie Dunn and Ann Morris (1995), and James Nagel (2001). On *The Thousand and One Nights*, see Tzvetan Todorov's essay, 'Narrative-Men', in *The Poetics of Prose* (1977) as well as Nicole

Ward Jouve's feminist response in *White Woman Speaks with Forked Tongue* (1991). On the Irish short story, see for example James F. Kilroy (1984), while the history of Celtic revivalism is discussed by Seamus Deane (1985). *The Atrocity Exhibition* is discussed in detail by Roger Luckhurst (1997). Elizabeth Freund offers a useful account of reader–response criticism in *The Return of the Reader* (1987). My reading of narrative and the event has been influenced by Jean-François Lyotard: see in particular Geoffrey Bennington's *Lyotard: Writing the Event* (1988).

11

Character Parts:
Identity in the Short Story

'What is character but the determination of incident? What is incident but the illustration of character?' (James 1987: 196–7). Henry James' question is particularly pressing for the short story since, despite the production of character studies such as James Lasdun's 'An Anxious Man' (2005) or Katherine Mansfield's 'The Stranger' (1921), the form is not necessarily suited to character development. As Edith Wharton has noted:

> Some of the greatest short stories owe their vitality entirely to the dramatic rendering of a situation . . . Type, general character, may be set forth in a few strokes, but the progression, the unfolding of personality . . . this slow but continuous growth requires space, and therefore belongs by definition to a larger, a symphonic plan. (Wharton 1997: 37)

Character, to use V. S. Pritchett's metaphor, is to be glimpsed from the corner of the eye or, as both L. A. G. Strong and R. K. Narayan suggest, to be glanced at as if through a window. Although the use of incidents such as an epiphany or single effect are often thought of as when character is most fully revealed, epiphanies are frequently deflated so that the protagonist's self-revelation is drained of significance. Gabriel Conroy, at the end of James Joyce's 'The Dead' (1914), remains as self-deluded as he ever was. Modernist short stories tend towards an ambiguous and paradoxical view of the self, in which psychological portraits such as Joyce's 'Clay' tend towards the static quality of the sketch.

As Wharton suggests in her essay, the short story's depiction of character as type relates the form to the classical epic. In *The Theory of the Novel* (1920), Georg Lukács contrasts the novel, where the 'inner action . . . is nothing but a struggle against the power of time' with the epic, where heroes age but the knowledge they acquire 'has the blissful time-removed quality of the world of gods' (Lukács 1971: 122). In a profane and increasingly secular age, 'traces of lost meaning are to be found everywhere' (Lukács 1971: 123). Heroes of novels endure the passing of time so that they may recover some of these lost significances. By contrast, the short story is not only closer to the epic than the novel, since chronological time cannot be fully rendered, but it is also more fully a product of the disenchanted modern age: 'the short story is the most purely artistic form' where 'meaninglessness *as meaninglessness* becomes . . . eternal' (Lukács 1971: 51).

To take Lukács' argument further, the protagonists of short stories cannot attain what, in *The Historical Novel* (1937), Lukács terms 'typicality': the capacity of characters, such as Walter Scott's Waverley, to embody the internal contradictions of their historical moment. Without the presence of chronological time, the heroes of short stories cannot age and develop in relation to historical change but are suspended at a single point in their lives. For Lukács, the incompleteness of narrative forms, such as the short story, is indicative of a pessimism that denies the revolutionary potential of art. By contrast, he suggests that nineteenth-century novelists, such as Honoré de Balzac and Leo Tolstoy, achieve a form of 'critical realism' insofar as their novels produce a fictional world that is so lifelike that it offers readers a vantage-point from which to dissect their own world.

Lukács' preference for the historical novel is indebted to the influence of G. W. F. Hegel, in particular his belief that the goal of philosophy was to arrive at a consistent world-view in which internal disagreements are resolved. The ambition of both Hegel and Lukács is for the mind to become one with the world that it perceives. The tension within this project is that it privileges unity above all else: the existence of the other is subject to the autonomy of the individual while conflict, which often exists as the expression of economic and social discrimination, is transcended in the interests of totality. By contrast, the tendency of the short story to focus upon individuals and communities submerged within the body politic runs counter to this objective. During the 1960s, Hegelian thought was contested by the rise of structuralism which, in its various critical orientations, cast the individual as a subject positioned in terms of social discourse and, therefore, inherently split. Yet, even before then, modernist writers such as D. H. Lawrence had sought to abandon 'the old stable ego of the character' often under the influence of new theories of identity proposed by, among others, Henri Bergson and Sigmund Freud. Lawrence goes on to describe fiction-writing as an experimental process that requires 'a deeper sense than any we've been used to exercise' (Lawrence 1981: 183). Implicitly, Lawrence places renewed emphasis upon observation and situational analysis, qualities that complement, as Wharton suggests, the writing of short stories. Consequently, in contradistinction to Lukács' argument, the short story is an effective medium for the exploration of new versions of identity and character.

Naturalism and the Self

The short story's predisposition towards outsiders is notably seen in Guy de Maupassant's 'Boule de Suif' (1880). The eponymous heroine is a prostitute from Rouen, who is attempting to flee the town before it falls to the invading Prussian army. Her fellow travellers include two businessmen and their wives, an aristocratic couple, two nuns and a political revolutionary, Cornudet. Unlike them, Boule de Suif (a nickname meaning 'Suet Pudding') has sensibly brought provisions which she invites her companions to share. After some hesitation, they agree, and for a time, a rapport develops that cuts across social barriers. Then, at a village outside Rouen, their carriage is stopped by a Prussian officer. He checks their travel permits but will not allow their journey to proceed until Boule de Suif has agreed to have sex with him. As a patriot, Boule de Suif refuses, but is pressurised by her companions into giving her consent. When the travellers depart the following day, she is shunned by them and, in a mirror image of the first half of the story, is excluded from the meal that they share. Cornudet's 'vengeful whistling' of the Republican anthem (Maupassant 1971: 67), while Boule de Suif sobs, implies that her suffering is a microcosm of the state's crime.

Maupassant's story originally appeared in *Les Soirées de Médan*, a volume of stories featuring Emile Zola and a group of his acolytes. Although Maupassant was more strongly influenced by his mentor, Gustave Flaubert, 'Boule de Suif' echoes the naturalistic method proposed in Zola's essay 'The Experimental Novel' (also 1880). Here, Zola compares the writer to a neutral observer, who 'presents data as he has observed them, determines the point of departure, establishes the solid ground on which his characters will stand', and the story to a scientific experiment, 'in order to show that the series of events therein will be those demanded by the determinism of the phenomena under study' (Zola 1963: 166). For Zola, character is not an innate or autonomous entity but, like human identity, is the product of social and environmental factors that can, like a machine, be 'take[n] apart and put together . . . piece by piece' (Zola 1963: 177). Although Maupassant did not share Zola's reformist ambitions, his story shows the formation of Boule de Suif's character in relation to her social background, her historical context, and the prejudice and hypocrisy that riddle the French class system.

For British and American writers, such as Theodore Dreiser and George Moore, naturalism exemplified a quasi-scientific method by which to explain the workings of character. Stephen Crane's 'Maggie: A Child of the Streets' (1893) also appears, at first sight, to be an exercise in naturalism, the title implying that Maggie is the offspring of her environment. Crane establishes a contrast between his own technique and the melodrama, to which Pete takes Maggie, where the audience 'hug[s] themselves in ecstatic pity of their imagined or real condition' (Crane 1993: 23). If the melodrama is an entertainment that distracts its viewers from the reality of their hardship then, by implication, Crane's objective method is meant to open his reader's eyes. Yet, Crane is also concerned with his protagonist's psychology: the play causes Maggie to wonder if she could acquire 'the culture and refinement she had seen imitated' (Crane 1993: 24) while also internalising feminine codes of dress and behaviour. Furthermore, Crane divides his story into chapters that intensify the photographic quality of the writing while, at the same time, fragmenting the link between cause and effect. The nonlinear narrative suggests that while, in one sense, Maggie is a product of the city, in another sense her character is not totally determined by its influence. Instead, like 'the ghost-mists of dawn' (Crane 1993: 10), there remains something spectral and unknown about her.

Psychology, Gender and Character

Maggie and Boule de Suif are two of the female figures that characterise the concerns of the *fin de siècle*. Greater social and economic freedom for women, the demand for political rights, the emergence of a lower middle and upper working class, and greater moral licence on the part of writers conspired to generate what commentators called 'the Woman Question'. In 1894, the romantic novelist Ouida coined the phrase 'New Woman' (originally intended as an insult) to describe women who rebelled against the social and sexual mores of their day. Whether or not these women were 'new', both male and female writers explored innovative methods with which to describe their fears and aspirations.

George Egerton, the pseudonym of Mary Chavelita Dunne, portrayed her characters' inner lives in a free indirect style that was influenced by the Norwegian novelist Knut Hamsun. In the dream sequence that dominates her most celebrated story, 'A Cross Line' (1893), Egerton's heroine imagines herself as, first, riding an Arabian stallion: 'Her thoughts shape themselves into a wild song, a song to her steed of flowing mane and satin skin.' Next, she sees herself as an exotic dancer 'with parted lips and panting, rounded breasts, and a dancing devil in each glowing eye' (Egerton 1993: 58). Then, her thoughts dissipate and she considers all the other women she has known or not known, a universal womanhood: 'Stray words, half confidences, glimpses through soul-chinks of suppressed fires, actual outbreaks, domestic catastrophes, how the ghosts dance in the cells of her memory!' (Egerton 1993: 59). Psychological sketches, such as 'A Cross Line', were extremely popular with writers of the 1890s, who were inspired by Walter Pater's depiction of subjective experience as a 'hard gem-like flame' (Pater 1912: 250). Yet, while Egerton toys with the notion of an elemental female consciousness, she also portrays femininity as a masquerade, a costume that in modernist stories either liberates, such as Jean Rhys' 'Illusion' (1927), or imprisons, such as Katherine Mansfield's 'Miss Brill' (1920). Mansfield's first published story, 'The Tiredness of Rosabel' (1908), develops the free indirect style of the 1890s, so that the conventional hierarchy of reality versus fantasy is reversed. Rosabel's dream of escape is, in many ways, more substantial than her real existence; yet, its release is predicated upon the confinement of her material condition. The inversion so that 'the work of art . . . should be something projected, not reflected' (Wharton 1997: 44) dramatises the extent to which women's psychological lives are shaped by the limitations of their social position.

The emphases upon dream and fantasy suggest a correlation with Sigmund Freud's exploration of the unconscious that became more widely known during the 1910s. As Egerton acknowledged, 'if I did not know the technical jargon current today of Freud and the psychoanalysts, I did know something of complexes and inhibitions, repressions and the subconscious impulses that determine actions and reactions' (Egerton 1932: 58). A discourse on human psychology had been developing, however, for several years before Freud's dissemination. As early as 1873, Pater had referred to consciousness as a 'stream' or 'dissolution of impressions, images, sensations', a 'continual vanishing away' (Pater 1912: 249). In 1890, William James described a 'stream of thought, of consciousness, or of subjective life' (in Ledger and Luckhurst 2000: 258). May Sinclair's use, in 1918, of the phrase 'stream of consciousness' to describe Dorothy Richardson's novels is often taken to be the first instance in English, and that her inspiration was the French novelist Edouard Dujardin, but her source could as easily have been Pater or James, among others. In the ending to Virginia Woolf's 'Kew Gardens' (1919), the stream of consciousness technique is infused with Henri Bergson's depiction of identity as a flux of past and present selves that coexist in a simultaneous state of becoming:

> It seemed as if all gross and heavy bodies had sunk down in the heat motionless and lay huddled upon the ground, but their voices went wavering from them as if they were flames lolling from the thick waxen bodies of candles. Voices, yes, voices, wordless voices, breaking the silence suddenly with such depth of contentment, such passion of desire, or, in the voices of children, such freshness of surprise; breaking the silence? (Woolf 2003: 89)

Woolf's final sentence, where the voices emerge above the din of the automated city, constitute a medley of sounds, a hybrid of speaking parts, in which the human and the mechanical, the natural and the artificial, the relaxed and the regimented coincide but do not supersede one another. Instead, Woolf's writing constitutes what poststructural critics have called *écriture féminine*, a discourse that dislocates without ever resolving the dominant, or masculine, discourse of logic and proportion. In her major fiction, Woolf's characters are fragmented and unknown, caught briefly as 'moments of being' (a short story title from 1928).

For many male writers, the New Woman and her descendants were a source of fascination. Around the time he was speculating upon the nature of character, D. H. Lawrence was revising his story 'Daughters of the Vicar', a tale that also fed into his novel *The Rainbow* (1915). Lawrence's balancing of the subjective and the objective is at its most effective in this story, so that the reader views Mary with detachment while, at the same time, experiencing her self-estrangement:

> She shut herself up, she shut herself rigid against the agonies of shame and the terror of violation which came at first. She *would* not feel, and she *would* not feel. She was a pure will acquiescing to him. She elected a certain kind of fate. She would be good and purely just, she would live in a higher freedom than she had ever known, she would be free of mundane care, she was a pure will towards right. She had sold herself, but she had a new freedom. She had got rid of her body. (Lawrence 1982: 121)

Lawrence's sympathetic restraint runs counter to the more chauvinistic responses that occur in his fiction. Equally, in 'Bernice Bobs Her Hair' (1920), F. Scott Fitzgerald undercuts a stereotype of modern womanhood – the flapper – that he himself had largely created. Desperate to join fashionable society, embodied by her cousin Marjorie, Bernice is tricked into the shaming spectacle of bobbing her hair. She exacts her revenge, though, by effectively operating on Marjorie:

> Bending over she found one of the braids of Marjorie's hair . . . she reached down with the shears and severed it . . . Bernice deftly amputated the other braid, paused for an instant, and then flitted swiftly and silently back to her own room. (Fitzgerald 1996: 78–9)

The unlawful 'amputation' mediates the proximity between sexual jealousy and physical mutilation, an uncomfortable insight into the intensity of female emotion that is belied by the story's ironic humour.

Gothic and the Abject

Modernist and proto-modernist strategies depict character as a psychological process rather than a social product. This change of emphasis, though, is prefigured by the Gothic where the fracturing of identity has been integral to the genre since its emergence in the mid-eighteenth century. The Gothic imagination turns upon a fear of objects, in particular the individual's anxiety of becoming subject to forces beyond its control. The fear of powerlessness, though, is paradoxical since it is also equated with sexual desire: the masochistic pleasure of becoming a plaything. It is in this tension between the subject and the object, fear and desire, that the Gothic has the potential of a political discourse (see Chapter 16).

Objectification in the Gothic can take a number of forms. The individual can be terrorised by predators such as Edgar Allan Poe's 'Ligeia' (1838), Sheridan Le Fanu's 'Carmilla' (1872) or the incubus in Maupassant's 'L'Horla' (1887): 'I felt somebody squatting on top of me, pressing his mouth against mine and drinking my life through my lips' (Maupassant 1971: 320). The predator is often a projection of the individual's private anxieties, such as the use of doubles in Poe's 'William Wilson' (1839) or Joseph Conrad's 'The Secret Sharer' (1910). In E. T. A. Hoffmann's 'The Sandman' (1817), the emotional divide of Nathanael's love for Clara and his desire for Olympia, a mechanical doll, is finally resolved by his suicide. Psychological fragmentation is also mirrored by the alienation of mind from body, for instance in Poe's 'The Masque of the Red Death' or 'The Pit and the Pendulum' (both 1842), where the individual is physically suspended between two kinds of certain death. In Nathaniel Hawthorne's 'The Minister's Black Veil' (1836), the dualism of internal security and external threat is inverted by the Reverend Hooper's decision to become the scapegoat for his community so as to illuminate the sins that he sees in 'every visage' (Hawthorne 1987: 157). In each of these stories, the comforting illusion of individual autonomy is disturbed and shattered.

From very early on, women writers were producers of the Gothic, such as Anna Letitia Aiken in 'Sir Bertrand: A Fragment' (1773). In her unfinished novel, *Maria, or the Wrongs of Woman* (1798), Mary Wollstonecraft realised the political potential of Gothic through her story of a woman wrongfully imprisoned in an asylum. At the end of the nineteenth century, during the resurgence of Gothic fiction, writers such as Charlotte Perkins Gilman reclaimed Wollstonecraft's literary as well as political legacy. 'The Yellow Wallpaper' (1892) is narrated by an unnamed woman who is confined to an attic room as a part of a rest cure following childbirth. She becomes fascinated by the wallpaper, the pattern of 'sprawling outlines' that 'run off in great slanting waves of optic horror' (in Ward 1996: 80), and which acts as a projection of her mental state. Gradually, she sees a figure in the pattern, 'a woman stooping down and creeping about' (in Ward 1996: 81), which eventually metamorphoses into 'a great many women' who are strangled by the pattern as they attempt 'to climb through' (in Ward 1996: 85). At last, having identified herself with the woman in the wallpaper and believing she has escaped from its confine, the narrator tears the paper from the wall in a bid to release the other women. Her husband enters the room and faints 'across' her 'path', so that she has 'to creep over him every time' (in Ward 1996: 88). The reversal of gender roles – it is he who is prone while she is dominant – suggests a kind of victory; yet, it is she who has lost her sanity. On the other hand, does the narrator's descent into madness expose the insanity of patriarchy where men and women are not treated as equal, and where male intellect is regarded as superior to the female body? Then, again, the narrator is not visibly hysterical: her thoughts are presented logically and eloquently while, at the same time, the content of her narration calls these rhetorical devices into doubt.

'The Yellow Wallpaper' has received considerable attention in recent years, not least because of its prefiguring of Julia Kristeva's theory of abjection. According to Kristeva, the subject defines itself by expelling all that is considered abject:

> Refuse and corpses *show me* what I permanently thrust aside in order to live. These body fluids, this defilement, this shit are what life withstands, hardly and with difficulty, on the part of death.

Abjection, by its definition in terms of ex-centricity, 'disturbs identity, system, order' (Kristeva 1982: 4). 'The Yellow Wallpaper' assumes an abject position by being narrated from the point of view of the Gothic subject. It is she who has become alien and whose foreignness contaminates the reading of the text. In other words, Gilman's narrator embraces a subject position disavowed by the dominant ideology and which cannot be accommodated by it. The abject emphasis upon psychological and linguistic fragmentation, as well as the instability of the body, develops the Gothic fascination with the grotesque but, unlike traditional Gothic, plays with the grotesque as a discursive tool that negates the ruling order. Katherine Mansfield's 'The Woman at the Store' (1912), for example, is set against the backdrop of a desolate New Zealand landscape where 'there is no twilight' and 'everything appears grotesque . . . as though the savage spirit of the country walked abroad and sneered at what it saw' (Mansfield 1984: 112). The desolation is mirrored in the 'extraordinary and repulsively vulgar' pictures of a 'diseased' 'kid's mind' (Mansfield 1984: 116). While her mother censors what her visitors are told, the child secretly shows them a picture of her 'shooting at a man with a rook rifle and then digging a hole to bury him in' (Mansfield 1984: 117). The abject imagery of the picture, coupled to the child's insanity, shatters the security of this apparent oasis.

Contemporary women writers, notably Angela Carter, have made extensive use of abjection in their fiction. 'The Loves of Lady Purple' (1974), for example, describes a marionette that nightly performs the history of Lady Purple, whose 'unappeasable appetites . . . turned her at last into the very puppet you see before you' (Carter 1995: 44). A libertine, sadist and murderess, Lady Purple was eventually consumed by the diseases she passed on to her lovers: 'Circe at last became a swine herself and . . . walked the pavements like a desiccated shadow.' Having 'abrogated her humanity' (Carter 1995: 47), Lady Purple turned into a doll, a magical transformation that calls into doubt whether this history is really a history at all, let alone whether the doll is actually Lady Purple. Instead, Carter's story describes the endless reproduction of narrative, where history and fantasy blur and where participation is not a choice, but in which the protagonists of later stories, such as 'The Tiger's Bride' (1979) or 'The Company of Wolves' (1977), can uncover a form of agency through voluntary self-abasement: 'She will lay his fearful head on her lap and she will pick out the lice from his pelt and perhaps she will put the lice into her mouth and eat them, as he will bid her, as she would do in a savage marriage ceremony' (Carter 1995: 219).

Kathy Acker's 'The Language of the Body' (1993) illustrates the dilemmas that surround the use of abjection. Acker's story distils many of the central themes in her work, in particular the reliving of physical trauma as psychic nightmare, so that the text functions by constant slippages that replicate the experience of dream and disturb the illusion of fiction as mimesis (or lifelikeness). Fleeing her abusive husband, Acker's narrator begins a quest to 'find the language of the body . . . where sex is lying' (Acker 1993: 407), that is to say, where sexuality both resides and dissimulates. This search for origins though is, as the narrator acknowledges in her 'Masturbation Journal', doomed to 'failure' since at the point of orgasm 'language is forbidden'. Only 'having crossed' is it 'possible to have language' (Acker 1993: 409). Consequently, the text can only retrace this ever-receding horizon of meaning while the narrator is trapped in an endless recirculation of her abject condition. Since 'here is no dialectic' where self has become other, 'and all that was inside is now outside' (Acker 1993: 408–9), the potential for revolutionary change becomes an impossibility. Instead, the abject itself becomes an empty, rhetorical gesture: a weak or attenuated version, despite its extreme imagery and formal disintegration, of the postmodern (see Chapter 18).

In contrast, ethnic and postcolonial writers tend to ground the abject in historical realities. In 'Going to Meet the Man' (1965), James Baldwin describes the abject spectacle of a mass lynching through the memories of a white racist. What he saw that day has affected him so deeply that he can now only make love to his wife by 'do[ing]' her 'like a nigger' (Baldwin 1991: 252). Even more horrific is the decay and decomposition of Cynthia Ozick's 'The Shawl' (1981), set amid a Nazi concentration camp. In stark contrast, the fairy tale opening of Janet Frame's fable 'Solutions' (1962) gives way to the grotesque as a would-be writer decides to rid himself of his body and liberate his mind. Eventually, having discarded everything but his brain, his 'shrivelled remains' are tipped into a dustbin where they are devoured by mice (Frame 1983: 120). Frame's darkly comic tale locates the split between mind and body, utilised by earlier Gothic writers such as Poe, as a projection of the male psyche rather than a universal condition.

Character and Sexuality

Character, then, serves to dramatise competing versions of identity, theories of the self that are ultimately grounded in the social and the historical. To this end, writers have been faced with the choice of either questioning the very basis of identity or revising its terms without dispensing with subjectivity altogether. This tension is particularly true of writers from sexual minorities since their positioning as social subjects highlights the extent to which subjectivity is a product of language.

In the wake of Oscar Wilde's imprisonment in 1895, a form of self-censorship was practised by male homosexual writers. Despite being socially taboo, male homosexuality had acquired linguistic recognition by the fact of its criminalisation: there was a public discourse in which it could be discussed. The homosexual, then, existed not only in terms of his sexual orientation but also as a linguistic invention (the word was coined during the 1890s). Paradoxically, the male homosexual was split from his identity since, in the moment of being outlawed, homosexuality was given a social presence while, at the same time, its expression was rendered indecent. By contrast, lesbianism was never legally recognised in Britain, so that lesbian women, unlike their male counterparts, had neither a social identity nor a potential voice. The historical importance of this disarticulation informs the work of modernist women, such as Mansfield and Woolf, and postmodernists, such as Acker and Jeannette Winterson.

In the stories published during his lifetime, E. M. Forster could only approach the topic of homosexuality through indirect means. In 'The Story of a Panic' (1904), he describes an adolescent boy's sexual maturation through a fantastical encounter with the demi-god Pan. 'The Point of It' (1911) begins with two young men in a rowing boat, Harold and Micky. Urged on by Harold to row faster, Micky suffers a heart attack and the last words he hears are: 'Don't you see the point of it? Well, you will some day' (Forster 1954: 149). Micky, though, survives and he grows up to lead a conventional and successful life, entirely forgetful of Harold. When at last he dies, Micky is shown a vision of Hell by an anonymous Christ-like entity: 'he who desires me is I' (Forster 1954: 164). Micky dies a second time, giving his assent, and reawakens in the river to be rescued by Harold, a blurred, cloudy figure comparable to the divine saviour. Without any sexual overtone, Forster implies that Harold has saved Micky from a routine future in which he is untrue to his own nature.

Since the inception of Gay Liberation in the 1960s, writers such as David Leavitt have responded to the self-censorship endured by their predecessors by seeking to naturalise gay experience for a general readership. Leavitt's 'Territory' (1983), for example, takes the familiar scenario of introducing a new boyfriend to the family with one crucial difference: here, Neil has to introduce Wayne to his mother. The embarrassment of a parent who is keen to please her child is recognisable to most readers: a day after learning of Neil's orientation, Mrs Campbell had joined 'an organisation called the Coalition of Parents of Lesbians and Gays. Within a year, she was president of it' (Leavitt 2005: 5).

In more recent years, Leavitt has had to respond to the reality of AIDS, a controversial and misunderstood disease that generated a new discourse with which to reinterpret the totality of sexual relations, but which also further demonised the gay sub-culture. In their joint collaboration, *The Darker Proof* (1987), the British writer Adam Mars-Jones and his American counterpart Edmund White offer a series of insights into the experience of sufferers and their loved ones living with AIDS. During a political era, when there was an intensely strong conservative coalition between the British Government and the American administration, White and Mars-Jones present a very different 'special relationship' with which to counter the judgemental attitude of politicians. In particular, they concentrate upon the minutiae of their characters' everyday lives, physical settings in London and Paris, and a series of allusions from poetry to television shows, which not only inform their characters' thoughts but are also recognisable to a general audience. Part of the collection's success, then, is in a kind of naturalism that avoids didacticism, demystifies stereotypes, and adheres to the strengths of time and place, the subject of the next chapter.

Further Reading

For a standard account of characterisation in the short story, see Valerie Shaw (1983). On the critical debate that surrounds the function of character, contrast the positions of Hélène Cixous (1974) and Alan Sinfield (1992). Douglas Tallack's *Critical Theory: A Reader* (1995) features a number of important interventions by, among others, Cixous, Louis Althusser and Jacques Lacan that contributed to the critique of Hegel and the poststructural re-evaluation of subjectivity. See also Catherine Belsey's chapter, 'Addressing the Subject', in *Critical Practice* (1980) and Jonathan Dollimore's account of discourse and 'sexual dissidence' (1991). There is a growing body of work on the New Woman: see, for example, Sally Ledger (1997) and Angelique Richardson's introduction to *Women Who Did* (2005). On the influence of Bergson and Freud upon modernism, see Randall Stevenson (1998). Fred Botting's *Gothic* (1996) is a useful starting-point, while for entries on David Leavitt and gay fiction, see *The Columbia Companion to the Twentieth-Century American Short Story* edited by Blanche Gelfant (2000).

12

Localities: Centres and Margins

As the previous chapter argued, the short story portrays human identity as a subject in process, so that characterisation tends towards only partial realisation. For the protagonists of short story cycles, such as Julia Alvarez's *How the García Girls Lost Their Accents* (1991) and Sandra Cisneros' *The House on Mango Street* (1984), part of this process involves a quest for origins. Although the short story has effectively described the experience of city-life (see the next chapter), it has also had a special role in depicting communities left behind by the movement towards urbanisation and industrialisation. Texts such as Ivan Turgenev's *Sketches from a Hunter's Album* (1852) and Sherwood Anderson's *Winesburg, Ohio* (1919) are iconic in this sense, but this chapter will extend the discussion to include writers that pre-date these authors as well as contemporary writers working against the backdrop of globalisation. Of particular note is that the search for authenticity implicated in the hunt for origins is always tentative and provisional, since the pursuit of origination is refracted through accumulated experience, historical ties that become more complex in periods of intense economic and cultural change.

Village Voices

The effects of land reform and the early Industrial Revolution encouraged Romantic writers to find a new pastoral style that described the lives and language of working men and women. In poems such as 'Michael' (1800) and 'The Ruined Cottage' (1797–8), William Wordsworth dramatised the depopulation of the English countryside. At the same time, in her posthumous novel *Northanger Abbey* (1818), Jane Austen evoked a vision of Middle England where 'murder was not tolerated, servants were not slaves, and neither poison nor sleeping potions [were] to be procured, like rhubarb, from every druggist' (Austen 2003: 188). The English village became mythologised as a sentimental retreat from the harsh reality of industrialisation.

Mary Russell Mitford's sketches of village life were first published in *The Lady Magazine* in the early 1820s and subsequently collected in five volumes under the general title of *Our Village* from 1824 to 1832. Like Austen, Mitford has a keen eye for social observation and a gentle, ironic wit. Furthermore, like her predecessor, she presents the village as a haven characterised by traditional customs and the turn of the seasons. To this end, Mitford is aided by the sketch form which tends towards a static rather than dynamic narrative. Yet, she paints a series of vivid portraits, for example in her description of the characters, humour and skulduggery that compose a village cricket match, 'a real solid old-fashioned match between neighbouring parishes, where each attacks the other for honour and a supper, glory and half-a-crown a man' (Mitford 1904: 167). Whereas the folktale tends to be concerned with fantastical events, the sketch allows Mitford to describe events realistically, thereby developing Austen's critique of the Gothic as romantic delusion. Despite her nostalgic qualities, Mitford is an important figure since she popularised an early form of literary realism. Among the writers indebted to her is Elizabeth Gaskell, whose novel, *Cranford* (1853), began as a single story in Charles Dickens' *Household Words* in December 1851 and continued as a series of missives from Gaskell's fictional small town. Like Alphonse Daudet's *Letters from My Windmill* (1869), *Cranford* overlaps with the epistolary novel (or 'novel of letters'), such as Samuel Richardson's *Clarissa* (1747–8) and Choderlos de Laclos' *Dangerous Liaisons* (1782).

Whereas Mitford's realism is coloured by her sentiment, the Italian writer Giovanni Verga offers a more unsparing treatment of rural life. Verga had been a supporter of Italian independence, but following the unification of Italy in 1871, he became disillusioned with the nation-state. His writing also changed from an early romantic style to a form of naturalism known as *verismo*. The story 'Gramigna's Mistress' (1880) features the proto-modernist remark that 'the work of art will seem to have created itself . . . without preserving any point of contact with its author' (Verga 1999: 94). Verga's dispassionate style was introduced in his tale 'Nedda' (1874), the story of a Sicilian peasant girl who retains her faith despite sickness, poverty and bereavement. Since the story is primarily told through its use of dialogue, with little or no authorial comment, the reader is left to decide whether Nedda's actions are correct. By treating its subject objectively, the story gives back to its unsophisticated protagonist a large degree of moral complexity. The same can also be said of Verga's most famous story, 'Cavalleria Rusticana' (1880), an uncompromising tale of jealousy, deceit and bloody revenge set again among the Sicilian peasantry.

Thomas Hardy, too, exchanged the melodramatic content of his *Wessex Tales* (1886) for the more subtle realism of *Life's Little Ironies* (1894). Although the supernatural elements in 'The Fiddler of the Reels' echo Hardy's earlier short fiction, it is more than balanced by stories such as 'On the Western Circuit'. Raye, a young solicitor, falls in love with Anna, housemaid to Mrs Harnham, after a chance encounter at a funfair. They meet again, Raye spending 'a few additional hours with his fascinating child of nature' (Hardy 1996: 102), before giving Anna a pseudonym and an address to which she can write. Since Anna is illiterate, the childless Mrs Harnham, who views Anna as her surrogate daughter, is persuaded to pose as Anna and to conduct a correspondence with Raye. In anticipation of Edmond Rostand's play, *Cyrano de Bergerac* (1897), Raye not only falls deeper in love with Anna but Mrs Harnham also falls in love with Raye, who represents an exciting alternative to her dull husband. On their second encounter, though, Raye had made love to Anna and she is now pregnant. Raye accepts his responsibility and agrees to marry Anna, only to discover that it was Mrs Harnham who had written her letters for her. Now both Raye and Mrs Harnham are locked into loveless marriages. Hardy's starkly ironic treatment of their unrequited love distils the many tensions – class, wealth, education, sexuality – that underwrite his Wessex fictions.

Hardy and Verga were important influences on D. H. Lawrence, especially his early stories set among rural and industrial communities. Whereas 'Love Among the Haystacks' (1913) remains heavily plotted, especially in its balancing of the two brothers, the intellectual Geoffrey and the physical Maurice, 'The White Stocking' and 'Odours of Chrysanthemums' (both 1914) make fine use of symbolism. The latter features a central motif, the laying-out of a corpse, which Lawrence reworked in both his play *The Widowing of Mrs Holroyd* (1913) and his novel *The Rainbow* (1915). Unlike the fictionalisation of his parents in *Sons and Lovers* (1913), the short story's concentrated form allows Lawrence to be even-handed. Faced with the body of her spouse, Elizabeth Bates realises that 'she had been wrong', that she had fought 'a husband who did not exist' and that, as a consequence, 'they had denied each other in life' (Lawrence 1982: 104–5). Despite her self-realisation, the moment of epiphany has come too late for Elizabeth: she shrinks 'from death, her ultimate master' (Lawrence 1982: 105), which will finally seal her fate. Lawrence's cool yet sympathetic treatment of working men and women was deeply influential upon later English writers, in particular A. E. Coppard.

In an important corrective to this tendency towards realism, Rudyard Kipling invested his new home of Sussex with a sense of mystery and enigma. Writing in 1902, Kipling described rural England as 'the most marvellous of all foreign countries that I have ever been in, (Kipling 1996: 113). The English Home Counties are rendered exotic and wondrous in what amounts to an inversion of imperial rhetoric. At the same time, as a new landowner, Kipling seeks to write himself into the history of this mysterious nation. In the opening to his story 'They' (1904), the automobile becomes a form of time machine:

> I found hidden villages where bees . . . boomed in eighty-foot lindens that overhung grey Norman churches; miraculous brooks diving under stone bridges built for heavier traffic than would ever vex them again; tithe-barns larger than their churches, and an old smithy that cried out aloud how it had once been a hall of the Knights of the Temple. Gipsies I found on a common where the gorse, bracken, and heath fought it out together up a mile of Roman road. (Kipling 1987d: 243)

Yet, instead of turning this history into a mythology, the narrator's ramble is more like a montage in which the detritus of history is randomly juxtaposed with one another. As the narrator discovers, his temporal and spatial journey is also an emotional quest, an unconscious exploration of submerged feelings and repressed memories, which ultimately disturbs the establishment of a coherent narrative. The catalyst for this disturbance involves a blind woman with second sight and the narrator's acknowledgement of a spirit-child. Instead of rationalising personal and national identity, Kipling seeks an accommodation with the mystical and the irrational: occult elements that, as in his story 'Wireless' (1902), Kipling associates with the workings of the imagination. Consequently, Kipling's Sussex is preoccupied with possession ('The House Surgeon', 1909), mediums ('The Dog Hervey', 1914) and hallucination ('Mary Postgate', 1915). Alongside writers such as May Sinclair, Kipling contributes to a mystical tendency within Edwardian literature that feeds into the equally mysterious work of Mary Butts, T. F. Powys and Sylvia Townsend Warner.

Frontier Tales

In an influential lecture delivered in 1893, the American historian Frederick Jackson Turner argued that the Frontier, 'the hither edge of free land', 'the meeting point between savagery and civilisation' (Turner 1962: 3), was the single most important factor in the creation of an American identity. According to Turner, the European settler had to 'accept the conditions' which the environment 'furnishes, or perish', but 'Little by little he transform[ed] the wilderness', so that 'the outcome [was] not the old Europe' but 'a new product that [was] American' (Turner 1962: 4). Despite the Darwinist echo of Turner's claims, he nevertheless points to the centrality of the landscape within American nationhood.

Yet, this 'new product' was viewed ambiguously by American writers. In Washington Irving's 'Rip Van Winkle' (1819), this ambiguity is sustained within the spectacle of the Kaatskill Mountains. On one side lies the river, 'the lordly Hudson . . . moving on its silent but majestic course', but on the other side lies 'a deep mountain glen, wild, lonely, and shagged, the bottom filled with fragments from the impending cliffs, and scarcely lighted by the reflected rays of the setting sun' (in Oates 1992: 22). The sublimity of the American landscape, its capacity for both beauty and terror, even manages to render Mark Twain's sceptical narrator speechless in 'A Visit to Niagara' (1869): 'Such a mad storming, roaring, and bellowing of warring wind and water never crazed my ears before' (Twain 1993: 22). The incomprehensible scale of the landscape, its propensity to disorientate the senses, meant that it was also an effective backdrop for Gothic horror, the physical and psychological dislocation of the haunted wanderers that occur in stories such as William Austin's 'Peter Rugg, the Missing Man' (1820) and Nathaniel Hawthorne's 'Ethan Brand' (1850). Nevertheless, even as it threatened to engulf the settlers, the landscape was a site of renewal, of vitality and possibility, which inspired both the expansion westwards and the formation of new communities, such as the settlement gently mocked by Louisa M. Alcott in her autobiographical tale, 'Transcendental Wild Oats' (1873).

As the land was increasingly settled, following the American Civil War (1861–5) and the decimation of the Native American tribes, so writers tended to romanticise the significance of the Frontier. In tall tales such as 'The Celebrated Jumping Frog of Calaveras County' (1867), Twain captured an authentic American idiom, a mixture of 'impressive earnestness and sincerity' (Twain 1993: 12). Initially working in close partnership with Twain, Bret Harte pioneered the cowboy story in tales such as 'The Luck of Roaring Camp' (1870). In his story 'The Bride Comes to Yellow Sky' (1898), Stephen Crane offers a memorable take on the cowboy formula. Jack Potter, having recently married, is returning to Yellow Sky where his old rival, Scratchy Wilson, waits for revenge. Disembarking from the train, Jack is challenged to a duel but Wilson is dumbfounded to discover that his opponent is unarmed. Upon learning that Jack is married, and that the woman beside him is his wife, Wilson decides that there is no longer any point to their antagonism. The bride symbolises the coming of domesticity, of civilising constraint, while Wilson is 'a simple child of the earlier plains' (Crane 1993: 88). In rehearsing a familiar cowboy scenario, Crane presents an incisive allegory for the end of the Frontier.

As the Frontier moved towards its official closure in 1892, so writers tended towards greater realism in their fiction. In stories such as 'Up the Coolly' (1891), Hamlin Garland focused upon lives left behind by the march of progress: 'I've come to the conclusion that life's a failure for ninety-nine percent of us. You can't help me now. It's too late' (Garland 1956: 85). In 'The Man Who Corrupted Hadleyburg' (1899), Twain debunked the myth of small-town America, the point of his story being that, despite its respectable pretence, Hadleyburg is *already* corrupt. Kate Chopin, in stories such as 'Désirée's Baby' (1893) and 'The Storm' (1898), explored the secret histories of race and sexuality while also capturing the lives of people living in the Bayou. Like Garland, Chopin can also be regarded as a writer of local colour, the most important exponent being Sarah Orne Jewett. Her most famous story, 'A White Heron' (1886), begins idyllically with a young girl, Sylvia, enraptured by the surrounding countryside and, in particular, the sight of a white heron. Then she encounters a hunts-man, whom she is attracted to, and to whom she promises to show where the heron lies. Yet, Sylvia is also alarmed by him and decides that she 'would have liked him vastly better without his gun' (in Ward 1996: 56). In the straightforward opposition between a feminine nature and a masculine culture, one defined by life and the other by death, Jewett hints at various forms of social and sexual initiation. The fact that Sylvia ultimately hides the heron from the huntsman, before returning to her grandmother, suggests that Jewett retreats from these possibilities, although she does also pose a series of questions to the reader. Nevertheless, Jewett was an influential writer, especially on the work of Willa Cather.

With the closure of the Frontier, writers had to find new territories in which to explore. In 1897, Jack London joined the Klondike Gold Rush to Alaska, an experience that inspired three volumes of short stories as well as his most famous tale, 'To Build a Fire' (1908). The spare prose and the even sparser plot – one man's struggle to survive amid freezing conditions – contribute to a story that assumes symbolic and existential overtones. In a brilliant *tour de force*, London changes the point of view in the final paragraph, so that the reader sees the dying man from the perspective of, first, his sole companion, his dog, and then that of the cosmos itself:

> As the twilight drew on, its eager yearning for the fire mastered it, and with a great lifting and shifting of forefeet, it whined softly, then flattened its ears down in anticipation of being chidden by the man. But the man remained silent. Later, the dog whined loudly. And still later it crept close to the man and caught the scent of death. This made the animal bristle and back away. A little longer it delayed, howling under the stars that leaped and danced and shone brightly in the cold sky. (London 2001: 271)

Regions, Borders and Provinces

The immortalisation of the Frontier as a cornerstone of American identity generated a tension at the start of the twentieth century.

Since American nationhood had largely been defined in terms of self-reliance, progress and outward expansion, the closure of the Frontier implied that there was no further possibility to this development. Instead, following the lead of authors such as Garland and Jewett, writers turned towards the many regions that constituted the United States, either to promote the spiritual sense of place (for example, in Cather's *O Pioneers*, 1913) or to demythologise the optimism of Manifest Destiny (Anderson's *Winesburg, Ohio*). This new-found regional awareness was especially important for the American South, since the Southern states were still scarred by the economic legacy of the Civil War and the inheritance of racial oppression.

Three notable women writers followed in the wake of William Faulkner: Katherine Anne Porter, Eudora Welty and Flannery O'Connor. Porter had spent time among the American émigrés in Paris and, in stories such as 'He' (1927) and 'Rope' (1928), she uses some of their experimental techniques, such as free indirect discourse, to create respective feelings of pathos and humour. Porter, though, was less avant-garde than her contemporaries and, in particular, she was motivated by both her political commitment and sense of place, beliefs that contribute to her best-known story, 'Flowering Judas' (1930), set amid the revolutionary politics of Mexico.

Welty deeply admired Porter's fiction but her own writing, with the exception of character studies such as 'A Worn Path' (1940) and 'Powerhouse' (1941), tends to be less political and more bizarre. As Sigmund Freud argues in his influential essay 'The Uncanny' (1919), notions of *heimlich* (the homely) are already inscribed with their obverse, *unheimlich* (the unhomely or unfamiliar). In pursuing the condition of *heimat* (the nebulous connotations of home and home-land), regional writers are often compelled to explore the unfamiliar aspects that act as an integral but disruptive element within cultural identity. Consequently, in 'Old Mr Marblehall' (1938), Welty explores the possibility of a double life, imagines a suspected rapist in 'Petrified Man' (1939) hiding out as part of a freak show, and in 'Why I Live at the PO' (1941) sympathises with a young woman who prefers living at the local post office to her dysfunctional family. Yet, by distorting the outward appearance of social reality, Welty's use of the absurd also acquires a political edge, for example in 'Keela, the Outcast Indian Maiden' (1941), the story of an African-American who has been horribly abused as part of a circus but who, having internalised his abuse, is only too ready to talk about it. His story, though, is instead narrated by two white men as they, hampered by their own verbal and social incomprehension, attempt to express its horror.

The grotesque is also a key element in O'Connor's work, where it is contextualised as part of her deeply held religious beliefs. A sense of apocalypse (literally meaning both an end and a revelation) runs throughout her fiction that, as in 'The Enduring Chill' (1958), often results in a violent climax. In what might be a parody of Gustave Flaubert's 'A Simple Heart' (see Chapter 9), the feverish, would-be intellectual, Asbury, sees an horrific vision of the Holy Ghost, 'emblazoned in ice instead of fire', and realises that he will continue to live, 'frail, racked, but enduring . . . in the face of a purifying terror' (O'Connor 1990: 382). O'Connor's unsparing treatment of her characters epitomises the vocabulary of 'Southern Gothic'. Despite individual attempts at self-improvement, O'Connor's characters are bound by the historical ties of racial and sexual discrimination: the inter-generational violence that spills over in stories such as 'A View of the Woods' (1957). Yet, to label O'Connor's fiction as exclusively Southern Gothic is to occlude the many tensions that make stories such as 'The Artificial Nigger' (1955) both fascinating and uncomfortable to read. At the same time, the violent tendencies in her work also obscure the use of black humour, for example in 'Good Country People' (also 1955).

Regionalist writing remains an important element in contemporary American fiction, whether as Garrison Keillor's nostalgic *Lake Wobegon Days* (1985), Annie Proulx's revisitation of the mythic American landscape in *Close Range* (1999), or Robert Olen Butler's inter-related tales of trauma and social dislocation, *A Good Scent from a Strange Mountain* (1992). A further strand of regionalist fiction has emphasised the importance of ecology, especially in relation to the survival of Native American culture, for example in Leslie Marmon Silko's story 'Lullaby' (1981):

> The sky cleared. Ayah saw that there was nothing between her and the stars. The light was crystalline. There was no shimmer, no distortion through earth haze. She breathed the clarity of the night sky; she smelled the purity of the half moon and the stars. (Silko 1981: 51)

Another tendency has been to emphasise the role of borders so that the writing exists at the fault-line between one cultural identity and another. Sandra Cisneros' 'Woman Hollering Creek' (1991) begins with Cleófilas crossing both 'her father's threshold' and the border between Mexico and North America as her husband's new bride (Cisneros 2004: 43). Cleófilas' self-division manifests in the discrepancy between her dreams of wedded bliss and the reality of an oppressive marriage. Her suppressed rage is symbolised by the creek, known as Woman Hollering, which demarcates the border and which, at the end of the story, she eventually crosses. In her volume *Crossing the Border* (1976), Joyce Carol Oates situates a series of stories at the border between Canada and North America. To cross the border is also to transgress the strains within the family relationships that predominate each of the stories.

Both Cisneros and Oates use the short story form in order to explore spaces that are *liminal* (literally 'on the threshold'), both emotionally and physically. For Canadian writers such as Margaret Atwood, her nation has appeared to occupy a liminal place overshadowed by the superpower just across the border. In novels such as *Surfacing* (1972), Atwood has sought to uncover a national identity distinct from the influence of North America. But, in later stories such as 'Wilderness Tips' (1991), Atwood suggests that this goal is far harder to achieve since her latter-day pioneers bring with them from the city their own baggage of personal and sexual antagonisms, including a private mythology of the Canadian landscape. The story's title is also that of a manual from 1905 offering practical advice on how to survive in the wilderness. But, for Atwood's characters, the wilderness is not only the physical territory but also their own emotional desolation. Similarly, in stories such as 'Meneseteung' (1990), Alice Munro dramatises the extent to which the Canadian borderlands have been mythologised and the resultant need for them to be reimagined, so that identities (especially females) excluded from the colonial narrative can be reinscribed.

This need for reinscription is also true of contemporary British literature, where a metropolitan view of the regions as peripheral has been countered in recent years. The short story has continued to play an important role in Irish literature, including writers such as John B. Keane, Mary Lavin, John McGahern and Bernard MacLaverty, although they have tended to be overshadowed by the prolific William Trevor. Despite Trevor's increasingly iconic status as a master of the short story, his mordant view of contemporary life, evident as far back as *The Ballroom of Romance* (1972) and still present in his most recent collection, *Cheating at Canasta* (2007), fixes Irish culture in a melancholic gaze. While Trevor has no sympathy for the legacy of Anglo-Irish rule, neither does he have any affinity for the Republic's economic expansion. Instead, Trevor's position resembles that of the poet Seamus Heaney, and the latter's wistful depiction of the Irish landscape.

Trevor's writing is in stark contrast with the renaissance in Scottish literature, where again the short story has played a vital role, for example in the work of writers such as Alasdair Gray, A. L. Kennedy, Ali Smith and Irvine Welsh. Arguably most important is the fiction of James Kelman. Although, due to their celebrity, writers such as Welsh have displayed a superficial engagement with politics, Kelman's work is both deeply political and devoid of the chauvinism that can result from a regional bias. A native of Glasgow, Kelman has criticised attempts to culturally renovate the city. Yet, in his depictions of horrific violence and crude language, Kelman is only too aware of the ugliness of Glasgow. Kelman's significance, though, lies not in his shock value but in his use of an ephemeral form, such as the short story, in order to describe the experience of a city impacted upon by economic and social deregulation. The characters of his first collection, *Not Not While the Giro* (1983), are usually restless, often seen trudging around the city on foot. Social and sexual relationships are either transitory or in the midst of transformation, as in, for example, 'Forgetting to mention Allende' from *Greyhound for Breakfast* (1987). By extracting particularities from the milieu that he knows best, Kelman constructs a social landscape that is applicable to most other British cities. To this end, Ra Page's Comma Press has published a series of anthologies set in northern cities such as Leeds, Liverpool, Manchester and Newcastle. Although inspired by the vitality of local regeneration, Comma Press has contributed to the gradual decentralisation of authority from the traditional heartland of London. As a consequence, these articulations of a regional identity are themselves bound up with the geopolitics of de- and neo-colonisation.

Colonial and Neo-Colonial Encounters in an Era of Globalisation

The tales of the nineteenth-century French author Prosper Mérimée offer a ready template for the colonial encounter between indigenous and imperialistic cultures. In stories such as 'Mateo Falcone' (1829), Mérimée's emphasis upon 'significant detail', equivalent to Poe's 'unity of impression' or Kipling's 'Higher Editing', influenced later writers such as Flaubert. The realist tendency in Mérimée's writing, though, was counterbalanced by his love of romance. In his most famous story, 'Carmen' (1845), Mérimée narrates the exploits of his *femme fatale* from two perspectives: an archeologist visiting southern Spain and Carmen's doomed lover, José. In each of these narratives, to which Mérimée later added a coda on the traits of Gypsy women, there is an attempt to define the female subject. The use of multiple perspectives, however, contributes to Carmen's enigma: her passionate defiance of male comprehension. As in his supernatural tale 'The Venus of Ille' (1837), Mérimée opposes an uncomprehending narrator, who represents the voice of civilised society, with a female subject that embodies a wild, excessive and primitive culture. The pedantic archeologist, who in passing introduces the story of Carmen, is nevertheless part of a colonial exercise whereby the Spanish landscape is treated as a site for excavation, a passive object for study, but which, in its embodiment as Carmen, confuses and distracts the narrator from his intended goal. Running in tandem with the development of nineteenth-century colonial discourse, and drawing upon a romantic view of history, Mérimée's short fiction establishes a pattern of binary oppositions through which to explore colonial relations.

Mérimée's narrative model holds good for late nineteenth- and twentieth-century fictions, although increasingly the outsider becomes either a witness or a participant within a horrific, often ritualistic, encounter between two cultures. The former scenario includes stories such as Kipling's 'The Mark of the Beast' (1890), Joseph Conrad's 'Karain: A Memory' (1897) and Charlotte Mew's 'A White Night' (1903). The latter category features stories such as Kipling's 'The Man Who Would Be King' (1888), Lawrence's 'The Woman Who Rode Away' (1925) and Paul Bowles' 'A Distant Episode' (1947). In his story 'The Air Disaster' (1975), J. G. Ballard inverts the pattern. A journalist, searching for the remains of a passenger jet that has crashed somewhere in the Mexican mountains, enters a peasant village. Believing if he bribes the villagers with enough money they will lead him to the crash-site, he is angered when they show him the carcass of a small military plane. Shouting 'there should be bodies everywhere, hundreds of cadavers' (Ballard 2001: 826), the journalist decides to leave the scene. But, as he drives down the mountainside, the villagers watch him go, standing next to the rows of corpses 'freshly jerked from their graves', while the journalist hands out to them 'the last of [his] money'. Although the journalist's amoral, neo-colonial attitude is contrasted with the villagers' sense of duty to the crash victims, the characters, including even the corpses 'at last earn[ing] their keep' (Ballard 2001: 827), are all ultimately players within the global cash economy.

In sharp contrast to Ballard's horrific satire, R. K. Narayan's tales of Malgudi, his fictional provincial city, are funny and heart-warming, even though Narayan's characters often survive in great hardship. In 'God and the Cobbler' (1976), Narayan recounts the meeting between a cobbler and a Vietnam veteran on the hippie trail through India. The traveller wishes 'he could be composed and self-contained like the cobbler', is 'struck by the total acceptance . . . of life as it came' and observes the cobbler's 'mystic joy in the very process of handling leather' (Narayan 2006: 234–5). But, when the hippie observes that 'flowers rain on you', the cobbler astutely replies, 'can I eat that flower? Can I take it home and give it to the woman to be put into the cooking pot?' (Narayan 2006: 237). Although Narayan's hippie is not as exploitative as Ballard's journalist, he is still guilty of romanticising a culture he does not fully understand, a symptomatic response to the guilt he feels about the villages he destroyed in Vietnam. He is far from being the god that the cobbler takes him for, lacking the latter's adroitness, although both are briefly brought together by the cash nexus that underwrites their lives. Their only difference is that the hippie can delude himself into thinking that there is a pure life beyond the influence of money, although it is only his ability to pay for the cobbler's services that ensures he can wander. The cobbler, by contrast, is tied to his material existence.

The impact of globalisation, an emerging economic reality since at least the early 1970s, but accelerating after the link-up of financial markets and the collapse of the Eastern Bloc at the end of the 1980s, has drastically altered the meaning of locality. To be local, as in Mitford's romantic vision of the village, is a practical impossibility when invisible economic processes routinely interpenetrate everyday social activities. In the integrated world of finance, data and capital, where everything and everyone is in transit, there are no longer any peripheries but neither are there any centres. For the short story, which traditionally has shown an affinity for the particular and the local, this new reality represents a significant challenge. Postmodern texts such as Douglas Coupland's *Generation X* (1991) are predicated upon this basis. Yet, in another sense, globalisation has merely intensified a condition that was always there: the relationship between the particular and the universal. In Irving's 'Rip Van Winkle', Rip wakes up to find himself in a society that, despite its democratic pretence, remains oppressive; the only difference is that he is now, to all intents and purposes, a ghost haunting the political system. In other words, while postmodern strategies are one response to the effects of globalisation, the short story has traditionally found ways of approaching the changing definition of locality.

Bharati Mukherjee's 'A Wife's Story' (1988) relocates Turner's Frontier thesis in relation to Panna, an Indian woman attending university in New York. She is preparing for a visit from her husband, a businessman still based in India. In the meantime, though, she is having an affair with Imre, 'a refugee from Budapest' who is also another member of 'the new pioneers' (Mukherjee 1989: 26–7). The story begins, however, with Panna's response to the racial abuse of David Mamet's play *Glengarry Glen Ross*. In an inversion of the Frontier thesis, she details how white Anglo–Saxon Protestant culture transforms its reception of racial minorities:

> First, you don't exist. Then you're invisible. Then you're funny. Then you're disgusting. Insult, my American friends will tell me, is a kind of acceptance. (Mukherjee 1989: 26)

Yet, it is Panna who is also changing in her language, her clothing and in her social conduct; changes that she does not notice until her husband arrives. While he indulges himself as a tourist in American culture, Panna comes to the realisation that 'whole peoples have moved before me; they've adapted' (Mukherjee 1989: 39), including herself. In the story's final scene, Panna gazes at herself in a bathroom mirror:

> I watch my naked body turn, the breasts, the thighs glow. The body's beauty amazes. I stand here shameless, in ways he has never seen me. I am free, afloat, watching somebody else's. (Mukherjee 1989: 40)

Despite the emphasis upon self-transformation, the symbolism of the mirror is double-edged, since it also implies self-division. In becoming 'somebody else', Panna is no longer herself but neither is she fully integrated as American: the racism that she describes at the start of the story has not been removed by her private metamorphosis. Instead, her liberation from her husband is only a partial freedom, a dichotomy that Mukherjee tends to gloss in Panna's rediscovery of her physical self, a conclusion that sidesteps the extent to which the iconography of the body has been censored within the dominant Protestant culture of the United States. In contrast, collections such as Junot Díaz's *Drown* (1996) and Jhumpa Lahiri's *The Interpreter of Maladies* (1999) emphasise the theme of self-division by dividing their content between different regions while, at the same time, reflecting upon the displacement of their characters.

Increasingly, it seems that dislocation, rather than locality, has become the dominant trait of the short story. In 'Metal' (2005), Matthew Kneale puts the well-worn device of the twist ending to effective use. An English businessman, travelling in an unnamed African state, is involved first in a car accident and then in a police beating. Welcomed into the household of a stranger, Toby has an epiphany – he will change his life and leave his career – but, gradually, his resolve fails as self-interest takes over: how can he explain his decision to his wife and children? In the final scene, Toby is shown selling armaments to the same government whose security police had previously attacked him and his driver.

Kneale's stateless businessman, whose own compromised morality is implicated in the states that he passes through, is emblematic of the ethical confusion that globalisation has brought in its wake. Yet, statelessness is itself the iconic imagery of globalisation, for example in the borderland between Russia and China where Ha Jin's *Ocean of Words*

(1996) is set. Although centring upon the lives of Chinese soldiers in the early 1970s, Ha Jin's use of location – merely a line on the map disputed by the two rival Communist nations – is also a product of the pre-millennial imagination. Yet, ironically, it was perhaps Kipling who, first of all, introduced this concept of statelessness into the short story in his depiction of the hillside city Simla in his *Plain Tales from the Hills* (1888). Here, and in subsequent stories such as the social satire 'A Wayside Comedy', Kipling depicted Simla as the prototype of the gated community from behind whose doors the British Raj ruled the surrounding territory. From Kipling to Ha Jin, it is possible to see a growing preoccupation with what William Burroughs termed 'interzones': the lost spaces within modern city-life.

Further Reading

A standard account of place and community is offered by Valerie Shaw (1983). For further discussion of the Frontier and American regionalism, see Martin Scofield (2006). For an introduction to James Kelman, see H. Gustav Klaus (2004). On Bharati Mukherjee and William Trevor, see the entries in *A Reader's Companion to the Short Story in English* edited by Erin Fallon et al. (2001). Ha Jin recounts the sources of his fiction in Dana Gioia and R. S. Gwynn, *The Art of the Short Story* (2006). For a short introduction to the issues surrounding globalisation, see Manfred B. Steger (2003). Sigmund Freud's 'The Uncanny' can be found in his essays on *Art and Literature* (1985).

13

Tales of the City

In 1887, the German sociologist Ferdinand Tönnies described the transition from countryside to city as the movement away from social networks connected by communal, familial, feudal and religious ties (*Gemeinschaft*) to human relationships that are individual, impersonal, commercial and secular (*Gesellschaft*). Social anonymity was intensified by the scale and volume of the modern city. For Gustave Le Bon, in his 1895 study of crowd psychology, the urban masses represented a loss of individual will. By contrast, for Georg Simmel in 'The Metropolis and Mental Life' (1903), the very crowdedness of the city encouraged individuals to differentiate themselves from their environment and to devise new methods for rationalising the shifting experience of the city. Throughout the nineteenth century, novelists such as Charles Dickens and Fyodor Dostoevsky, and poets such as Charles Baudelaire, sought innovative means of describing the urban milieu. The short story was a further device that allowed the writer to adopt the role of a detached and impartial observer.

Flânerie and the Modern City

Edgar Allan Poe's 'The Man of the Crowd' (1840) begins with the first-person narrator sitting in a coffee house in London coolly observing the various classes, types and manners within the passing crowds. As night looms and 'the general character of the crowd materially alters', the narrator spies 'a countenance which at once arrested and absorbed my whole attention' (Poe 1998: 87–8). Fascinated by the stranger, and by the hidden history that his agonised expression seems to suggest, the narrator pursues him throughout the rest of the night and into the following day. Tracing and retracing his steps, secreting himself into marketplaces and gin-dens, the stranger is in constant pursuit of crowded spaces, so that eventually the narrator abandons his quest of discovering the stranger's secret: 'He refuses to be alone. *He is the man of the crowd*. It will be in vain to follow' (Poe 1998: 91). Like a closed book, the stranger's story remains unread. At the same time, his wanderings through London map out the city as a place of circuitous routes and hidden haunts. The narrator's ironic references to his own isolation and fevered mental state suggests that the stranger may instead be a projection of the narrator's mind, a doppelganger through which the labyrinthine city acts as an impression of the narrator's own psychological condition. In the stories that compose *Goodbye to Berlin* (1939), Christopher Isherwood takes Poe's device of the disaffected narrator to its limits by positing his narrator as a constant, impersonal 'Camera Eye'. In the modern urban experience 'there is no longer a city . . . only a man walking through it' (Williams 1973: 243).

Poe's story partially inspired Baudelaire's influential notion of the *flâneur* or idle stroller. Baudelaire describes the *flâneur* as a 'passionate spectator':

> It is an immense joy to set up house in the heart of the multitude, amid the ebb and flow of movement, in the midst of the fugitive and the infinite. To be away from home and yet to feel oneself everywhere at home; to see the world, to be at the centre of the world, and yet to remain hidden from the world . . . The spectator is a *prince* who everywhere rejoices in his incognito.
> (Baudelaire 1995: 9)

In his analysis of Baudelaire, Walter Benjamin elaborates upon the *flâneur* by arguing that it is an identity, a mask, which intermingles with the spectacle of the marketplace: 'The intoxication to which the *flâneur* surrenders is the intoxication of the commodity around which surges the stream of customers' (Benjamin 1983: 55). Baudelaire imagines the city as a site of fleeting encounters, bizarre juxtapositions, ennui and introspection. The French avant-garde, among them Guillaume Apollinaire in his poem 'Zone' (1912) and Louis Aragon in his novel *Paris Peasant* (1926), took Baudelaire as their starting-point. Yet, in his story 'Nevsky Prospect' (1835), Nikolai Gogol had already described St Petersburg as a phantasmagoria in which 'the whole city turns into a rumbling and brilliance, myriads of carriages tumble from the bridges, postillions shout and bounce on their horses, and the devil himself lights the lamps only so as to show everything not as it really looks' (Gogol 2003: 278). Furthermore, in 'Bartleby, the Scrivener' (1853), Herman Melville inverts Baudelaire's aesthetic so that it is the object, the stray or errant 'dead letter' (Melville 1997: 41), who is the story's title-character. Subtitled 'A Story of Wall Street', Melville incisively evokes a series of alienated economic relations where the narrator's altruism towards Bartleby is shown to be naïve, while it is the polite but non-compliant worker who realises his status as a mere unit within the shifting network of financial exchange systems. In a premonition of more recent accounts of late capitalism, the memory of Bartleby returns as a ghost that haunts the narrator.

The rise of literary naturalism and the growth of modern sociology, both of which emphasised the importance of culture and environment upon the formation of human identity, resulted in a more explicitly realistic depiction of the city, for example in Stephen Crane's 'Maggie: A Child of the Streets' (1893). British short story cycles, such as Arthur Morrison's *Tales of Mean Streets* (1894), took not only a more objective approach to the subject of working-class poverty but also, as in the case of Clarence Rook's *The Hooligan Nights* (1899), derived much of their vividness from the new forms of tabloid journalism. Although, on the one hand, aesthetic writers such as Hubert Crackanthorpe, Arthur Symons and Oscar Wilde were inspired by Baudelaire's *flâneur*, on the other hand, representation of the urban poor was influenced by a new type of documentary realism. While this approach tended to objectify the working classes, to treat them as a case study in order to arouse middle-class pity and fear, the long-term effect was to highlight the myriad communities that make up the modern city. In New York, despite the commercial nature of his writing, O. Henry did much the same by drawing attention to the speech and conduct of his lower-class characters.

Indebted to this naturalistic style, although strongly revisionary, is Mary Butts' 'In Bayswater' (1923). The opening sequence, describing a young man, Alec, moving into his new lodgings, appears realistic enough but once Alec is lured into sexual intrigue involving his landlady's son, Charles, Charles' lover, Festus, and the girl, Billy, whom Charles' mother hopes to tempt him with, the naturalistic frame explodes into a psychological drama in which sexual identity is continuously under assault. Butts' modernist technique not only calls the fidelity of naturalism into doubt but it also inverts one of the key dialectical components of city literature. Whereas for both Baudelaire and Gogol the deceptive surface of the city is equated with the dissimulation of female attractiveness, Butts switches the point of view so that it is the male object, whose taboo and repressed sexual desire is equated with urban violence. In 'The Golden Bough' (also 1923), Butts applies J. G. Frazer's anthropological study of ritual and sacrifice to the change in sexual roles in postwar London, while in 'Mappa Mundi' (1938) the male object of desire disappears into the shadowy, other world of Paris.

Butts was not the only modernist woman for whom city life was a vicarious existence. As Raymond Williams has argued, the metropolis was central to the development of modernism since it was both the embodiment of technological modernity and the centre of economic and artistic activity (Williams 1989: 37–49). In order to be published and to be known, writers gravitated towards the city. Yet, urban and mass culture was also frequently described in degraded, feminine terms (Huyssen 1986: 44–62). Furthermore, women writers lacked the social and sexual mobility with which the mask of *flânerie* provided for their male counterparts (Wolff 1990: 34–50). Consequently, the experience of a woman writer resident in the city was marked by ambivalence and the concomitant need to express that uncertainty in forms, such as the short story, which were equivocal and not overdetermined in terms of their narrative structure.

The heroine of Virginia Woolf's 'Mrs Dalloway in Bond Street' (1923) finds liberation in the city: 'I love walking in London . . . really it's better than walking in the country!' (Woolf 2003: 147). Yet, the cityscape she experiences is marked by social boundaries: it is predominantly aristocratic and comfortably middle class. Other urban stories by modernist women, such as Mansfield's 'Life of Ma Parker' (1921), persist in portraying working-class conditions as irredeemably grim. Although her respectable status allows Mrs Dalloway to walk certain parts of the city, she also reads that terrain from the point of view of a woman, the *passante* or female passer-by as opposed to the all-consuming eye of the *flâneur*. Mrs Dalloway's vision lights upon minute details of dress and behaviour that only a person of her class and gender would notice, and instead of extracting these incidents from their social context, she experiences them through a myriad of other impressions: 'the stream was endless' (Woolf 2003: 148). Woolf's refusal to order the narrative according to a hierarchy of experience, so that the detached third-person narrator is itself incorporated within Mrs Dalloway's interior monologue, makes for an unsatisfying effect in comparison with the fiction of her nearest rival, Mansfield. In that sense, the story necessitates its expansion into a novel. But, in another sense, however, by inverting public and private experience, so that the city becomes a projection of Mrs Dalloway's wandering eye, Woolf not only calls into question the gender relations that conduct the city but also the conventions that underwrite the short story.

In contrast with Woolf's protagonist, Jean Rhys' characters experience the city as a place of entrapment. Like Butts, Rhys lived in Paris during the 1920s as part of the émigré community of British and American writers that emerged around Gertrude Stein, in particular, and the salons of the Left Bank more generally. For women of different ethnic backgrounds and sexual orientations, the more liberal atmosphere of Paris represented a temporary respite from prejudice and discrimination. Yet, as Rhys' stories make clear, this comparative freedom was both precarious and uncertain. In the absence of traditional social ties, such as marriage and motherhood, Rhys' contemporaries were both more liberated and more alienated than their immediate predecessors. In stories such as 'Mannequin', from her collection *The Left Bank* (1927), Rhys exposes the economic and sexual exploitation of working women. At the same time, the incongruous appearance of stories such as 'Mixing Cocktails', set in Rhys' homeland of the Caribbean, imply that the social life of Paris is implicated in the economics of colonialism. Rhys' fiction complements the work of Colette, once an actress in Paris, whose backstage stories, such as 'The Quick-Change Artist' (1941), play with the notion of femininity as a masquerade while also emphasising the economic subjugation of women. Mansfield too, although a visitor rather than a resident of Paris, places a similar emphasis in her story 'Je ne parle pas français' (1918), where her narrator, the avant-garde poet Raoul Duquette, funds his dilettantish lifestyle by working as a pimp for English-speaking tourists. Without the baggage of the novel, the short story form allows women writers to surf the social and economic landscape of the city in which they themselves are players.

The City at War

The fall of Paris to the Nazis in 1940 marked the beginning of its end as the dominant culture capital during the early twentieth century. After 1945, the centre of artistic activity would shift to New York. London, ravaged throughout the war years by aerial bombardment, experienced a form of siege mentality but in which artistic experimentation was sustained. The precariousness and unreality of life during wartime inspired the artistic imagination, in particular the use of nontraditional forms such as the short story.

In stories such as 'The Demon Lover' and 'In the Square' (both 1941), Elizabeth Bowen presents a transfigured city-space. Familiar routes through the city, and by implication conventional means of reading the city, are impeded by blockades, bomb craters and devastated buildings. At the start of 'Mysterious Kôr' (1944), the city has become its mirror-image: 'London looked like the moon's capital – shallow, cratered, extinct.' The spatial transformation is mirrored by the emotional pressure upon the inhabitants: 'People stayed indoors with a fervour that could be felt: the buildings strained with batteneddown human life' (Bowen 1999: 728). As Bowen's protagonist, Pepita, comments, London has become Kôr, H. Rider Haggard's mythical kingdom, 'a completely forsaken city, as high as cliffs and as white as bones, with no history' (Bowen 1999: 729). Pepita continues: 'if you can blow whole places out of existence, you can blow whole places into it . . . Kôr may be the only city left: the abiding city.' Like a pagan equivalent to Jerusalem, Kôr is both timeless and ever-present: 'you mean we're there now, that here's there, that now's then?' (Bowen 1999: 730). Bowen's characters, living an ephemeral existence governed by the privations of war, the requirements of service and warwork and the odd rhythms of wartime, experience life as a dream:

> I could have sworn she saw it, and from the way she saw it I saw it, too. A game's a game, but what's a hallucination? You begin by laughing, then it gets in you and you can't laugh it off. (Bowen 1999: 738)

In 'The Wall' (1944), William Sansom also plays with the discontinuities of wartime by focusing upon the three seconds that follow after the front of a burning building becomes detached and threatens to collapse upon the firemen below. Sansom's concentrated prose prefigures similar experiments in time delay such as Tobias Wolff's 'Bullet in the Brain' (1995).

Bowen's sense of alienation is also picked up, although in a very different mode, by Julian Maclaren-Ross, a key figure within the drinking dens and artistic haunts of wartime Soho. Casting himself in the role of *flâneur*, Maclaren-Ross' crisp and laconic style is indebted to Americans such as Ernest Hemingway and Dashiell Hammett. Despite criticisms of his anecdotal style, Maclaren-Ross makes effective use of the comic form in order to suggest the blurred priorities of life under wartime conditions so that, in 'The Virgin' (1944), the narrator views the rare encounter with a sexually innocent woman to be as dramatic as the fall of Italy. In 'Welsh Rabbit of Soap' (1946), Maclaren-Ross' use of modernist reference-points such as T. S. Eliot, James Joyce and Gertrude Stein in the context of his low-life characters suggests a collapse of 'high' and 'low' culture that also conveys the transience of wartime where such distinctions no longer seem viable.

If Maclaren-Ross is gesturing beyond the immediate effects of the War towards the emergence of an homogeneous mass culture, in 'The Destructors' (1954) Graham Greene is concerned with another aspect of the War's legacy. The gang of children, who pursue a nameless vendetta against the adult they call 'Old Misery', are products of the scarred and cratered postwar landscape. The ascent to power of the new boy known only as 'T', allied by Blackie's attempts to maintain the solidity of the group, signal that the story should be read as a political allegory with Old Misery acting as their scapegoat. The boys' dismantling of his house from within effectively completes what the Nazi bombardment has failed to achieve. Yet, the story is also presented as black comedy with the adult deserving his comeuppance. As T observes, 'all this hate and love . . . it's soft, it's hooey. There's only things' (Greene 1972: 338). The house's disintegration into a pile of rubble evokes the entry into a world of interchangeable objects in which moral distinction is also lost.

Multiculturalism and the Postcolonial City

Stories such as 'The Destructors' depict the decline of London as an imperial heartland. In retrospect, however, beginning with mass immigration from the Caribbean in the late 1940s, London has not deteriorated but has been transformed by its immigrant populations. Courttia Newland's recent sequence, *Society Within* (1999), describes an impoverished, predominantly black housing estate in West London which, despite its hardships, erects a sense of its own identity, symbolised in particular by the friendship between Elisha, the newcomer, and Boozy, a married woman only slightly older than herself. Newland's stories are part of a dual process, first, in which the grandchildren of immigrants have come to redefine common British identity, and second, in which working-class communities have sought to overturn earlier artistic representations.

The theme of assimilation has been of particular importance for Jewish-American writers, such as Saul Bellow, Bernard Malamud, Cynthia Ozick, Grace Paley, Philip Roth and Isaac Bashevis Singer. Born in Poland, Singer migrated to the United States in 1935 and wrote most of his fiction in Yiddish. (Bellow was one of his first translators.) Singer's story 'The Cabalist of East Broadway' (1971) begins not only with a portrait of modernity versus tradition, 'the synagogues became churches, the yeshivas restaurants or garages', but also of multiculturalism as an index of modernity: 'in former times one could meet Yiddish writers, journalists, teachers, fund raisers for Israel . . . now the place catered mainly to Negroes and Puerto Ricans' (Singer 1982: 381). The narrator, a journalist, becomes fascinated by Joel Yabloner, an expert on Jewish mysticism, who leads an isolated life in New York although admired in Israel. Then, by chance, the narrator encounters Yabloner again, this time delivering a lecture in Tel Aviv where his fortunes have been 'resuscitated' by 'the Jewish state' (Singer 1982: 383). Yabloner embodies an older, more mystical Jewish identity with which his admirers seek to connect, not least his new wife who effectively acts as his minder. The narrator encounters Yabloner one last time, an émigré once more in New York, but this time his appearance is dishevelled, his manner 'hostile' and his faith spent (Singer 1982: 386). Yabloner is a man out of joint both temporally and geographically. His final resting place is unknown and the narrator is left only with questions.

Singer's sense of the arbitrariness of immigrant existence is true also of Malamud, for example in his most celebrated story 'The Magic Barrel' (1954). Finkle, a rabbinical student, hires a marriage-broker,

Salzman, to find him a wife, since he has been told that as a married man he would be preferred for a congregation. Finkle's inability, though, to select a bride from Salzman's list calls into question why he had decided to become a rabbi. Unable to choose, because 'he had never loved anyone', in what way is Finkle fit to 'love God' (Malamud 2003: 205)? He breaks his bargain with Salzman, declaring that he will only marry someone he loves, but then discovers a picture of a girl among Salzman's discarded photographs: a girl Finkle later learns is Salzman's daughter, Stella. Throughout the story, the relationship of Finkle, torn between sacred and profane love, and Salzman, the commercial animal, is treated as if it were a Faustian pact, with Salzman vanishing and reappearing as if he were the Devil. Again, the tradition of devotion to which Finkle aspires is undercut by Salzman's modernity, in which such ties are regarded only as commodities.

Roth's 'Epstein' (1958) acts as an effective counterpart to 'The Magic Barrel'. Here, the title-character has done all that could be expected of him as both a devout Jew and an American citizen: he has worked hard, bought a home, married and raised a family. Yet, Epstein feels that life has passed him by, a feeling accentuated by the sexual freedom of his daughter and his nephew. As in Grace Paley's 'A Conversation with my Father' (1974), the story turns upon the tension between generations, one enjoying the freedoms that the other had striven for, but it also reveals the anxiety within the older generation as their traditional beliefs in marriage and hard work begin to shatter. Roth's fiction expresses similar feelings of despair as in the work of American writers such as John Updike, but the desperation of his characters is mediated through their divided sense of cultural identity.

Self-division is also a key theme in Rohinton Mistry's *Tales from Firozsha Baag* (1987). As in Vikram Chandra's *Love and Longing in Bombay* (1997), Mistry's milieu is the contemporary Indian city, and while Chandra uses the convention of stories retold within a local bar, Mistry centres his stories round the residents of an apartment block. This device adds to Mistry's use of the short story cycle, since the compartmentalised lives of the inhabitants ultimately intersect, thereby revealing the tensions that underpin their existence. These anxieties are not only religious, economic and class-based but also grounded in the history of Empire. The Parsi residents of Firozsha Baag were once privileged subjects of the British Raj, and even in their impoverished state they continue to mimic their former role. The neighbouring area of Tar Gully is regarded as a 'menacing mouth', its migrant population as 'satanic animals and fiends' (Mistry 1992: 16, 31), while workers such as Jacqueline, the spectral servant who narrates 'The Ghost of Firozsha Baag', are mistreated by their Parsi employers. In an elegant twist to this theme, the final story is narrated by Kersi, the son whose development is also mirrored in the collection. Now resident in Canada, Kersi is subject to racist abuse just as his parents have abused local incomers. The irony of this situation attests to both the ambiguity of power relations and the heterogeneity of cultural identity: movement in and out of the postcolonial city is unstoppable, and with it, the transformation of the people that compose the polis.

Interzones: The Postmodern City

The urban ethnic experience shares an affinity with postmodern representations of the city insofar as both describe an unstable locus. If, for the modernist writer, the city existed as a space onto which s/he could map their own psychological terrain, for the postmodern writer the city is experienced as a rapidly changing domain in flight from what Michel de Certeau has described as the 'Concept-city' of rational and official discourse. In place of a centralised and regulated social order, the postmodern city works against an absolute or totalising political structure, in which power is experienced everywhere but emanates from nowhere, in which the city is experienced as, in Ian McEwan's 'Psychopolis' (1978), 'vast, fragmented . . . without a centre . . . a nexus of change or stagnation' (McEwan 1995: 301).

The early short stories of William Burroughs are a convenient starting-point, since Burroughs developed his preoccupation with lost centres from a reading of Dada, Surrealism, and modernist poets such as T. S. Eliot. Burroughs' hybrid city, Interzone, is a contraction of the International Zone, the European quarter of Tangier. In a sketch from 1954, Burroughs describes the city as existing 'on several dimensions' where 'fact merges into dream, and dreams erupt into the real world' (Burroughs 1989: 58). He praises the city as 'a sanctuary of noninterference' but also describes it as 'a vast penal colony' (Burroughs 1989: 59), an allusion not only to the fiction of Franz Kafka but also, as in a mirror image, to the real-life gulags described, for example, in

Varlam Shalamov's *Kolyma Tales* (1980). Commerce penetrates every aspect of Tangier: it 'is a clearinghouse', 'a vast overstocked market', 'where no movement is possible because all energy is equally distributed' (Burroughs 1989: 54). There are no fixed borders, 'anyone can enter Tangier' (Burroughs 1989: 52), but the city is also the 'last stop' where all its inhabitants 'will be frozen in a final, meaningless posture' (Burroughs 1989: 49).

Burroughs' apocalyptic tableau of Tangier resonates in the work of J. G. Ballard. Unlike other city writers, Ballard has found his milieu in the outskirts of London, the ring of suburbs linked by the motorway system. For Ballard, suburbia is another kind of interzone: leafy, comfortable and bourgeois on the outside, but sufficiently shielded from the urban heartland to explore its own private obsessions. Raised as a child of Empire in Shanghai, Ballard has imported the colonial gated community, described for instance by Rudyard Kipling in his tales of Simla, to the urban periphery. In 'The Enormous Space' (1989), for example, Ballantyne establishes his island retreat within his own suburban home. Estranged from his work and his ex-wife, Ballantyne maintains the outward appearance of a conventional suburbanite while first living off rations and then his neighbours' domestic pets. Whether as a symptom of madness, malnutrition or the haunted remains of 'the old Croydon aerodrome' (Ballard 2001: 1134), the geometry of the house begins to expand and accelerate: 'Sooner or later the process will halt . . . revealing the true dimensions of the world we inhabit' (Ballard 2001: 1137). Losing all perspective with the outside world, Ballantyne retreats into the contours of his own unconscious mind.

For other writers, the city itself becomes the limitless expression of the imagination. In Donald Barthelme's 'City Life' (1970), Ramona admits, 'we are locked in the most exquisite mysterious muck', which 'heaves and palpitates', yet nevertheless is touched with 'sublimity' (Barthelme 1993: 158). Barthelme's most succinct description of the sublime within the mess of urban living is his story 'The Balloon' (1968). A gigantic balloon mysteriously expands throughout New York, covering vast tracts of the city. Unable to explain its origins, the inhabitants write on it, play on it, explore it and fantasise about it. The interpretations and uses of the balloon are endless because it is 'not limited, or defined.' It constantly shifts 'its shape', adapting itself to each attempt to navigate its surface. In that sense, the very plasticity of the balloon becomes an extension of the observer's imagination. Yet, since no part 'could be ignored', the balloon also defies absolute comprehension: its meaning residing within the meeting of 'each intersection' just as the city's meaning resides within the meeting of each block and avenue (Barthelme 1993: 57).

As Barthelme suggests, the urban sublime is closely equated with the fantastic. In Will Self's story 'The North London Book of the Dead' (1991), a grieving son is startled to discover that not only is his dead mother residing in a flat in Crouch End but that whole communities of dead people are inhabiting unfashionable parts of the city, running 'dead businesses' or intermingling with the living: 'It just goes to show you how big and anonymous the city really is' (Self 2006b: 14–15). Self's painfully funny story conceals its emotional undertow, as does Haruki Murakami's 'Super-Frog Saves Tokyo' (2001), in which Katagiri encounters a gigantic frog intent on saving the city from an enormous, burrowing worm. Part of Murakami's sequence, *after the quake* (2003), the story describes in oblique terms the trauma felt within the Japanese psyche following the massive Kobe earthquake of 1995. Similarly, in China Miéville's 'Looking for Jake' (1998) the melancholic fixation upon a lost friend is described in terms of an apocalyptic scenario drawn from science fiction. Something has, apparently, happened to London: the streets are deserted, the rubbish mounts, the telephones are tapped, the mass media has either been silenced or taken over, and the birds have been killed by 'unseen flapping things' (Miéville 2006: 12). The inexact nature of the apocalypse, though, suggests that all of these details may instead be the paranoiac delusions of the narrator. Unable to live without the mysterious Jake, the narrator heads off for the former Gaumont cinema in Kilburn, an iconic structure from his childhood, which he assumes to be at the heart of the unnamed disaster. Despite their fantastical trappings, each of these stories is concerned with the effects of trauma and with the city as a place of hidden secrets. This latter theme is taken up in Miéville's bizarrely comic 'Reports of Certain Events in London' (2004), in which the science fiction tropes of time travel and alien invasion are played out as a battle between streets while the physical geography of London morphs and unfolds.

The city as a site of metamorphosis is graphically described in Iain Sinclair's 'The Griffin's Egg' (1996). Sinclair has, throughout his writing, closely pursued the principles of Situationism, a postwar grouping of French intellectuals and activists who, inspired by Baudelaire and the pre-war avant-garde, drifted across the landscape of Paris in order to map out, what they termed, a 'psychogeography' of the city. As if in imitation of the unfolding cityscape, Sinclair has mixed literary forms – novel, essay, poem – while also playing upon his own persona. His collaboration with the artist Dave McKean and the photographer Marc Atkins further dismantles the role of the omniscient author. In contravention of traditional comic-strip form, Sinclair and his collaborators construct a palimpsest in which text (in various typographies), photographic image and pen and ink drawing bleed into one another (see over). The technique recalls the illuminated manuscripts and marginal glosses of early modern literature but, in effect, it foregrounds London as an 'unedited city' (Sinclair and McKean 1996: 43). Within the cyclical plot design, the narrative prefigures events and echoes others in order to create a feeling of simultaneity, that is to say, what is to come has always already occurred: a concatenation of past and future into the present. Narrative order is further disturbed by the master-servant relationship of the two main characters: Turner, a photographer, hired by Norton, a writer, in order 'to gain access to . . . the riverside penthouse apartment' of Lord Kawn (Sinclair and McKean 1996: 44), a thinly veiled caricature of the novelist and political operator, Jeffrey Archer. Their mutual attempts to penetrate Kawn's inner sanctum, just as the reader seeks permission into the text, dramatise the conflict between word and image displayed also in the story's construction. Their private contest becomes more concerned with spying on each other than on Kawn or, as the text remarks, 'surveillance is the art form of the millennium' (Sinclair and McKean 1996: 50).

Surveillance, though, takes on an altogether different meaning in Deborah Eisenberg's story 'Twilight of the Superheroes' (2006). The narrative, told in a series of titled sub-sections, moves back and forth in time while describing the interactions within a group of friends. The non-chronological and contiguous arrangement is gradually explained since the view from their luxury apartment had suddenly become a perfect vantage-point from which to see the attack on the World Trade Center on 11 September 2001:

Iain Sinclair and Dave McKean, 'The Griffin's Egg', in *It's Dark in London*, ed. Oscar Zarate (London: Serpent's Tail, 1996), 50.

These days they rarely see – as for a time they invariably did – the sky igniting, the stinking smoke bursting out of it like lava, the tiny figures raining down from the shattered tower as Lyle faints.

But now it's unclear what they are, in fact, looking at. (Eisenberg 2006: 16)

The events of that day have dramatically affected each of the protagonists, their relationships to one another, and their understanding of the city. The narrative moves non-continuously because the shock to New York and its inhabitants has undermined the certainties of cause and effect. Life continues, but the trauma reiterates itself within the minds of the characters, so that they are no longer the superheroes they once saw themselves as. Although Eisenberg uses postmodern tropes such as non-linearity and a flat, unaffected style, she does so in order to suggest the ethical dilemmas that have underlined postmodernity, concerns that are framed by an awareness of historicity. Eisenberg's poignant and unsentimental response to '9/11' re-emphasises the suitability of the short story to evocations of the metropolis. Their effectiveness, though, suggests a more fundamental, aesthetic relationship between the short story and the fragment, in which the city is grasped as an incalculable loss. As the narrator of Barthelme's 'See the Moon?' (1968) remarks, 'fragments are the only forms I trust' (Bartheleme 1993: 98).

Further Reading

Tönnies' social theories are translated as *Community and Association* (1955). See also James Donald's overview, *Imagining the Modern City* (1999). Extracts from Le Bon and Simmel can be found in Sally Ledger and Roger Luckhurst's reader on the *fin de siècle* (2000). *Flânerie* and the role of women is the subject of Deborah Parsons' *Streetwalking the Metropolis* (2000). The culture of wartime London is described by Robert Hewison (1977). On the Jewish-American short story, see Martin Scofield (2006). Michel de Certeau's influential essay, 'Walking in the City', can be found in *The Practice of Everyday Life* (1984). On the work of Iain Sinclair, see Brian Baker (2007) and on the influence of Situationism, see in particular Simon Sadler (1998).

14

Romance and the Fragment

In the preceding chapters, a tendency towards fragmentation has been noted within the short story: character viewed as an incomplete object, rural communities evoked as they verge on vanishing, the city dramatised as an irrecoverable absence. In this chapter I want to explore in more detail the aesthetic relationship between the short story and the fragment.

Although it was Edgar Allan Poe who argued that the artistic success of the short story lay in its 'unity of impression', Poe also contended in the same review of Nathaniel Hawthorne that the structure of the short story tended towards a 'single effect', in other words, a fragment upon which the whole turned. As suggested in Chapter 9, it was relatively straightforward to graft Poe's single effect onto the early modernist notion of the epiphany, the moment of illumination that was itself foreshadowed by Romantic aesthetics, for instance William Wordsworth's belief in 'spots in time'. Mary Rohrberger, summarising her influential study of Hawthorne, makes a similar connection. Following Hawthorne's own distinction between realism and romance in his preface to *The House of the Seven Gables* (1851), Rohrberger associates his tales with romance narrative: 'the allegorical framework of myth, the historical past, and patterns of images creating metaphors, symbolic identifications' (in Winther et al. 2004: 4). Yet, she also reads Hawthorne's aesthetic through the critical language of modernism: 'Hawthorne's best stories . . . clearly ended in epiphany' (in Winther et al. 2004: 5). Despite the many ambiguities that surface in Hawthorne's writing, for example in 'Young Goodman Brown' (1835) or 'The Minister's Black Veil' (1836), Rohrberger still seeks to draw out the underlying unity favoured by New Criticism and by modernist poets such as T. S. Eliot. Nevertheless, in citing Hawthorne as a progenitor of the short story and in linking his tales to romance, Rohrberger opens up a critical pathway.

Robert Louis Stevenson, writing in his 'Gossip on Romance' (1882), notes the childlike desire for 'the brute incident':

> Crusoe recoiling from the footprint, Achilles shouting over against the Trojans, Ulysses bending the great bow, Christian running with his fingers in his ears, these are each culminating moments in the legend . . . This, then, is the plastic part of literature: to embody character, thought, or emotion in some act or attitude that shall be remarkably striking to the mind's eye. (Stevenson 2006: 142)

As Stevenson suggests, romance narrative is built around fragments: significant details that seem to encompass the totality of the work while, at the same time, standing alone. The fragment is at once the masterstroke that completes the text while remaining the most memorable and self-sufficient part. Although, in one sense, Stevenson parallels Poe's emphasis upon the centrality of the single effect to the structure of the short story, in another sense, Stevenson presents the single effect as *ex-centric*: a fragment that breaks – breaks free from – the whole.

V. S. Pritchett once defined the short story as 'something glimpsed from the corner of the eye, in passing'. Writers such as Raymond Carver have concentrated upon the notion of the glimpse, the detail 'that illuminates the moment' (in May 1994: 277). In this instance, though, I am more interested in the element of motion: the glimpse and the object pass, according to Pritchett, in relation to one another. Consequently, neither observer nor observed is in a fixed or stable position: the glimpse can only look towards what is already moving out of view. There is a strong similarity here with what, in Chapter 3, Charles Baudelaire described as 'mnemonic art' or with what the South American writer Julio Cortázar describes as the paradox inherent to photography: 'cutting off a fragment of reality, giving it certain limits, but in such a way that this segment acts like an explosion which fully opens a much more ample reality' (in May 1994: 246). As Cortázar implies, the short story too can be read as 'a fragment of reality' in which 'certain limits' are imposed. Yet, following Pritchett's definition of the short story as a form that is itself in movement, the short story can be seen as embodying dual meanings of the fragment as 'a part broken off or otherwise detached from a whole' and as 'a part remaining or still preserved when the whole is lost or destroyed' (*The Oxford English Dictionary*).

Dictionary definitions suggest a structural similarity between the fragment and the aphorism. In terms of etymology, the aphorism is derived from the Greek 'apo' (meaning away) and 'horos' (meaning a boundary). Consequently, although the aphorism appears to be tightly structured, as in the witty maxims of Oscar Wilde, it is striven with bisection; the aphorism is literally a breaking or separating off from an imposed limit. In that sense, the fragment and the aphorism are closely aligned, a fact that Wilde and other aphorists, such as Blaise Pascal, Friedrich Nietzsche and E. M. Cioran, understood by their use of paradox. I want to suggest then that, as a type of fragment, the short story has an aphoristic structure. While it appears on the surface to be solidly organised, as for example in the model of the well-made story (see Chapter 4), beneath its trappings the short story tends towards fragmentation as, for instance, in modernist short stories such as Ernest Hemingway's 'Hills Like White Elephants' (1927). Just as the aphorism is often perched precariously between profundity and banality so, as Chapter 9 explored, modernist short stories hover between significance and the loss of meaning.

This tendency is further compounded by the short story's ambiguous relationship to the folktale, since in another sense internal contradiction echoes the mutability of storytelling, and in particular the twinning of the oral and romance traditions during the twelfth century. Medieval romance differs from its classical predecessors. Whereas romantic encounters such as Calypso's imprisonment of Odysseus or Dido's seduction of Aeneas distract the classical heroes from the narrative goal (Odysseus' return to Thrace, Aeneas' founding of Rome), medieval romance turns upon such encounters, raising questions about the relationship of duty to desire, for example in Lancelot's romancing of Guinevere in Sir Thomas Malory's *Le Morte d'Arthur* (1469–70). Medieval romance narratives function on a principle of divergence and distraction, so that they develop episodically and are often disrupted by the interweaving of parallel storylines. The heroes of medieval romance are lost in a world of signs and wonders, in which divine intervention is hinted at, but in which they have to wander and interpret for themselves. It is for this reason that postmodern narratives, preoccupied also with the reading of signs, have frequently employed the structures of romance as part of their compositional design. The *Exemplary Stories* (1613) of Cervantes, a key reference-point for the twentieth-century avant-garde, self-consciously use the conventions of romance in order to criticise its ideological values. Romance becomes, for Cervantes, a viable mode of artistic and satirical expression.

During the late eighteenth century, the romance evoked by classical antiquity and the Middle Ages acts as a source of fascination for the Romantic movement. Despite Ian Reid's suggestion that the psychological impulse to assemble short story cycles 'has its origin in the very nature of imagination itself, a "coadunating" power as Coleridge described it' (Reid 1977: 46), Coleridge was himself the author of fragments such as 'Kubla Khan' (1816). As Chapter 10 also showed, short story cycles operate between the fragment and the whole, while texts such as J. G. Ballard's *The Atrocity Exhibition* (1970) delight in the dissident potential of aphoristic forms such as the sub-title, the caption and the list. During the Romantic period, the aphorism is reworked as the literary fragment and as part of a pervasive interest, for example in P. B. Shelley's 'Ozymandias' (1817), in ruins and decay. The fragment operates here as part of a paradox. Its apparent lack of completion captures the movement of thought; its incompleteness seems to crystallise and distil the writer's imagination. The fragment is at once broken and static, complete and dynamic. For German Romantics, such as Novalis and Friedrich Schlegel, the fragment was not only a more authentic expression of authorship but it was also a necessary preparation for both the writer and the reader for the longer texts to come. There is a parallel here with the common view of the short story as forming part of a writer's apprenticeship, although crucially, the fragment is regarded by the German Romantics as a central aspect of the reading culture that they sought to create. In the wake of the Napoleonic Wars, and a revived interest in national literatures, the folktale collections of, for example, the Grimms survive as fragments, vestiges of an earlier culture. Walter Scott's literary adaptations of folk sources, such as his ghost story 'The Tapestried Chamber' (1829), exist as fragments in their own right.

Yet, as poems such as 'Ozymandias' and paintings such as Henry Fuseli's *The Artist Overwhelmed by the Grandeur of Antique Ruins* (1778–9) suggest, the fragment also acts as a reflection of the writer's self-image. The spectator is only a step away from the descent into the unconscious, as in the surreal apparitions of Fuseli's *The Nightmare* (1781), the sexual imagery of 'Kubla Khan' and the dream-like structure of Thomas de Quincey's *Confessions of an English Opium-Eater* (1822). Théodore Géricault's drawings of *Severed Limbs* (1818–19) dovetail with a Gothic fascination for body parts, instruments of terror and the sequencing of single effects as, for example, in Anna Letitia Aiken's early Gothic horror 'Sir Bertrand: A Fragment' (1773). Despite several critics' attempts to design taxonomies of the form, for instance in distinguishing between intentional and accidental fragments, the story of Honoré de Balzac's 'The Unknown Masterpiece' (1837) confounds such distinctions. The artist, Frenhofer, works for many years to capture the portrait of a young woman. In the end, there is only a mass of paint from which a solitary fragment – a luminous foot – is identifiable. Frenhofer's arrival at this detail is neither intentional nor accidental: it is the only possible way of expressing his unattainable goal. As Balzac's tale also indicates, a post-Romantic emphasis upon the epiphany as the moment of illumination is negated by a Romantic aesthetic that pulls in opposite directions at once.

This reciprocal movement can, for instance, be seen in the tension between economy and fragmentation that surfaces in the German *Novelle*. Ludwig Tieck's 'Blond Eckbert' (1796), an example of art-tale in its self-conscious use of fairy-tale conventions, juxtaposes the domestic setting of its telling with the uncanny content of the story. Tieck's contradictory impulse between realism and romance prefigures the splitting of the *Novelle* into supernatural tales, most notably E. T. A. Hoffmann's 'The Sandman' (1817), and tales of heightened realism, such as Heinrich von Kleist's 'The Marchioness of O. . .' (1808). Kleist's use of initials in order to identify his characters and the pretence of an unmediated narration presents the story as a type of case-history. Yet, the depersonalisation only serves to heighten the emotional content of the taboo material, the revelation of which fragments the social consensus that underwrites the story's pursuit of truth. 'The Sandman', too, sub-divides between the epistolary form at the start of the story and then the more conventional prose narrative, the mirroring of Nathaniel's two loves, Clara and Olympia, and Coppelius' reappearance as Coppola. In a sense, Hoffmann's story reiterates itself while at the same time suspending the forward motion of linear narrative. Like 'The Marchioness of O. . .', 'The Sandman' does not so much accumulate meaning as accrete it: each of the story's fragmented parts compacting significance within the whole. Georg Büchner's tale of a doomed artist, 'Lenz' (1839), effectively integrates Kleist's realism with Hoffmann's Gothic fantasy through its modulation of first- and third-person narrative, its complex layering of experience, and its fragmentation of syntactic structure: devices that convey the artist's slide into insanity.

Alexander Pushkin's 'The Queen of Spades' (1834), perhaps the most celebrated Russian short story until the emergence of Anton Chekhov, takes the model of the German *Novelle* as its inspiration. Like other stories of the period, for example Poe's 'The Man of the Crowd' (1840), the tale begins with an epigram: 'The queen of spades indicates some covert malice' (Pushkin 1997: 69). In other words, the tale not only proceeds in fragments but is also announced by a fragment. The claim that the epigram derives from a recent book on fortune-telling is itself a false trail: the pseudo-scientific explanation is undercut by its own modishness, the culture that Pushkin's hero, Hermann, inhabits and in which references to Mesmer and Mephistopheles jostle with one another. The epigram invites a way of reading the story – a reasoned explanation for the irrational – that effectively redoubles Hermann's own quest: his desire to conquer chance at the card-table by penetrating to its underlying logic. Pushkin veils the meaning of the story in realistic and supernatural causes that distract the reader's attention just as the narrative alternates between episodes and, in which, Hermann's character is established from rival points of view. Pushkin's economic and suggestive prose holds the composition together while, at the same time, implying that there is an unfolding pattern at work. Yet even at the end of the story, when Hermann has descended into madness, there remains the sense that resolution is to be found not within the text but from elsewhere.

The decentred quality of the fragment, in which the heart of the text – the key to its mystery – is extrinsic to its structure, results in the proliferation of fragments. Rudyard Kipling's story 'Mrs Bathurst' (1904) is compiled from fragments, multiple points of view offered by each of the narrators, in which the eponymous character is narrated but does not speak; an absence in the midst of her own story. As Roland Barthes notes in his autobiography:

> To write by fragments: the fragments are then so many stones on the perimeter of a circle: I spread myself around: my whole little universe in crumbs: at the centre, what? (Barthes 1995: 92–3)

In contrast, Virginia Woolf's praise of the essay form as springing from 'unity and a mind at harmony with itself' (Woolf 1935: 177) is countered by Theodor Adorno's observation:

> Even in the manner of its presentation, the essay may not act as though it had deduced its object and there was nothing left to say . . . it has to be constructed as though it could always break off at any point. It thinks in fragments, just as reality is fragmentary, and finds its unity in and through the breaks and not by glossing them over. (Adorno 1991: 16)

Writing in 1922, though, Woolf sounds closer to Adorno's position when she comments of her contemporaries that they can aspire to composing no more than 'fragments – paragraphs – a page perhaps: but no more' (Woolf 1976: 598). In her pessimism, Woolf prefigures Samuel Beckett's close friend, E. M. Cioran, when he writes: 'No need to elaborate *works* – merely say something that can be murmured in the ear of a drunkard or a dying man' (Cioran 1993: 4). Yet, as Adorno suggests, fragmentary writing is not only produced by desperation but as a thoughtful response to the generalisation of thinking in totalities. The range of devices employed in modernist short stories – impressionism, stream of consciousness, narrative framing, ellipsis – operate not only as a fragmentation of the well-made story but also as a negation of the assumptions – symmetry, single effect, unity of impression – sustained by commercial short fiction. In this respect, modernist writing begins to dovetail with the critique of modernity proposed by Frankfurt School thinkers, such as Adorno, Walter Benjamin and Siegfried Kracauer, in which the idea of totality is no longer sustainable since, on the one hand, modernity is experienced as discontinuous while, on the other hand, the modern world is itself the product of social and economic ties that are *reified* (lost or forgotten) in the interests of capital. The world comes to us as fractured and hollow, a point remade in Benjamin's unfinished masterwork *The Arcades Project*, in which it is the fleeting and transitory fragment that acts as the microcosm to this new society.

Yet, part of the vertigo of modern living, as the quotation from Barthes indicates, is the exploration of new identities. This theme was of paramount importance to the New Woman writers of the late nineteenth century, for example in the dreamlike, fragmentary sections of George Egerton's 'A Cross Line' (1893) and in Victoria Cross' equally controversial 'Theodora: A Fragment' (1895). Whereas male Decadent writers, such as Ernest Dowson and Oscar Wilde, delighted in the idea of the fragment as an example of art for art's sake, resistant to moral readings, Cross' story breaks off when she can no longer contemplate the full implications of her protagonists' transgressive desires for one another. In other words, the text terminates at the point at which Cross reaches the outer edge of late Victorian codes of sexual conduct. Equally, despite the relative explicitness of Kate Chopin's 'The Storm' (1898), the strength of her story lies in its use of ellipsis to suggest more than she can tell, especially the way in which the adulterous affair successfully slips the society's mores. Chopin's talent for formal innovation is apparent also in 'The Story of an Hour' (1894), where she compresses the significant details of her character's life into a three-page description of her dying hour. In a prefiguration of what has variously been described as 'sudden', 'flash' or 'micro fiction', Chopin's fragment aspires to the condition where, to paraphrase Friedrich Schlegel, everything is italicised.

In contrast with the apparent exuberance of Chopin, Cross and Egerton, 'The Yellow Wallpaper' (1892) by Charlotte Perkins Gilman achieves much of its intensity through not only the episodic structure of the narrative but also the fragmented movement from sentence to sentence, in which the point of view shifts, and the reader becomes increasingly disorientated as to whether the descriptions are real or not. The narrative, as a reflection of the narrator's mind, comes to resemble the wallpaper: 'a lack of sequence, a defiance of law . . . a constant irritant to a normal mind' (in Ward 1996: 82). Nevertheless, even though the writing borders upon hysteria in its disruption of cause and effect, the logical mind embodied by the narrator's medical husband, its transgression is not necessarily liberating. Instead, the accumulation of fragmented thought structures mirrors the pattern of the wallpaper through which the imaginary women attempt to pass:

And she is all the time trying to climb through. But nobody could climb through that pattern – it strangles so; I think that it is why it has so many heads.

They get through, and then the pattern strangles them off and turns them upside down, and makes their eyes white! (in Ward 1996: 85)

The suffocating pattern operates simultaneously as an externalisation of the narrator's unconscious mind, as an image that distils her narrative and as a metaphor for her confinement under patriarchy. The disarticulation of the narrator even as she tells her story shatters the social order under which female identity is defined and constricted. Her self-mutilation is painful and disturbing to read, her emancipation provisional at best. Gilman's jarring use of fragmentation, in order to recollect the disordered subjectivity of her protagonist, prefigures similar experiments by avant-garde writers such as H. D. and Djuna Barnes (see Chapter 17).

In Jorge Luis Borges' 'Funes the Memorious' (1942), recollection is itself the basis for fragmentation. Unable to forget anything, Funes' memory 'is like a garbage heap' (Borges 1970: 92). Here, where everything is in a state of difference from everything else, Funes' memories become useless to him, a sprawling mass of broken fragments, in which no connections can be made. Funes' early death is itself an incidental detail to be amassed with all the others. Borges' delight in fiction as a field for thought experiments results in him not only playing with ideas, as in his tale of parallel worlds 'Tlön, Uqbar, Orbis Tertius' (1940), but also in extending the logicality of those ideas to the point of fragmentation, for example in 'The Garden of Forking Paths' (1941). Embedded within this story is the idea of a labyrinthine novel in which variations of the same decision and its effects are played out. Each variation has its own repercussions, entailing further decisions, each with its own range of possible effects. Consequently, the novel expands exponentially to incorporate 'an infinite series of times', a 'dizzying net of divergent, convergent and parallel times' (Borges 1970: 53). The propensity for the imagined novel to endlessly depart from itself not only prefigures experiments in hypertext (see Chapter 7) but also Barthes' ideal, in 'From Work to Text' (1971), of the Text that can snap at any point and run in paradoxical lines. Yet, both Barthes' ideal and Borges' fiction sustain the riddling quality of the oral tradition.

It is in this sense, then, that the postmodern use of fragmentation replenishes, rather than exhausts, the uses of storytelling even while it denies the determination of a structural pattern. Angela Carter's *The Bloody Chamber* (1979), for example, uses fairy tales and other cultural material as a form of *bricolage*, that is to say, the sources are treated as fragments, remnants of elite and folk cultures whose distinctions have collapsed into one another, and then put to work, constructing new texts out of old ones. John Barth's 'Frame-Tale', the opening piece in his collection *Lost in the Funhouse* (1968), presents the reader with a vertical strip running down the right-hand side of the page on which is written the words, 'ONCE UPON A TIME THERE'. This strip is mirrored over the page by another that states 'WAS A STORY THAT BEGAN'. Directions for cutting out and tying them into a Moebius strip, one that has only one edge so that it runs continuously, are placed in the middle of the first page. Below these directions in brackets is a single word, 'continued', which is repeated in the lower right-hand corner of the second page (Barth 1968: 1–2). The story teases its reader: is s/he really meant to follow the directions and extract the text? For, in ruining the page, the reader would not in effect be producing a continuous text; rather s/he would be following a literal reading of the text that imposes a limit on its play of meaning: the fragment as self-sufficient unit. Leaving the page intact would not mean submitting to the authority of the printed book but, instead, investing the page with its own visual delight. Like Carter, Barth replenishes the printed word.

Donald Barthelme, for whose aesthetic the fragment was integral, furthers the play of word and image in collage stories such as 'The Flight of Pigeons from the Palace' (1972). Usually, where words appear alongside images in books, the text is either there to support the image or to be reinforced by what the image represents. Either way, the juxtaposition of word and image confers authority upon the context of what is being described. In Barthelme's story, though, the images have clearly been removed from their original contexts, for example the profile of a naked man taken from a medical textbook. It is the *obviousness*, though, which underlines Barthelme's conceit: the naked man is read literally as 'the amazing Numbered Man.' Whereas, in the original image, the numbers are there to indicate body parts, in the accompanying text the numbers act as part of his performance:

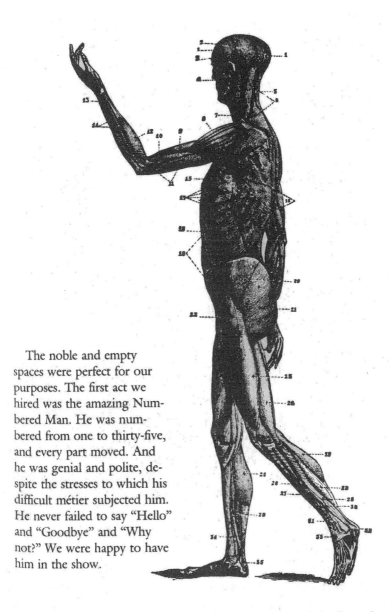

The noble and empty spaces were perfect for our purposes. The first act we hired was the amazing Numbered Man. He was numbered from one to thirty-five, and every part moved. And he was genial and polite, despite the stresses to which his difficult métier subjected him. He never failed to say "Hello" and "Goodbye" and "Why not?" We were happy to have him in the show.

Donald Barthelme, 'The Flight of Pigeons from the Palace', in *Forty Stories* (New York: Penguin, 1989), 131. © Donald Barthelme, 1987. Reproduced by permission. All rights reserved.

'He was numbered from one to thirty-five, and every part moved.' Again, whereas in the original image the man is simply a specimen study, in the text he is given his own subjectivity: 'he was genial and polite . . . he never failed to say "Hello" and "Goodbye" and "Why not?"' (Barthelme 1989: 131). Instead of explaining one another, word and image diverge, but instead of producing an oppositional effect, as might be expected, for example, in modernist texts where the word tends to be privileged over the image, the creative tension of Barthelme's collage stories produces a playfulness of meaning as new juxtapositions and new contexts are brought into focus. As in Iain Sinclair's graphic short stories (see previous chapter), the reader is invited to read into the gaps and silences that open up between the fragments of word and image.

The visual play of writers such as Barth, Barthelme and Sinclair turns upon the dialectic of absence and presence, which is inherent to the fragment, poised between a narcissistic sense of form (hence, its appeal for metafictional writers like Barth and Borges) and self-dissolution. Fragmented texts, such as Robert Coover's 'The Babysitter' (1969), invite the reader to speculate upon the presence of a disguised, underlying pattern while pointedly emphasising the absence of any such structure. James Kelman's 'Acid' (1983) not only describes a man accidentally falling into a vat of acid but is also formally dissolved. Lasting no more than a single paragraph placed in the middle of the page, the story ends with a co-worker submerging the man since 'only the head and shoulders . . . which had been seen above the acid was all that remained of the young man' (Kelman 1989: 115). As if mimicking Hemingway's remark on the graceful movement of the iceberg where only one-eighth is visible, the horror of Kelman's story rests upon its partial visibility. So much is left unsaid, consumed by the final horrific image. Instead, 'Acid' graphically depicts Beckett's ideal of a 'total object, complete with missing parts' (Beckett 1965: 101). In this respect, Kelman's story complements Franz Kafka's decision to publish 'Before the Law' (1914) separately from *The Trial* (1925), Hemingway's labelling of the vignettes that punctuate *In Our Time* (1925) as 'unwritten novels' and Ballard's description of the stories that compose *The Atrocity Exhibition* as 'condensed novels'.

In his own fragmentary study of the possibilities of writing, *The Writing of the Disaster* (1980), Maurice Blanchot observes that 'writing is per se already (it is still) violence: the rupture there is in each fragment, the splitting, the tearing of the shred – acute singularity, steely point' (Blanchot 1995: 46). Blanchot also quotes the object of his friend, the philosopher Emmanuel Levinas, 'to save a text from its book misfortune' (Blanchot 1995: 101). The irreducibility of the fragment, even as it reduces itself, opposes the authoritarian structure of the book: the need for coherence and comprehensibility. Although, in one sense, Poe's formulation of the short story became the basis for commercial short fiction, in another sense, Poe emphasises the singularity of the short story: its resistance to greater comprehensiveness and the demand that it places upon the reader. For example, in Julio Cortázar's 'Blow-Up' (1959), the photographer's pursuit of the hidden significances within a sequence of photographs that he has taken results in him shrinking from what he imagines to be there: 'I covered my face and broke into tears like an idiot' (Cortázar 1978: 131). The fragmentation of the short story, like the enlarged details that feature in Cortázar's narrative, places an additional responsibility upon the reader: an ethical imperative that underwrites the activity of reading. William Gibson's hybrid text 'Agrippa: A Book of the Dead' (1992) – part prose-poem, part short story, part family memoir, part electronic experiment – encapsulates this demand. In its original design, the story was packaged on a CD-Rom that was programmed with a computer virus, which locked the user's keyboard, forcing them to read the text as it scrolled down at its own pace. At the end of its run, the virus scrambled the text, rendering it unreadable. The experience of reading 'Agrippa' was, therefore, meant to be unrepeatable just as the snatches of family life were ultimately irretrievable. As the text processed to its conclusion, the final moment of erasure, the reader performed a solemn meditation on its possible meanings, among them the disappearance of an older form of existence within the glare of the digital landscape. Yet, as Gibson implies, the various spectres that constitute his fragment do not only include his characters and narrative persona, but as J. G. Ballard suggests, in the *tour ed force* that concludes his story 'Now: Zero' (1959), the reader also:

> As you read these last few lines you will be overwhelmed by horror and revulsion, then by fear and panic. Your heart seizes, its pulse falling . . . your mind

clouds . . . your life ebbs . . . you are sinking, within a few seconds you will join eternity . . . three . . . two . . . one . . .

Now!

Zero. (Ballard 2001: 105)

Further Reading

Camelia Elias' *The Fragment* (2004) is a book-length study devoted to the form. For the origins and development of romance, see Barbara Fuchs (2003). On the Romantic fragment in philosophy, see Kathleen Wheeler (1984), in literature, see Elizabeth Wanning Harries' essay in Michael Ferber's *Companion to European Romanticism* (2005), and in the visual arts, see Linda Nochlin's *The Body in Pieces* (1994). Stories by Büchner, Kleist and Tieck are available in *Eight German Novellas* edited by Andrew J. Webber (1997). On the role of the fragment in Marxist and Frankfurt School thought, see David Frisby (1985) and Naomi Schor (1987). Roland Barthes' essay 'From Work to Text' is available in *Image Music Text* (1977). On sudden, flash and micro fiction, see the respective anthologies edited by Robert Shappard and James Thomas (1988), James Thomas et al. (1992) and Jerome Stern (1996).

15

Ghost Stories and Other Hauntings

John Berger observes in his series of short philosophical speculations that border upon fiction and poetry, *and our faces, my heart,
brief as photos* (1984), that in 'the modern era of quantification . . .
it follows that one no longer counts what one has, but what one has
not. Everything becomes loss' (Berger 2005: 38). It is no coincidence
that the ghost story, like science fiction, was a product of the early
nineteenth century and the impact of industrial capitalism. Where
science fiction looks forward to the future, even if only to warn, the
ghost story looks backward and dwells upon what was and what might
have been. This chapter will examine, first, the development of ghost
fiction and second, the inherent haunting of what Nadine Gordimer
has seen as the 'fragmented and restless form' of the short story (in
May 1994: 265).

A ghost, unlike a revenant or reanimated corpse such as
Frankenstein's Creature or Sheridan Le Fanu's Vanderhausen in
'Strange Event in the Life of Schalken the Painter' (1839), is the
spirit of someone or something. It is literally a thing without substance. According to tradition, ghosts become attached to persons,
places or objects where there has been some form of trauma, where
the business of life at its end has not been settled either where it has
been terminated too soon, for example in the form of murder, secrets
left unspoken or the living left unaccounted, or where the proper ceremony of death has not been obeyed. Although descriptions of ghostly
visitations occur in many cultures, the ghost story did not emerge
as a distinct literary genre until the 1820s. Apparitions manifest in
the work of classical writers like Apuleius, Lucian and Pliny, and in
medieval texts such as Geoffrey Chaucer's 'The Nun's Priest's Tale',
but these incidents are drawn from the folk culture that these writers
used as source material. Even the first recognisable ghost story, Daniel

Defoe's 'A True Relation of the Apparition of Mrs Veal' (1706), is an embellishment of a reported incident that seeks to create a feeling of realism rather than terror or suspense. Ghost stories designed to induce fright only begin to develop with the Gothic novel, for example in the tale of the Bleeding Nun embedded within Matthew Lewis' *The Monk* (1796). As discussed in the next chapter, Gothic reacted against Enlightenment values of reason and progress, and operated in either melancholic evocations of the medieval past or vicarious pleasures designed to excite the imaginations of its readers. The ghost story was instrumental in both these goals but, until the start of the nineteenth century, it lacked a distinct existence of its own.

In 1824, however, the novelist and folktale collector Walter Scott inserted 'Wandering Willie's Tale' into his novel *Redgauntlet*. Although original to Scott, his tale of a poor tenant who visits Hell in search of a receipt from his dead landlord draws upon the resources of Scots dialect and local legend so as to create a sense of authenticity. Scott's entrapment of the reader into believing that this might be a genuine folktale establishes 'Wandering Willie's Tale' as the first distinctive ghost story that can also be read outside of its intended context. Later attempts though, such as 'The Tapestried Chamber' (1829), reveal the deficiencies of Scott's method. Borrowing the figure of the female spectre from *The Monk*, Scott recounts how Browne, an English army officer, spends a fitful night at Woodville Castle during which he is visited by the evil spirit: 'all manhood melted from me like wax in the furnace' (in Blair 2002: 48). The following morning he is informed by his host that the ghost was 'a wretched ancestress of mine', only to veil the nature of her crimes since their 'recital . . . would be too horrible' (in Blair 2002: 51). In other words, for reasons that might be social, sexual or artistic, there is no real story to speak of in Scott's tale, merely the relation of an incident that has no bearing either upon Browne's character.

During the course of the 1830s and 1840s, the English ghost story remained wedded to the Gothic, the vestigial influence of which is apparent in the savage landscape and labyrinthine mansion in Elizabeth Gaskell's 'The Old Nurse's Story' (1852). Nevertheless, Gaskell's supernatural fiction introduces anxieties surrounding class, race and home that are integral parts of the Victorian ghost story. In particular, the climax to 'The Old Nurse's Story' defuses the Gothic narrative by averting repetition of the past crime and opening up a conclusion in which wrongs are righted and history is corrected. Although Gaskell's ending is in some sense compensatory, it nevertheless emphasises the flaws within the official record. The ghost returns in order to indicate what has been repressed, a residue that, as Virginia Woolf writes of Henry James' supernatural tales, 'remains unaccounted for' (Woolf 1988: 325). The ghost story, then, became an effective means for nineteenth-century writers to register their unease with the apparent progress of society in ways that the dominant form of the novel – social realism – could not encompass.

Although ghosts featured in American and European literature of the period, it was the Victorians who most developed the genre. The economic, legal and technological changes that affected the print industry from the mid-1850s onwards (see Chapter 5) encouraged a new generation of periodicals, such as *The Cornhill* and *Macmillan's* (both 1859), *Temple Bar* (1860), *The Belgravia* (1866), *Tinsley's* (1867) and *Cassell's* (1868). These journals, which were often published by printing houses or edited, like *The Belgravia*, by well-known writers such as Mary Elizabeth Braddon, gave fresh prominence to shorter and serial fiction that sought to entertain rather than educate the readership. Christmas editions were an especially fruitful occasion for ghost stories, a tradition that went back to Scott's inclusion of 'The Tapestried Chamber' in the Christmastime annual *The Keepsake*. Charles Dickens, who had encouraged the development of the ghost story not only in 'A Christmas Carol' (1843) but also by publishing the work of others, such as Wilkie Collins' 'A Terribly Strange Bed' (1852), made particularly effective use of the Christmas numbers of his journals *Household Words* (1850) and *All the Year Round* (1859). Besides publishing tales by Gaskell, Le Fanu, Amelia Edwards and Rosa Mulholland, Dickens published his finest short story, 'The Signalman', in the special Christmas issue of *All the Year Round* in 1866.

On this occasion, the magazine was given over to seven inter-related stories, the first three of which (written also by Dickens) set the scene. A mysterious stranger disembarks from his train at Mugby Junction, 'a place replete with shadowy shapes' (Dickens 2005: 4). Like the prototypical detectives of Collins' *The Woman in White* (1860) and Braddon's *Lady Audley's Secret* (1862), the traveller decides to investigate the surroundings. He comes to the conclusion that the Junction is one 'of many branches, invisible as well as visible' that has 'joined him to an endless number of byways' from which he decides not to escape but to explore further (Dickens 2005: 29). Pursuing the length of the first branch line, the stranger meets with the signalman employed 'in as solitary and dismal a place as ever I saw' (Dickens 2005: 55). Ushered inside the signal box, the stranger learns of the man's impoverishment and his work built around the 'telegraphic instrument with its dial face and needles' (Dickens 2005: 57) that connects him to the outside world. He learns also of the ghostly figure, and the suggestion of an accident, which the signalman had previously, inexplicably, encountered in the tunnel. The signalman fears reporting the incident to his employers in case he is considered mad and replaced. Later, upon returning to the spot, the stranger meets with the spectre as he had been described to him. The signalman has been killed in a freak accident and the spectre – a railway employee – has been signalling for help. The stranger speaks with the engine driver, who repeats not only the words used by the signalman but also the words that the stranger had intimated in the signalman's gesture. It is as if a telepathic communication has been enacted between the trio across time and space, a ghostly act of transference that shadows the signalman's alienation from human society and the spectral technology of telegraphy.

Dickens' enigmatic tales based around Mugby Junction link the spectral with modernity: the estrangement of human beings from one another represented by modern methods of communication, the dehumanisation of society embodied in the industrial organisation of the railway network, and the hollow spaces – symbolised by the signal box and the Junction itself – that open up within the workings of capitalism. Instead of ghost stories about past wrongs, guilty secrets and haunted places, Dickens seems to be proposing a language of spectrality that would express the condition of modernity. In this respect, Dickens complements his near-contemporaries, such as Charles Baudelaire's descriptions of Paris in which the city and its inhabitants are experienced as a series of fleeting apparitions, or Nikolai Gogol's phantasmagorical representation of St Petersburg in stories like 'The Overcoat' (1842). Gogol's tale of an office clerk who haunts the city in search of the overcoat that was stolen from him is embedded with ambiguity and contradiction, for as Gogol's narrator writes, 'all those houses and streets, has so mixed and merged together in our head that it is very hard to get anything out of it in a decent fashion' (Gogol 2003: 410). As in the stories of Herman Melville and Edgar Allan Poe, the metropolis emerges as a site of hauntings and disappearances. For Spencer Brydon returning to New York after several years abroad in Henry James' ghost story 'The Jolly Corner' (1908), the city looms before him like a 'vast ledger-page, overgrown, fantastic, of ruled and criss-crossed lines and figures' (James 1990: 163). Assaulted by the 'uncanny phenomena' of the city, where 'proportion and values were upside-down' (James 1990: 162), Brydon encounters his double, the ghost of who he might have been if he had stayed. As Woolf again perceptively notes of James' phantoms:

> They have their origins within us. They are present whenever the significant overflows our powers of expressing it; whenever the ordinary appears ringed by the strange. (Woolf 1988: 324)

Woolf's insightful comments on James indicate a fracturing within the tradition of the ghost story. While, on the one hand, the genre became a staple ingredient of late Victorian and Edwardian popular fiction associated, most notably, with writers such as Algernon Blackwood, M. R. James, W. W. Jacobs and Saki, on the other hand, it became associated with writers who used the form for psychological investigations, especially women writers like Vernon Lee, May Sinclair and Edith Wharton. Contemporary writers of ghost stories, such as A. S. Byatt or Jane Gardam, tend to make use of both of these tendencies. A third strand, though, can also be detected involving writers who pursued the connection between spectrality and modernity.

As with the titles of so many of Joseph Conrad's stories, 'Karain: A Memory' (1897) is a pun. The frame narrative is a reminiscence of Karain, a great African chief, but the embedded story related by Karain is also a memory, that of Matara, the friend whom he killed over the love of his sister, and who he believes pursues him as a phantom. Yet, Karain is himself a memory, a ghost that haunts the first-person narrative even as it attempts to recall and reorder his presence. In other words, the frame narrative performs a complex role in this story. It relives Karain's narrative in the present, thereby complementing the timelessness that the narrator attributes to Karain's people: 'they had forgotten all the past, and had lost all concern for the future' (Conrad 1997: 39). Yet, quite plainly, Karain has not forgotten the past and is deeply concerned for his personal future, so that the narrative also tries to recuperate his story for a Western view of chronological time, symbolised by 'the two ship's chronometers' set to Greenwich Mean Time, and which seem 'a protection and a relief' (Conrad 1997: 58). GMT had only been instituted as international standard time thirteen years before Conrad's story, so that its time-scheme is undercut by pre-modern and non-Western ways of thinking about the passage of time. Although reliving Karain's tale, the first-person narrator attempts to distance himself from it by setting it backwards in time within a mythic depiction of Africa as a 'motionless fantasy of outline and colour' (Conrad 1997: 40). However, in the coda that follows Karain's tale, set within the busy London metropolis, the narrator encounters one of his fellow travellers, Jackson, who ponders upon the authenticity of Karain's story: 'I mean, whether the thing was so, you know . . . whether it really happened to him'. The narrator attempts to persuade Jackson of what is authentic and real by encouraging him to look around:

> Our ears were filled by a headlong shuffle and beat of rapid footsteps and an underlying rumour – a rumour vast, faint, pulsating, as of panting breaths, of beating hearts, of gasping voices. Innumerable eyes stared straight in front, feet moved hurriedly, blank faces flowed, arms swung. (Conrad 1997: 67)

As in the stories of Gogol, James and Poe, the metropolis dissolves into fantasy, an hallucination composed from disconnected fragments, a ghostly presence that appears vital yet without substance: 'it pants, it runs, it rolls; it is strong and alive; it would smash you if you didn't look out; but I'll be hanged if it is yet as real to me as . . . as the other thing . . . say, Karain's story.' The narrator puts Jackson's denial of modernity's proof as having 'been too long away from home' (Conrad 1997: 68). But Jackson's home is no longer homely and familiar; instead, it is a site or spectacle of deception like the 'Jubilee sixpence' that the Westerners persuade Karain is a lucky charm (Conrad 1997: 64). Imperialism, and the modernity that it underwrites, is presented as a magic spell that binds its subjects just as Karain, in his traditional role as storyteller, weaves a spell over his audience. Karain's submission to the glamour of the imperial coin indicates the decline of his belief-system in the face of Western modernity. Yet, as Jackson's hesitant response suggests, modernity is haunted by the ghosts of what it either suppresses or absorbs: 'displaced, discarded, or sublated ("abolished") concepts' not fully 'laid to rest' (Rabaté 1996: x–xi; xvi). Modernity's constant need to renew itself, 'to transcend the present' (Osborne 1992: 76), creates openings within the empty passage of time that modernity otherwise presents as a linear or progressive succession. Through these breaches, the ghost – the disembodied figure of anachronism and temporal discontinuity – can invade the present.

Like Conrad, Rudyard Kipling used the image of the ghost to question the practice (if not the theory) of British imperial rule, for example in his satire of a wastrel haunted by his dead mistress in 'The Phantom Rickshaw' (1885) or 'The Return of Imray' (1891), where the far-sightedness of the natives' supernatural beliefs is contrasted with the arrogant views of the imperial masters. In his story 'Mrs Bathurst' (1904), Kipling produces a ghost out of the machinery of cinema:

> There was no mistakin' the walk in a hundred thousand. She came forward
> – right forward – she looked out straight at us with that blindish look which
> Pritch alluded to. She walked on and on till she melted out of the picture –
> like – like a shadow jumpin' over a candle. (Kipling 1987d: 277)

This is the only time that the title-character appears in the story formed from both the light-particles that constitute the technology of cinema and the interlocking narratives that compose Kipling's story, a projection – in both senses – of men's desire. For Vickery, with whom Mrs Bathurst has had an affair, the effect is mesmerising; he returns again and again to witness the spectacle. It is almost as if Vickery is attempting to relocate himself within the movement of time (Pyecroft compares his visage to a pickled foetus), but in whose eternal moment he becomes frozen: 'Vickery began to navigate the town at the rate o' knots, lookin' at a bar every three minutes approximate Greenwich time' (Kipling 1987d: 280). Fearing that he will either go mad or commit murder, Vickery dissolves – like Mrs Bathurst – from the narrative frame: '"The rest," 'e says, "is silence"' (Kipling 1987d: 283).

The story's dissolution into non-significance though, symbolised by Hooper's frustrating lack of evidence, is contrasted with the excesses in meaning embodied not only by Mrs Bathurst but also the minor characters, such as Boy Niven, the vagrants and the orphans, who are considered surplus to the story of Empire.

In stories such as 'They' (1904) and 'Wireless' (1902), Kipling invests a ghostly quality within technologies such as the motor car and telegraphy. But, in 'A Madonna of the Trenches' (1924), he places a haunting within a battlefront that, as the narrator of 'The Gardener' (1925) comments, was also 'manufactured' (Kipling 1987a: 281). Unlike the jingoism of Arthur Machen's 'The Bowmen' (1914), where German scientific efficiency is overwhelmed by the sudden apparition of Henry V's archers, 'A Madonna of the Trenches' uses the ghost story in order to question the reality of subjective experience since, as the narrator of 'The Bull that Thought' (1924) asserts, 'after the War . . . everything is credible' (Kipling 1987a: 160). Strangwick's shell-shock is shown to be the result of a vision, in which he sees his aunt and her lover resurrected in the trenches on the same day that she dies in London from cancer and he takes his life. Strangwick is not only appalled by the thought of his aunt as a sexual being but also by the idea that suicide and profane love can be redeemed within the afterlife: 'If the dead *do* rise – and I saw 'em – why – why *anything* can 'appen?' (Kipling 1987a: 190). Instead of the idea of resurrection acting as a source of comfort, as within Christian theology, it is the point at which Strangwick's naïve beliefs in what constitute the real collapse, a break-down also implicated in the seismic effect upon human consciousness by the War. Strangwick's raving that 'the reel thing's life an' death' is juxtaposed with Dr Keede's observation that '*that's* the real thing' (Kipling 1987a: 191) as Strangwick descends into sleep. As the voice of reason, Keede is implicated within the rationalisation of human lives that underpinned the War. By contrast, Strangwick's vision communicates a sense of the numinous that goes beyond human understanding, but in which, as for Helen Turrell in 'The Gardener' or Grace Ashcroft in 'The Wish House' (1924), there is no certain prospect of forgiveness, only the life that endures through the pain.

As has been suggested (Armstrong 1998: 94), the short story can be read as an extension of the *fort-da* game that Sigmund Freud describes in his essay 'Beyond the Pleasure Principle' (1920). Freud observes the masochistic pleasure that a young child takes in repeatedly discarding and retrieving its favourite toy. Similarly, part of the delight associated with the short story is the way in which it retrieves something from what is otherwise lost: a fragment of the whole. In other words, what is present in the short story is predicated on what is absent, which would be another way of rephrasing Ernest Hemingway's comparison of writing to the elegant movement of the iceberg. Yet, it is possible to go further since, as Freud suggests, the child's pleasure is based upon the wilful abandonment of the object. Presence can slide into absence, meaning into insignificance. This elision is shrouded in the disembodiment of the ghost. There may also be a pleasure in reading and writing short stories that is drawn towards the emptying of significance, the hollowing-out of experience. As suggested in Chapter 9, modernist short stories turn precisely upon this tension between meaning and non-meaning. Another way of reading James Joyce's use of ellipsis, for example, would be to say that where the text fragments, where an abridgement is formed, a spectral effect occurs. The textual phantom appears where, as Woolf says above, 'the significant overflows our powers of expressing it; whenever the ordinary appears ringed by the strange.'

The uses made of fragmentation by postmodern writers frequently invoke the spectral. William Boyd's collection *Fascination* (2004) not only includes a story entitled 'A Haunting', in which the protagonist believes his personal disasters are due to the spectre of an unacknowledged nineteenth-century scientist, but also include stories that are compiled from detritus, loose bits of information that constitute the ghostly residue of contemporary culture. So, for example, 'Lunch' is composed from a series of restaurant reviews that describe not only the narrator's social pretensions but also the parlous state of his professional and sexual relations. His identity is no more than the fragments that he assembles around himself, becoming, like Patient 39 in 'The Ghost of a Bird', 'an endless series of labyrinths' (Boyd 2004: 178).

J. G. Ballard takes this theme further in his story 'The Index' (1977). The text purports to be 'the index to the unpublished and perhaps suppressed autobiography' of Henry Rhodes Hamilton, of whom 'nothing is publicly known', but who 'exerted a profound influence' on the history of the twentieth century. The index, though, is haunted by the 'shadowy figure' of the possibly 'deranged lexicographer' who 'has taken the unusual step of indexing himself into his own index' (Ballard 2001: 940). Ballard's text, which runs from A to Z, referencing many of the key cultural and political events of the last hundred years and with individual entries that read like fragmented narratives in themselves, resembles one of Poe's hoaxes. It is impossible to formulate a coherent picture of the subject. Joining up the dots, symbolised by the entries, produces an image of Henry Rhodes Hamilton that is so excessive and contradictory that it disappears under the welter of details. At the same time, the lexicographer's indexing of himself not only undercuts his authority, which suggests that the index might just be a grand illusion, but it also leaves the text radically indeterminate; the reader cannot simply dismiss it as a falsehood. The objectivities of truth and reality are violently destabilised as the spectral images of Hamilton and his lexicographer loom out of the media landscape in which historical events flit like electronic ghosts.

Yet, of contemporary Anglo-American writers, it was Donald Barthelme who made most conspicuous use of the fragment. 'The Explanation' (1970) is composed of an interview between two nameless protagonists. Q appears to be testing a product on A. The product is a new machine which is represented on the page as a large black square that dominates the text. A observes that 'it offers no clues'; Q responds that 'it has a certain . . . reticence' (Barthelme 1989: 36). In other words, the machine not only resembles Barthelme's text, which is equally enigmatic, but also the short story form's characteristic reticence, its emotional restraint and withholding of information (Shaw 1983: 293–4). Q asks A what will replace the dying novel. A responds, 'it is replaced by what existed before it was invented' (Barthelme 1989: 36), that is to say, by the folktale, the form that most clearly haunts the modern short story. And, indeed, A's responses are littered with the ghosts of emotional memory that contrast with Q's account of the machine's efficiency and which indicate A's mistrust of the machine: 'They're not like films. With films you can remember, at a minimum, who the actors were' (Barthelme 1989: 38). The short story, in other words, is an imperfect recording device in that what is salvaged as memory also recalls what is lost and which returns to haunt the narrative.

The most curious element of 'The Explanation', though, is that the reader is invited to see what A sees: the black square, which purports to be a machine despite any obvious utilitarian function, and which interrupts the interview on a further three occasions. The square acts as the catalyst for Q and A but its meaning remains irreducible. It haunts the text by distracting the reader's attention in a way that complements A's deflections of Q. The square's enigma resembles the mystery of Vereker's secret in Henry James' 'The Figure in the Carpet' (1896) that Tzvetan Todorov has compared to a spectre: 'for this ever-absent cause to become present, it *must* be a ghost' (Todorov 1977: 154). At one point in the story, James' narrator imagines the contest between Vereker and Corvick, his fellow literary detective, as a chess game:

> On the other side of the table was a ghostlier form . . . who leaned back in his chair with his hands in his pockets and a smile on his fine clear face . . . [Corvick] would take up a chessman and hold it poised a while over one of the little squares, and then would put it back with a long sigh of disappointment. (James 1986: 376–7)

The failures of both Corvick and the narrator to grasp Vereker's secret is due to their impatience: their desire to interpret Vereker for what he signifies rather than to wait upon what apparition crosses the threshold, the space between which the participants are suspended.

This is precisely what occurs in the astonishing conclusion to 'In a Bamboo Grove' (1921), the sequel to Ryunosuke Akutagawa's 'Rashomon' (1915), where the ghost of the murder victim *speaks*. The ghost's account transforms the testimonies previously given by the wife and the bandit, but who can we believe: a dead man over the voices of the living? Akutagawa's objective reporting of the various accounts collapses the distinction between what is true and verifiable, and what is true by being believed. The result is not the same as Poe's use of the hoax with its implicit demand for scepticism. Instead, the fragmented points of view of 'In a Bamboo Grove', their inability to cohere as a single narrative, introduce what Jean-François Lyotard has called a *différend*: the contestation of two or more perspectives for which there can be no final adjudication. Each account registers an indescribable event – in Akutagawa's story, the possible betrayal and murder of the husband – but which is untranslatable within the terms of the other. Like a haunting, the event disorders narrative, so that reading its effects compels us to engage with its otherness. Barthelme's square, Vereker's secret and Akutagawa's spectre all impose limits upon representation, and yet, it is where representation fragments that an ethical exchange with the Other can begin. The short story's propensity for fragmentation and for haunting reminds us that writing, like a séance, is always conducted through a medium of words, in which meanings can slip and slide, return to the abyss from whence they came, in which voices are heard 'as though they were speaking out of the air' (Faulkner 1963: 19).

Further Reading

For histories of the English ghost story, see Julia Briggs (1977) and Jack Sullivan (1978). Excellent anthologies include those edited by Michael Cox and R. A. Gilbert (1986) and Richard Dalby (1988). On the relationship between spectrality and modernity, see in particular Jacques Derrida (1994) and the psychoanalytic essays by Nicolas Abraham and Maria Torok (1994) that partially inspired him. Freud's essay on the pleasure principle can be found in *On Metapsychology* (1984). The ghostliness of modern technology is explored by Erik Davis (1999). For a discussion of Lyotard and *le différend*, see Geoffrey Bennington (1988). See also Emmanuel Levinas' essay 'Ethics of the Infinite' in Douglas Tallack's *Critical Theory: A Reader* (1995) as an introduction to his influential account of the Other and the ethics of representation.

16

Popular Short Fictions

Following the previous discussion of the ghost story, this chapter offers a brief survey of five popular sub-genres: Gothic, detective fiction, contemporary romance, humour and science fiction. The choice is not random. The Gothic tradition began to divide into romantic and crime sub-genres during the middle of the nineteenth century while science fiction has also been seen as an outgrowth of the Gothic form. Even the more surreal and darkly comic elements of Gothic might be said to feed into contemporary humour. Although some of these sub-genres, such as romance, have closely defined conventions, others like science fiction exist as *modes* of writing with a vocabulary of images that have informed cultural thought. Indeed, what connects these sub-genres is their preoccupation with *effects*, not necessarily in terms of the epiphany, but in ways that subvert their canonically low status.

The Gothic Tradition

The key starting-point for Gothic fiction is usually taken to be Horace Walpole's short novel *The Castle of Otranto* (1764). Like other eighteenth-century figures, Walpole was intrigued by signs of decay, in particular the ruined castles and desecrated churches that dotted both the English countryside and the European continent. The dense brutality of their structures, offset by collapse and fragmentation, inspired a nostalgic interest in early modern culture. *The Castle of Otranto*, like Anna Letitia Aiken's early tale 'Sir Bertrand: A Fragment' (1773), accumulates supernatural effects rather than developing either character or plot. The suspension of linear narrative in both texts evokes a sense of atavistic incomprehension in stark contrast with the rational beliefs of the eighteenth-century Enlightenment.

As the Gothic form developed, especially in the novels of Ann Radcliffe, it became a means of debating reason versus unreason. In Radcliffe's *The Mysteries of Udolpho* (1794), the mysterious effects are only thought to be supernatural and are used by the villain to unsettle the heroine's mind. By contrast, the structure of Gothic short fiction, which was mainly distributed through cheap productions known as 'blue books', worked by sequencing sensationalistic effects. The blue books, such as those cited in Jane Austen's *Northanger Abbey* (1818), traded upon the public appetite for Gothic fiction and tended to be derivative and repetitive. Their influence, though, is apparent in Walter Scott's 'The Tapestried Chamber' (1829) which, as discussed in Chapter 15, lacks any substantial story: it is built solely around the ghostly incident and its effect upon the witness.

Instead, it was American writers such as Nathaniel Hawthorne and Edgar Allan Poe who, unencumbered by the props of medieval history, redefined the form by translating its conventions to the American landscape and by concentrating more upon the psychological effects of horror, especially the depths of guilt and madness within the legacy of Puritanism. Poe imports the Gothic conventions of degenerate aristocrats, decaying mansions, burial chambers and sinister women but in his many horror stories, such as 'The Tell-Tale Heart' (1843), delights in the ambiguity of what is real and what is not. Hawthorne's horror stories, even while drawing upon seventeenth-century realities of witchcraft and superstition as in 'Young Goodman Brown' (1835), tend towards allegory and symbol embodied, for example by the doomed wanderer of 'Ethan Brand' (1850). The successes of Hawthorne and Poe, though, have tended to obscure their closest British counterpart, Sheridan Le Fanu. In the early 'Strange Event in the Life of Schalken the Painter' (1839), Le Fanu avoids the rhetorical extravagances associated with the blue books in order to create, like Hawthorne and Poe, a plausible context for the incidents to unfold. The telling is notably restrained as in the story's chilling climax:

> Shriek after shriek burst from the inner chamber, with all the piercing loudness of despairing terror. Schalken and Douw applied every energy and strained every nerve to open the door; but all in vain.
>
> There was no sound of struggling from within, but the screams seemed to increase in loudness, and at the same time they heard the bolts of the latticed window withdrawn, and the window itself grated upon the sill as if thrown open.

One LAST shriek, so long and piercing and agonised as to be scarcely human, swelled from the room, and suddenly there followed a deathlike silence. (in Blair 2002: 86)

Despite the vocal anguish, what makes this passage effective is its surrounding silence. Like Schalken and Douw, the reader is forbidden from entering the chamber: its secrets, like the marriage bed, can only be shared between Rose and her demonic husband, Vanderhausen. Le Fanu's use of the Gothic – its taboo and implied imagery – indicates what cannot be expressed within polite social discourse, in this instance the bartering and sexual domination of women. As in his later stories, such as 'Green Tea' (1869), Le Fanu uses rhetorical devices such as implication and ambiguity to create a horrifying sense of mystery that goes beyond the unsophisticated effects of earlier Gothic short stories.

During the Victorian era, Gothic runs parallel with other supernatural forms, such as the ghost story, in shadowing – and, as in Charlotte Brontë's *Villette* (1853), exploding into – literary realism. Towards the end of the period, as imperial pressures both home and abroad began to accumulate, Gothic had a new lease of life, for example in the work of writers such as Robert Louis Stevenson and Bram Stoker. Despite the potential dissidence of these fictions, for instance the macabre ending to Stevenson's 'The Body Snatcher' (1884), their work appeared as the literary marketplace was splintering into recognisable sub-genres. The demarcation of Gothic horror as just one of many competing genres tends to diminish its transgressive power; it becomes a safety-valve in which readers can indulge their worst fears before returning to social normality. In the United States, however, Ambrose Bierce and Charlotte Perkins Gilman found new opportunities for Gothic by setting their stories within familiar landscapes and by exploring the form's potential for social and psychological critique.

The tendency of Gothic for equivocation complements the partial viewpoint of the short story form, so that what appears to be an external reality may actually be internal, what should be kept on the inside is externalised. The chief anxiety of Gothic is possession, so that personal identity is dismembered, either by invasion of the body, as in Le Fanu's 'Carmilla' (1872), or by physical transformation, as in Poe's 'The Masque of the Red Death' (1842). At the same time, these fears border upon erotic desires since objectification can also induce desire: the ecstasy of losing oneself within the other. This contradictory impulse may be read as the projection of internal conflicts – the tension between the reasoning *ego* and the irrational *id* – so that self-identity is rendered uncanny: the individual is no longer at home with him/herself but is a stranger. In its more politicised forms, Gothic acts as the antithesis to Enlightenment notions of the self as stable and knowable. Instead, Gothic fiction presents the self as split into subject and object, each desiring and fearing the other, each perpetually sliding into one another.

The mirror-image encapsulates this tension since the reflection offers both narcissistic freedom and the threat of seduction and entrapment. The double, in stories such as E. T. A. Hoffmann's 'The Sandman' (1817), Poe's 'William Wilson' (1839) and Joseph Conrad's 'The Secret Sharer' (1910), is a physical extension of the mirror-image. Each story, though, also features an intricate symmetrical structure, so that the doubling that forms an integral part of the content is reflected in the narrative design. Hoffmann's Nathaniel, lost in a world of doubles represented both by the antagonist, Coppelius/Coppola, and his twin desire for Clara and Olympia, ultimately commits suicide. Repelled yet secretly attracted by his double, William Wilson kills his doppelganger, effectively murdering himself. Conrad's nameless sea-captain finally spares his double, the fugitive Leggatt; better it would seem to live a life of service than no life at all. In relinquishing his other, Conrad's hero reveals the limitations of a humanistic model of the self in which a viable social identity can only be predicated upon what it denies. By contrast, the taboo desires of Nathaniel and Wilson have no place within social norms: death is their only form of release.

Although by the start of the twentieth century, Gothic horror had become a mainstream sub-genre, its form and content had also become a literary mode that could be adapted by writers working outside the genre. The language of Gothic has been a constituent element within the work of writers from Isak Dinesen and Daphne du Maurier through to Angela Carter. The postmodern fascination for the form, witnessed by *The Picador Book of the New Gothic* (1992), may be partially explained by the growth of the consumer society, in which the individual is beset by interchangeable products, mass media and reproducible images; by the intensification of bureaucracy, in which the individual exists as an objective unit; and by the inherent anxiety of the labour market, where the individual can be replaced by another adequately skilled worker, effectively a double.

Shirley Jackson's 'The Lottery' (1948) is an important historical marker. The story takes as its inspiration commercial lotteries that were then a regular feature of small-town America. Jackson's lottery, though, is used by the local citizens to pick a sacrificial victim as a means of ensuring a successful harvest. The use of ritual killing connects the story with the culture of witchcraft that pervades Hawthorne's Gothic tales, as does the name of the victim, Tess Hutchinson, invoking the figure of Anne Hutchinson, who was expelled from the Puritan settlement at Plymouth Plantation for preaching the word of God. Tess' distractedness, 'clean forgot what day it was', and her subsequent protest, 'it wasn't *fair*' (in Ford 1998: 64, 68), mark her out as an enthusiast who thinks that by her good nature other people will listen to her. Instead, she is deserted by her family as the collective mentality asserts itself: the villagers 'had forgotten the ritual' but 'they still remembered to use stones' (in Ford 1998: 69). Jackson's blurring of past and present not only roots American mass culture in ritualised behaviour but also in the myths (which is to say ideologies) that have underwritten American history. Her use of anachronism implies that the American nation has, from its foundations, defined itself by what it excludes from the body politic: the victims upon whose sacrifice the state has been built. In questioning linear progress, Jackson's use of the Gothic prefigures the postmodern 'incredulity towards metanarratives' (Lyotard 1984: xxiv).

Detective and Crime Fiction

In the Gothic romances of Ann Radcliffe, there are two key narrative strands. One is the thwarted love of the protagonists; the other is the guilty secret of the supposedly haunted location. During the nineteenth century these strands began to unravel, for example in the exploration of the criminal underworld in the so-called 'Newgate novels' of the 1830s, and an increasing interest in the role of detection, most notably in the 'sensation novels' of the 1860s. Although William Godwin had introduced an element of detective work in his Gothic novel *Caleb Williams* (1794), the major advance was made by Poe in 'The Murders in the Rue Morgue' (1841).

Although Poe was sceptical of humanistic values, his Gothic horrors explored the darker recesses of the human psyche in order to understand more fully what it meant to be human. His stories featuring the prototypical detective, Auguste Dupin, were an extension of this principle with an even greater emphasis upon the powers of reasoning. Unlike the empirical detectives of later writers, Dupin is effectively an artist who imagines 'himself into the spirit of his opponent' (Poe 1998: 93). Dupin has no need to move outside his apartment in order to detect the crime: he can project himself into the criminal mind by making a close study of the news reports. Unlike other literary detectives, then, who *deduce* an explanation from a close observation of the facts, Dupin *induces* a theory that, however unlikely, explains the evidence. As Dupin comments, 'it is only left for us to prove that these apparent "impossibilities" are, in reality, not such' (Poe 1998: 110). The chief problem, though, with Poe's stories is that they are effectively treatises disguised as fictions: they are primarily concerned with problem-solving and lack narrative action. The impoverished and reclusive Dupin, whose almost telepathic ability may be the product of 'a diseased intelligence' (Poe 1998: 96), recalls the degenerate aristocrats of Poe's horror stories. Despite Wilkie Collins' introduction of the professional investigator in his novel *The Moonstone* (1868), the detective heroes of the mid-nineteenth century tend to be amateurs who duplicate Dupin's mixture of imagination and pseudo-science, for example Dr Hesselius in Le Fanu's collection *In a Glass Darkly* (1872). Nevertheless, Poe establishes the idea of the detective as someone who can navigate the city by reassembling it from its fragments (Benjamin 1983: 48): albeit, in the case of Dupin, at a distance.

The transformation of the detective hero occurs with the first appearance of Sherlock Holmes shortly after the launch of *The Strand Magazine* in 1891. Arthur Conan Doyle had originally introduced the character in a novel, *A Study in Scarlet* (1887), but to little success. The short story, by contrast, fitted the character admirably since each story featured a self-contained problem whose ingenious solution created an appetite for further stories. The development of the stories into a series meant that the readers could follow the growing relationship between Holmes and Dr Watson, an overriding frame that gelled with Holmes' deductive method of piecing together the evidence. The importance of Watson as both narrator and intermediary can be best understood by a brief comparison with Jacques Futrelle's clone, Professor Van Dusen, who appeared in several stories, most notably 'The Problem of Cell 13' (1907). As his nickname of 'the Thinking Machine' suggests, Van Dusen is little more than an overgrown calculator. Stripped of the characterisation that arises from the friendship of Holmes and Watson, Futrelle's stories are no more than crossword puzzles. In other words, despite the short story's propensity towards situation rather than character, characterisation is vital to the enduring interest of a detective series.

Despite the ideological role that Holmes plays for his middle-class readers by offering the comfort of a reasoned explanation in a world devoid of logic (London was still reeling from the Whitechapel Murders of 1888), Holmes is not a reassuring figure. In addition to his introspection and drug use, Holmes can be indolent, caustic and cerebral. At the start of 'The Blue Carbuncle', he is observed 'lounging upon the sofa in a purple dressing-gown' (Doyle 1981: 144), an archetypal decadent pose. His 'extreme languor' is contrasted with his 'devouring energy' (Doyle 1981: 66), a mania that invokes other split personalities such as Stevenson's Jekyll and Hyde and Oscar Wilde's Dorian Gray. Holmes embodies the mirror-image of decadent aestheticism and gentlemen's clubs, the exclusive fraternity symbolised by his friendship with Watson. It is Watson though, as Holmes' partner, who is instrumental in revealing the other side of Holmes' character: his defence of justice even if it means using methods outside of the law. Although Watson effectively humanises Holmes, women act as a continual enigma that exposes the limits of Holmes' empiricism (Belsey 1980: 109–17). Yet, it is also possible to see figures such as Irene Adler in 'A Scandal in Bohemia' as contributing to the depth of Holmes' character. Where exactly, in this story, is the scandal? Near the beginning the reader is told that Holmes 'loathed every form of society with his whole Bohemian soul' (Doyle 1981: 9). If it is Holmes' Bohemianism that is scandalised, then Irene Adler, '*the* woman' (Doyle 1981: 32), performs a significant role in developing Holmes as a character that readers would want to follow.

The success of Holmes, then, depended upon self-contained problems, the pseudo-scientific claims of deduction and, above all, Doyle's use of characterisation. There were numerous imitators of Holmes, among them E. W. Hornung's Raffles, Grant Allen's Colonel Clay and G. K. Chesterton's Father Brown. The form turned to parody, though, in E. C. Bentley's *Trent's Last Case* (1913), and thereafter the clue-driven narrative pioneered by Agatha Christie, which demanded the length of the novel rather than the short story, has dominated British detective fiction. The short story has tended to become the province of crime, as opposed to detective, fiction where actual detection plays less of a role, for example in Roald Dahl's crime stories such as the ingenious 'Lamb to the Slaughter' (1953).

In the United States, however, the detective story endured within the conventions of the pulp magazine that began with the relaunch of *Argosy* in 1896 as an all-fiction title designed for a light-reading, adult audience. The most important pulp in the history of American detective fiction was *The Black Mask* (founded 1920) which, through successive editors, became associated with the 'hard-boiled' style of contributors such as Carroll John Daly and Dashiell Hammett, the latter drawing upon his own experience as a private eye. Like Doyle, Hammett realised the importance of character for sustaining a series, but unlike Watson's external descriptions of Holmes, Hammett created his characters through his taut and muscular use of language, a stylistic technique partially inspired by the methods of Ernest Hemingway: 'a big bruiser of a man, something over two hundred pounds of hard red flesh, and a czar from the top of his bullet head to the toes of his shoes that would have been at least number twelves if they hadn't been made to measure' (Hammett 2001: 35). The Confidential Op's keen eye for observation, his laconic wit and his reticence – the reader is confided with information that the Op, quite sensibly, keeps from his clients – create an attitude and a sensibility that convince within the context of what he does and where he works. The Op's pragmatic response – as an employee of the agency, he has to work with clients he dislikes but has to respect – does not ameliorate the condition of his employment though. Like Holmes and Dupin, the Op's personal integrity is contested by the moral and social corruption of the cases that he investigates. His language use becomes a kind of armour: an ironic and defensive shield against the contagion of his work but which, at the same time, appears shallow and superficial; a linguistic conceit that hides genuine loss. The void at the heart of the Op's existence, signified by his anonymity, mirrors the dark and fragmentary state of his urban environment.

Although *The Black Mask* went into decline in the mid-1930s, some journals survived recession and the competition of new media, most notably *Ellery Queen's Mystery Magazine* (1941–). Part of its success was due to the fact that the magazine has never solely published detective fiction but crime stories of all types including, in the postwar era, the psychological thrillers of Patricia Highsmith. Like Shirley Jackson working in the Gothic genre, Highsmith prefigures some of the concerns associated with postmodern literature, in particular shifting or shadowy states of consciousness. In 'A Dangerous Hobby' (1960), for example, Andy Forster has a curious fetish: he approaches women, flatters and dates them, and then steals some insignificant item. His behaviour suggests a sexual insecurity that contrasts with his outward appearance as a successful salesman, a father and a husband. Andy justifies his conduct as an extension of his profession: selling and ingratiating himself in the company of unsuspecting women is no different from the vacuum cleaners that he sells. In other words, his private fetish is justified on the basis of commodity fetishism – the perceived magic of ownership – that, according to Marxist analysis, oils the commercial process by seducing the consumer. Andy's latest seduction, though, leads him into a tale of murder and intrigue in which ultimately only himself stands in the way of escape. Highsmith's pursuance of story rather than revelation, let alone epiphany, creates an overall effect that is morally and psychologically ambiguous.

Contemporary Romance

While one strand of the Gothic romance became the basis for the detective story, another strand – that of thwarted love and the heroine's right to choose her partner – became the template for contemporary romance. Despite publishers' claims that short stories do not sell, there is one market where they do: the mass circulation women's magazine. In Britain, for example, short stories designed for light readers feature regularly in titles such as *Chat*, *Prima* and *Woman's Own*. Yet, despite this presence, romantic short stories have received little critical attention. Academic interest in romance fiction has tended to focus upon the novel rather than the woman's magazine and, as a consequence, has neglected the short story. At the same time, the preference within short story criticism for stories that are recognisably 'literary' has further marginalised the contemporary romance, even though this is the form in which most short stories are consumed and consequently understood by the majority of readers. In this brief overview, I can only register the need for greater critical work to be performed.

The literary agent Cari Crook has defined romantic short stories as 'cheerful and plot-driven, with heroines who triumph over adversity. They make people feel better about their lives.' Crook's emphasis upon cheerfulness is tempered by the comments of Della Galton, one of the most successful magazine writers, who notes that her own stories tend to be 'poignant' rather than 'funny' (quoted Taylor 2003: 10). Nevertheless, the overall tendency is towards optimism, which is mirrored in the stories' forward movement towards resolution. The emphasis upon formal and ideological closure, so that the story compensates for the lack in the reader's own life, tends to mean also that the romantic short story acts, in Wilkie Collins' terms, like a 'little novel'. The defence, from the late nineteenth century onwards, that the short story is not to be regarded as an abbreviated novel is a commonplace within short story criticism, which explains further why there has been scant critical attention devoted to the contemporary romance. There also remains the perception, fostered again in the late Victorian period, of the magazine writer as a hack tied to a perpetual treadmill, even though Galton's short interview reveals a writer who is entrepreneurial and fully aware of the competitive market in which she has chosen to work.

A more profitable approach is offered by J. G. Cawelti in his study of adventure, mystery and romance as 'formula stories'. The contemporary romance follows a prescribed series of formulae, which are acknowledged by both the writers and the readers, and which form part of their appeal. Although constrained by the formula, insofar as it has to be satisfied by the narrative, the success of the writing depends upon how the formula can be negotiated. In many respects, this is the same dilemma that confronted O. Henry (see Chapter 4), one of the architects of the commercial short story. This technical aspect, though, is also significant for the readers since it allows them to compare and contrast individual stories, to establish their own criteria for preferring one kind of romantic story to another, and for creating a fan base. In other words, the relationship between the writer and the reader of romance fiction is not passive but is constituted through an active negotiation of likes and dislikes. This dynamic contributes to the success of writers such as Galton, who is far from being an anonymous hack, but is identifiable to her readers. The mutual sense of identity and belonging has been enhanced by the packaging of recent romantic anthologies and series, which also introduce a degree of playfulness that again involves the readers.

National Humours

Humour, like romance, would seem to be as old as human nature, but instead I want to suggest that as popular genres became established within the publishing industry of the late nineteenth century, so humour became a means of registering differences between national cultures. Although there is a type of humour that functions by stereotyping non-indigenous people, humour can also operate as a particular kind of written discourse that creates a national self-image, which in turn can be actively reproduced within other cultures.

Mark Twain offers a useful starting-point since his fame was based originally upon tall tales such as 'The Celebrated Jumping Frog of Calaveras County' (1867). In his essay 'How to Tell a Story' (1895), Twain distinguishes American humour from English and French comic traditions. In a comment that prefigures the formalist distinction between *sjuzet* and *fabula*, Twain writes that 'the humorous story depends for its effect upon the *manner* of the telling; the comic story and the witty story upon the *matter*.' Twain continues: 'The humorous story may be spun out to great length, and may wander around as much as it pleases . . . but the comic and witty stories must be brief and end with a point' (Twain 1993: 195). Not only does Twain locate the humorous story in an American oral tradition but he also suggests that the expansiveness of the telling complements the vastness of the continent. England and France, by contrast, are known and closed cultures so that their comic writing is equally punctuated. Whatever the validity of Twain's observations, the important aspect here is how comic writing acts as a discursive construct of its culture: 'The humorous story is told gravely; the teller does his best to conceal the fact that he even dimly suspects that there is anything funny about it' (Twain 1993: 196). The apparent lack of irony, which non-American readers often mistake as a genuine absence, creates a mocking self-image of Americans as unduly serious, even puritanical. Twain's deadpan delivery and ear for detail, which conceal the vicious satire of stories such as 'The Man That Corrupted Hadleyburg' (1899), act as cornerstones for American humorous writing from James Thurber's tales of male angst to Damon Runyon's depictions of urban street-life and Garrison Keillor's melancholic evocations of a mid-West community in *Lake Wobegon Days* (1985).

The tall tale surfaces elsewhere though, for example in the writings of Henry Lawson and Stephen Leacock. Lawson, one of the key architects of Australian literature, not only wrote poignant tales of the outback, such as 'The Union Buries Its Dead' (1894), but also anecdotes like 'The Iron-Bark Chip' (1900), in which a group of railway construction workers attempt to fool a government inspector. The trick ending, though, indicates Lawson's ultimate respect for the natural world and the folly of mortal games. The jesting, companionship and anti-authoritarian content of the piece all contribute to Lawson's discursive representation of the Australian working man: a cultural construction as significant and as long-lasting as his more serious works. Leacock, whose family settled in Canada when he was six years old, produced self-conscious fictions characterised by a generous, absurd humour. Whereas Lawson turns to the Australian landscape as the basis of national identity, Leacock gently satirises the attempts of city-dwellers to reinvent the Frontier experience: 'If any moose comes to our lodge, we'll shoot him, or tell the butler to' (Leacock 1923: 235). Leacock's parodies of social custom and Anglo-European literature are marked by self-deprecation, a sense of Canada as a hinterland located somewhere between the Old and New Worlds. In this respect, Leacock establishes a literary representation of the Canadian psyche that informs the work of later writers such as Margaret Atwood and Alice Munro.

Leacock's humour echoes the absurdist tendencies of Edwardian comic writers, such as G. K. Chesterton in *The Club of Queer Trades* (1905) and Saki in *The Chronicles of Clovis* (1911). Their maverick celebration of characters with double lives and social dilettantes, such as Saki's Clovis and Reginald, tear at the social restrictions of their own Victorian childhoods. The destructive force of these stories which, as in Saki's 'The Toys of Peace' (1914), devastate sentimental idealisations of home and family prefigure the postmodern satires of writers such as Will Self where a love of disproportion and illogic is also paramount. However, by comically veiling their motivations – and, in Saki's case, their possible sexual orientations – the Edwardian humorists also avoided public censure. As P. G. Wodehouse demonstrated, in his various writings about Psmith, Jeeves and Wooster, Blandings and Mr Mulliner, it was possible to defuse the more anarchic strains within Edwardian humour and then successfully market an affectionate, farcical and increasingly nostalgic view of the English upper classes not only to the United States but also to other parts of the British Empire. The extent to which colonial subjects gained their understanding of the motherland from popular writers such as Wodehouse requires further exploration.

Just as Lawson and Leacock used humour for the expression of cultural identity, so Jewish-American writers fashioned a comic tradition that became one of the characteristic discourses of modern America. Leo Rosten's *The Education of H*Y*M*A*N K*A*P*L*A*N* (1937) captures this sense of cultural hybridity since, by giving voice to an evening class of European immigrants, Rosten dramatises their underlying need to voice themselves in another's language, to claim American citizenship by proving their proficiency in English while at the same time inscribing and merging their own identities within the dominant American culture. Rosten subverts the Frontier thesis of historians such as Frederick Jackson Turner, whereby the settler loses his/her European identity and becomes recognisably American, by showing that it is the European-ness of the students, especially that of the title character, which enriches American cultural identity and makes it a viable, democratic and attractive alternative to the totalitarian regimes of pre-war Europe.

Kaplan's inventive use of language and rhetorical play, so that the signifiers of his discourse shift and slide in their positions, is matched by S. J. Perelman's comic interventions. Whereas Perelman's contemporary at *The New Yorker*, James Thurber, presents a view of the Protestant male as beleaguered by contemporary mores, Perelman depicts an external reality that, in some sense, is already a pastiche. His characters, for example in the private eye skit 'Farewell, My Lovely Appetizer' (1947), perform roles that have already been acted out either in cinema or popular fiction, a diminishing of authentic experience that coincides with the Hollywood satire *The Day of the Locust* (1939), written by Perelman's brother-in-law Nathanael West. The blurring of art and reality, in which both are repackaged for the needs of mass culture, is a recurring theme for Perelman's successor, Woody Allen, for instance in short stories such as 'The Kugelmass Episode' (1977). Allen's college professor, a parody of the frustrated heroes of Philip Roth and John Updike, enters a magic cabinet from which he is projected into the pages of *Madame Bovary* (1857). There he begins an affair with Flaubert's heroine, which not only radically alters the novel so that Emma even begins to talk like a late twentieth-century New Yorker, but also acts as a commentary on the writing of fiction. Kugelmass, though, is a travestied version of Emma's lovers and eventually he becomes prey to her romantic desires: she persuades Kugelmass to take her back to New York only to be stuck there. Allen's farcical play on the historical differences between sexual and romantic desire dovetails with the metafictional concerns of postmodernism.

Science Fiction: From Romantic Gothic to New Worlds

Allen's story is also notable in that it is an example of how tropes associated with science fiction – time travel and alternate realities – have entered into other areas of contemporary culture. The origins of science fiction, though, are hotly contested. Although the genre could not flourish until there was sufficient cultural anxiety surrounding the effects of mechanisation (Luckhurst 2005: 3–6), Paul O'Flinn has convincingly shown how Mary Shelley's *Frankenstein* (1818) coincided with machine-breaking and riots orchestrated by the rural poor (O'Flinn 1995: 24–30), thereby linking science fiction with the late Romantic Gothic. For our purposes, the interlocking of the novel's frame-narration, which counterpoints the assemblage of body parts, relates the novel to the oral tradition. Like later science fiction, the narrative turns upon a single yet unrepresentable incident: the reanimation of the Creature. Edgar Allan Poe, in 'The Facts in the Case of M. Valdemar' (1845), is also attracted to this scenario (Valdemar's body disintegrates as his life is restored) as if, from very early on, science fiction was not only concerned with the possibilities of technological modernity but also with the limits that it imposed upon representation. Poe's scientific romances – the term itself was not popularised until 1886 – parallel his detective stories by testing out the boundaries of reason and intuition. Like 'The Balloon Hoax' (1844), Poe inserts impossible descriptions, for example of the inside of Valdemar's lungs, which are there to fool the reader into believing their plausibility. Despite either the Gothic content of Poe's proto-science fiction or its cover as a treatise on mathematics ('A Descent into the Maelström', 1841), Poe introduces the pretence of authenticity that H. G. Wells, in particular, works into his later fiction.

Whereas Poe sought to tease his readers, Wells wanted to seduce them by becoming a 'Realist of the Fantastic' (Conrad 1986: 126). The idea of literary realism though, as it was being redefined during the course of the late nineteenth century, was a contestable notion for Wells. He later made his preference clear for 'abundant and irregular forms' such as the anecdote, declaring also that his stories were 'a miscellany of inventions' (Wells 1914: viii, ix). Wells' stories are short on character and plot but expansive on ideas. 'The Star' (1899), for example, begins with the solitary observation of a comet and then expands to chronicle its approach, the reaction of mass populations and the destruction of the Earth's surface before finally assuming a universal perspective as Martian observers dispassionately note the comet's physical effect. Wells' story, tinged with irony, not only demonstrates the insignificance of human beings in the face of cosmological forces, but also shows the close affinity between science fiction and the short story where both are concerned primarily with ideas: 'the idea as hero' (Amis 1960: 137) or the *novum*, the novel and estranging concept as coined by Darko Suvin. During the highpoint of American pulp science fiction from the late 1930s to the early 1950s, it became a commonplace to refer to science fiction as a 'literature of ideas', although ideas were taken to mean *techne*: technology or technique. By contrast, the word 'idea' is derived from the Greek *eidein* meaning 'to see'. Ideas are literally the putting of thought into vision, and in Wells' science fiction the perception of alternate realities is a recurring trope, for instance in 'The Remarkable Case of Davidson's Eyes' (1895), 'A Slip under the Microscope' (1896) and 'The New Accelerator' (1901).

Wells' visual sense was often lost amid the early American pulps where *Argosy*, like *Weird Tales* (launched in 1923 and most associated with the Gothic fantasies of H. P. Lovecraft), often published scientific romances as part of its general remit. In 1926, however, Hugo Gernsback launched *Amazing Stories* with a commitment to publishing what he originally termed 'scientifiction' in the tradition of Poe, Verne and Wells. Gernsback had built his career by publishing popular science magazines, and his ambition for *Amazing Stories* was to generate public interest in science and technology with well-told stories. Gernsback's dilemma, though, was how to sustain demand while also supplying his prospective readers with sufficient quantities of fiction. He began initially by reprinting stories and by employing hacks from other pulp magazines. These hack writers, versed in writing romance, horror, detective stories and westerns, imported scenarios of intrigue and adventure into a science fictional setting. Gernsback's second response was to solicit readers' contributions and, in particular, by encouraging their responses through a letters page. Gernsback found that his audience was primarily young and male, and was more interested in gadgetry and heroism than scientific instruction. Gernsback redirected the magazine to serve their interests, effectively inventing pulp science fiction.

The fan base that Gernsback had initially encouraged increasingly became not only a discerning readership but also active producers of the genre. Readers, such as Isaac Asimov and John W. Campbell, eventually became writers and editors. Like the readers of contemporary romance, they recognised science fiction to be a formula but that it could also be developed; in 'A Martian Odyssey' (1934), for example, Stanley Weinbaum emphasises the other-worldliness of the environment and the need for communication between species. Campbell and the writers, such as Asimov and Robert Heinlein, he published in *Astounding Science Fiction* (relaunched 1938) brought terseness, economy and a laconic humour to what they wrote. They also shared Campbell's vision of a future technocracy, for example in the scientific planning of society in Heinlein's 'The Roads Must Roll' (1940). If for Gernsback ideas had meant gadgetry, for Campbell ideas meant social and technological progress.

In the wake of the Jewish Holocaust and the atomic bomb, such beliefs were harder to sustain. A new set of magazines, most notably *Galaxy* (launched 1950), published stories such as Frederick Pohl's 'The Tunnel Under the World' (1955) that were intensely suspicious of the ideals of mass consumerism and small-town America as covers for what Dwight D. Eisenhower termed the military-industrial complex. Philip K. Dick's prolific output (more than half of his short stories appeared in five years between 1951 and 1956) blur the distinction between what is authentic and what is not. The later story 'We Can Remember It for You Wholesale' (1966) is a fine exposition of Dick's recurrent theme of memory as the basis for experience. A bored clerical worker, Quail, purchases the memory of a spying mission to Mars. It transpires, though, that he really is a spy who has just returned from the planet. An attempt is made to erase Quail's memory but his secret identity returns. The security services refashion his memory again with the story of how, as a child, Quail had prevented an alien invasion by a show of kindness. However, this false memory is also shown to be true and that if Quail was now to be eliminated, the aliens would invade. Dick not only satirises the invasion of private identity by bureaucracy but he also calls into question the objectivity of the reality that the bureaucracy seeks to defend. In a gesture reminiscent of nineteenth-century libertarians, such as Henry David Thoreau, Dick proposes empathy and altruism as incalculable human virtues.

Dick's delight in simulacra prefigures the British 'New Wave' of the 1960s, which is where I shall end this overview. Ted Carnell relaunched the pre-war fanzine *New Worlds* in 1946 and throughout the 1950s the magazine represented the interests of writers such as John Christopher, Arthur C. Clarke and John Wyndham. Carnell, though, also promoted younger writers, such as Brian Aldiss, J. G. Ballard and Michael Moorcock, and in April 1964 he passed the editorship of *New Worlds* on to the latter. Moorcock's redirection of the journal had just been anticipated by publication of Ballard's 'The Terminal Beach', a fragment that responded to the imminent threat of nuclear destruction by compressing narrative time into sub-titled segments, removing the linkages of linear storytelling and interpolating other texts. Much of the meaning of 'The Terminal Beach' arises from its appearance. For Ballard, deeply influenced by collage and by surrealism, ideas in science fiction meant images: possibly his only point of contact with the Wellsian tradition.

Under Moorcock's stewardship, image as well as political commitment was a defining characteristic of *New Worlds*. Pamela Zoline's 'The Heat Death of the Universe' (1967), possibly the archetypal *New Worlds* story, appeared in a new digest format that encouraged stylistic play. Zoline's story of how a young housewife, Sarah Boyle, slides into madness is narrated in fifty-four numbered paragraphs including seven inserts on topics such as entropy and systems analysis. The form attempts to order Sarah's thoughts just as she attempts 'to index, record, bluff, invoke, order and placate' the household (Zoline 1983: 150). Yet, the form also describes how Sarah's identity is processed through commercial and technical discourses: 'she imagines *in her mind's eye* the headlines, "Nation's Small Fry Stricken, Fate's Finger Sugar Coated, Lethal Sweetness Socks Tots"' (Zoline 1983: 149). As the text moves, cutting and splicing linguistic registers, subjectivity itself appears as no more than an invented discourse, in which the unconscious is no refuge, but from which the outbreak of madness emerges as the inevitable entropic result. The look of the text conveys much of its significance as Zoline adumbrates and abridges the everyday spectacle of advertising, mass consumerism and the commodification of lifestyle.

By 1970, *New Worlds* had largely abandoned science fiction and become an avant-garde magazine like other titles within the counter-culture. Yet, its influence has remained considerable on later movements such as cyberpunk, magazines such as *Interzone* (1982–) and China Miéville's advocacy of what he has termed the 'New Weird'. By returning to the idea as image, although now as part of the iconography of the spectacular society, science fiction had also shown its ability for devising a vocabulary for thinking about social, psychological and technological change. In addition, the New Wave represented a synthesis with the classical avant-garde, in which the short story also played a significant role, and to which I shall now turn.

Further Reading

J. G. Cawelti's *Adventure, Mystery and Romance* (1976) is a ground-breaking study in genre fiction. The critical industry around Gothic has expanded exponentially in recent years: see Fred Botting (1996) and Jerrold E. Hogle (2002) as starting-points. On Gothic as a literary mode, see Rosemary Jackson, *Fantasy* (1981), and on the influence of the uncanny, see Nicholas Royle (2003). The role of doubles in literature is explored by Karl Miller (1987). On the history of detective fiction, see Martin Priestman (2003), and for theoretical, especially structuralist, approaches, see Tzvetan Todorov's 'The Typology of Detective Fiction' in *The Poetics of Prose* (1977). Janice Winship offers a brief but suggestive account of romantic short fiction in *Inside Women's Magazines* (1987). Besides Roger Luckhurst's cultural history of Anglo-American science fiction (2005), see also Edward James and Farah Mendlesohn (2003). Darko Suvin articulates his notion of the *novum* in *Metamorphoses of Science Fiction* (1979), while Mike Ashley (2000) offers a detailed survey of the early pulp magazines. Useful anthologies of Gothic, crime and science fiction stories include, respectively, David Blair (2002), Bill Pronzini and Jack Adrian (1995), and Tom Shippey (1992).

17

The Experimental Text

In his essay 'The Painter of Modern Life' (1859), Charles Baudelaire defined modernity as 'the ephemeral, the fugitive, the contingent, the half of art whose other half is the eternal and the immutable' (Baudelaire 1995: 12). As Chapters 9 and 10 described, modernist writers used forms such as the short story and the interlinked cycle as ways of ordering the apparent insignificance of modern life; in Georg Lukács' terms, elevating meaninglessness to the level of artistic form. The modernist aesthetic conserves notions of tradition, perspective and analysis even as it acknowledges the impossibility of objective understanding. Integral to the development of modernism, though, was an avant-garde ethos that pursued fleeting moments of subjective experience without seeking to conserve. For these writers and artists, conservation was associated with the hierarchical structures of the museum, the gallery and the mainstream press, social organisations diametrically opposed to the new arrangements of modern society. For the avant-garde, artistic institutions divided the experience of art from the experience of life. The avant-garde sought to negate the power of the institutions by producing art-works that shocked traditional criteria, which could not be displayed or reproduced conventionally, which highlighted and called into question the ruling frames of reference, and which often made use of technological methods of manufacture. In particular, as Tristan Tzara asserts in his 'Dada Manifesto' (1918), the avant-garde desired the abolition of meaning: 'precise works which will be forever misunderstood' (in Kolocotroni et al. 1998: 279). From the battle-cry of Dada to the contrasting methods of Samuel Beckett and William Burroughs, the classical avant-garde used forms, such as the fragment, the cut-up and the short fiction, in an aesthetic that ultimately resolved itself in terms of silence.

Baudelaire's prose-poems prefigure the avant-garde's need for new forms with which to express the fleetingness of existence. Like his more conventional verse, the prose poems describe what Baudelaire saw as the legacy of the 1848 revolutions: the division of society into an imposed civil order, in which human beings are defined by their economic role, and the remnants of the traditional polis, in which human beings function as moral creatures. The most extreme example of this tension is 'Let's Beat up the Poor!' (1865), in which Baudelaire's narrator attacks a beggar and then rejoices when his victim retaliates. Declaring that they are now equals, the protagonist happily shares his purse and advises the beggar to apply his theory 'to all your confederates' (Baudelaire 1991: 105). Baudelaire's dandies, though, who commit all kinds of social violence while justifying themselves (an ironic mirror-image of the bourgeoisie), are haunted by the emptiness of their existence: 'Memories, Regrets, Spasms, Fears, Anguish, Nightmares, Rages, and Neuroses' (Baudelaire 1991: 36). Although Baudelaire establishes the basis for the avant-garde artist, his alter-egos are trapped by their despair – their *ennui* – at the loss of meaning within the objectified polis. By contrast, his successors such as Stéphane Mallarmé would more fully celebrate the 'simultaneous vision' (in Rothenberg and Joris 1994: 53) of blankness and inscription to be found in texts such as 'A Throw of the Dice Never Will Abolish Chance' (1897).

The avant-garde movements of the early twentieth century such as Cubism, Dada and Futurism all play with notions of fragmentation. In his long prose poem, *Zang Tumb Tuuum* (1914), Filippo Marinetti discards Baudelaire's adherence to narrative for a syntax that invokes an accelerated, mechanised rhythm: 'exploding roasting + speed + ferocity of the tires coal dust of the street thirst thirst of the rubber cactus' (in Rothenberg and Joris 1994: 205). Despite its formal experimentation, Marinetti's text is still no more than a list of parts, a celebration of automatism insofar as other descriptive elements, suggesting some form of emotional depth, have been stripped away. Marinetti does not play with the internal possibilities of language as, for example, in sound-texts such as Hugo Ball's 'Caravan' (1917), but instead treats language as if it were a mathematical equation. By contrast, in 'Kora and Ka' (1930), the poet and novelist H.D. draws upon Cubist principles of collage and palimpsest to create a complex and ambiguous study of sexual identity. John Helforth, recovering from a nervous breakdown, is apparently possessed by an ancient Egyptian shade, Ka. He puts his recovery down to his lover, Kora, but he also states:

Sometimes I call Kora, Ka, or reverse the process and call Ka, Kora. I am on familiar terms with Kora, with Ka, likewise. We are, it is evident, some integral triple alliance, primordial Three-in-One. I am Kora, Kora is Helforth and Ka is shared between us. Though she repudiates affiliation with Ka, and refuses to discuss it, yet the fact remains. Ka is Kora, Kora is Ka. The waif must be shared between us. (in Adams and Tate 1991: 193–4)

H.D.'s slippages in point of view, indicating the impossibility of establishing a fixed identity in language, contrast sharply with the monocular viewpoint of Marinetti, in which all external objects are absorbed into his static gaze just as the motor car devours time and distance.

Having been a member of the Imagist circle in London, alongside Richard Aldington and Ezra Pound, H.D. became one of Gertrude Stein's close friends in Paris. As mentioned in Chapter 9, Stein intersected the Parisian avant-garde with the American expatriate community. A friend and a collector of artists such as Henri Matisse and Pablo Picasso, Stein applied the avant-garde techniques of Cubism and Post-Impressionism to her first published work, *Three Lives* (1909). Before its publication, though, Stein had already written her vast novel *The Making of Americans* (1906–8), in which she explored the 'continuous present and using everything and beginning again' (Stein 1993: 499). Stein's technique is different from the stream of consciousness perfected by Dorothy Richardson and Virginia Woolf, since her prose impedes and forces the reader to recommence a '"layering" of one phrase against another' that 'draws attention to the words themselves' (Nicholls 1995: 205). In so doing, Stein exposes the arbitrary link between the word and the object that it names, for example in her anachronistic use of the word 'gay' in 'Miss Furr and Miss Skeene' (1911). Although the word did not then have homosexual connotations, it was used in American slang to denote a sexually loose woman. Stein's extensive repetition confers upon it sexual intimations before, finally, losing all significance:

They stayed there and were gay there, not very gay there, just gay there. They were both gay there, they were regularly working there both of them cultivating their voices there, they were both gay there. Georgine Skeene was gay there and she was regular, regular in being gay, regular in not being gay, regular in being a gay one who was one not being gay longer than was needed to be one being quite a gay one. They were both then there and both working there then. (Stein 1993: 255)

The other feature of this passage is its use of qualification. Each qualifier, implying an attempt to be more precise (more 'regular'), confounds the reader's attempt to read the story as if it were a linear narrative. The indirection adds to the whimsicality of the writing in stark contrast with the demand for precision, and it is this opposition, on top of the repetition, which creates the humour. In other words, there is a delight on Stein's part in drifting away from sense-meaning that, in generic terms, synthesises the anecdote with the fragment. As Stein writes in 'Ada' (1910):

She was telling some one, who was loving every story that was charming. Some one who was living was almost always listening. Some one who was loving was almost always listening. That one who was loving was almost always listening. That one who was loving was telling about being one then listening. (Stein 1993: 103)

Stein's seemingly mechanical prose performs an ironic twist by recalling the short story's origins within the oral tradition. Love is not here an object that can be named. Instead, it surfaces within the reciprocation between teller and listener: the shifting dynamic embodied by Ada as both lover and loved one. The simultaneous pleasure of telling and listening suspends time and memory, the usual co-ordinates by which identity is established but which, as in her war story 'Tourty or Tourtebattre' (1919), Stein associates with a mythical pursuit of origins and essences:

What did he ask for.
Why I don't know.
Why don't you know.
I don't call that making literature at all.
What has he asked for.
I call literature telling a story as it happens.
Facts of life make literature.
I can always feel rightly about that. (Stein 1993: 324)

Although the women part in 'Miss Furr and Miss Skeene', the suspension of cause and effect means that there is little pathos. Instead, the accent falls upon the continuous reinvention of language as, for example, in the climax to 'As a Wife Has a Cow: A Love Story' (1923) that scatters sense-meaning by the impossibility, according to patriarchal and heterosexual logic, of same-sex desire:

> Happening and have it as happening and having it happen as happening and having to have it happen as happening, and my wife has a cow as now, my wife having a cow as now, my wife having a cow as now and having a cow as now and having a cow and having a cow now, my wife as a cow and now.
> (Stein 1993: 462)

Sherwood Anderson's derivation from his reading of Stein that words could be used as tonal colours, although important in terms of American regional writing, diminishes the radicalism of her work. Similarly, Ernest Hemingway's 'Mr and Mrs Elliot' (1924), modelled upon 'Miss Furr and Miss Skeene', domesticates Stein's ethos in ways that are interesting both in terms of modernism's relationship to the avant-garde and contemporary sexual politics.

Another important member of Stein's circle was Djuna Barnes. Her early short stories appeared in the mainstream New York press for which she carefully tailored her fictions as if they were news reports. The stories tend to be chronological but, although beginning in definite times and places, they tend to end abruptly, vanishing 'like a puff of smoke' (Barnes 1996: 154). Barnes' naturalistic sensibility, extending to her early Paris stories such as 'Spillway' (1919), presents her characters as social types whose lives continue even after the text has finished. The stories are held together by Barnes' objective pretence that is undercut by the ingratiating authorial figure, the writer as reporter: 'It takes circumstances alone to make them either friend, lover, enemy, thief, brawler, what–not. It may be a hand on the shoulder, a word whispered in the ear, a certain combination of apparently unimportant incidents' (Barnes 1996: 99). Although lacking the experimentation of her later work, Barnes' early stories show an ear for detail, a tight and compact use of language not unlike Dashiell Hammett. The comparison with American crime fiction can be extended further since Barnes privileges incident over psychology:

And then the crash comes. A man and his wife somewhere on the border of town die suddenly, and the cause has been traced back to poison found in a loaf of bread. As Jennie and Trenchard are the only bakers in the town, they are immediately pounced upon by the marshal, and both of them landed securely in . . . jail. (Barnes 1996: 224)

As Jorge Luis Borges has observed, the adventure story can delight in its own artifice and not pretend 'to transcribe reality' (Borges 2003: 6). Consequently, Barnes' early stories feature the ingredients of her later fiction: a jarring sense of discontinuity, characters regarded as objects, an unstable authorial role, and a self-referential use of language and form. 'Katrina Silverstaff' (1921), for example, draws its socially frustrated protagonist from the plays of Henrik Ibsen and August Strindberg, but unlike naturalistic drama, both the causality and Katrina's motivations are unclear: 'some people drink poison, some take a knife, and others drown; I take you' (in Adams and Tate 1991: 132). The story's incoherence means that Katrina cannot be rationalised as another specimen of modern womanhood, therefore contradicting the principles of her scientific training, but instead, it nullifies the arbitrariness of social discourse.

Barnes' story mediates the negative emphasis of the avant-garde movements that emerged in or around World War One. Surrealism, which grew jointly from Cubism and Dada, sought a more positive response by exploring the terrain of the unconscious. As André Breton, the group's leader, wrote, 'the marvellous is always beautiful . . . in fact only the marvellous is beautiful' (in Kolocotroni et al. 1998: 309). Nevertheless, Breton's project of resolving 'dream and reality' into an 'absolute' state could only be achieved by negating current social conditions: the tyranny of logic and reason (in Kolocotroni et al. 1998: 308). English émigrés, such as Leonora Carrington, already possessed an archive of Gothic tales, folk legends and anthropomorphic myths that could be used as the basis for Surrealist experiment. With illustrations by her lover, Max Ernst, Carrington published a pamphlet, *The House of Fear* (1938), and a collection, *The Oval Lady* (1939). The fake naïvety of Carrington's prose belies her ability to locate 'the extraordinary within the rhythms of the everyday' (Nicholls 2004: 407). In other words, Carrington uses the language of fantasy in order to read the hidden patterns within normative behaviour. 'The

Debutante', for example, describes the friendship of a young girl and a hyena. An intimate bond is struck, so that on the eve of the girl's coming-out ball, the hyena agrees to take her place. The girl's double creates a mask by eating the maid and wearing her face, only to be discovered at the party because of its strong smell. The doubling of the girl and the hyena suggests that the animal is the girl's sexual self, the initiation into adulthood that the ball celebrates while repressing its darker aspects. Carrington's story works, though, because of its quintessentially modern, that is to say, flippant, attitude towards the cruelties of the bourgeoisie: 'I can't eat any more. Her two feet are left over still, but if you have a little bag, I'll eat them later in the day' (Carrington 1988: 47).

Carrington's wit contrasts with the morbid and intense imagery of Edward Upward's 'The Railway Accident' (1928) and Dylan Thomas' 'The Burning Baby' (1934) which, although surrealistic, prefigures the introspection of the English Surrealist movement. Franz Kafka, whose writings began to be translated during the mid-1930s, was arguably more of an influence on English Surrealists than their French counterparts. 'Metamorphosis' (1915) and 'In the Penal Colony' (1919) described a world of pain, violence and torture that seemed to counterpoint the political horrors of the decade. This literal reading of Kafka, though, evades both the humour, which is another aspect of his writing, for example in 'Investigations of a Dog' (1922), and his affirmation of the avant-garde ethos. The critical tendency to turn Kafka's fiction into an allegory of either his religious identity, tensions with his father or the rise of nascent fascism glosses the recurring trope of negation, as in the closing of the door in 'Before the Law' (1914), or nullification, as in the protagonists' deaths in 'Metamorphosis', 'A Hunger Artist' (1922) and 'Josephine the Singer, or the Mouse Folk' (1924). In these stories, there is a gravitational pull towards non-significance that acts as political and social dissent (Gross 2002: 80–94). Like Herman Melville's Bartleby, the alienated subject can only register his/her opposition by withdrawing into themselves, an acknowledgement of their own estrangement that can only resolve itself in self-dissolution. In psychoanalytic terms, Kafka's fiction describes a desire for wholeness, a remaking of the self beyond the limits of the social order, which can only be achieved through the objectification of death (Jackson 1981: 159–62). Yet, in 'Metamorphosis', Gregor's demise comes only after the family has lost interest in him. The implication is that Gregor's needs have always been secondary to his economic usefulness. His transformation into a gigantic insect merely reveals the extent to which he has always been 'other' within the family unit. Once his grotesque form is no longer worthy of comment, he shrivels and decays. In prefiguring contemporary theories of the abject body, Kafka's negative fictions – his 'smudges' (Adorno 1967: 245) – reveal how apparently transgressive forms are always already entangled in invisible networks of power.

The Italian dramatist and short storywriter Luigi Pirandello presents a comic take on this same theme in 'The Tragedy of a Character' (1911):

> Everything turns, therefore, on whether we can be what we want to be. Where that power is lacking, our desire must of necessity appear ridiculous and quite futile.

The tragedy of Pirandello's character is that he refuses 'to recognize that this is how things are' (Pirandello 1987: 94). The fictional Dr Fileno believes that he will find an author who will make proper use of him and reveal his true purpose. Pirandello's narrator informs Fileno that his hopes are misplaced since authors are another kind of absence: 'under your inverted telescope . . . you would no longer see anything or anybody' (Pirandello 1987: 102). For Pirandello, life is an endless series of masks that conceal the nothingness which is an irreducible component of existence. Pirandello's comic vision of the futility of meaning prefigures not only the existentialism of Albert Camus and Jean-Paul Sartre but also the so-called 'Theatre of the Absurd' with which Samuel Beckett was temporarily associated after the premiere of *Waiting for Godot* in 1954.

Despite being better known for his plays, Beckett considered his short fiction to be his more important work. Beckett began under the influence of his mentor, James Joyce, for example in the short story cycle *More Pricks than Kicks* (1934), which followed the adventures of an itinerant student, Belacqua, modelled upon Joyce's Stephen Dedalus. Nevertheless, the opening story, 'Dante and the Lobster', prefigures aspects of Beckett's later style. The story begins with Belacqua studying *The Divine Comedy*, principally Beatrice's defence of divine power and her refutation of Dante's narrow logic. Belacqua's insistence that he will get to 'the meanings of the words, the order in which they were spoken' (Beckett 1993: 9) indicates his failure to understand the premise of the argument since Beatrice's defence is founded upon a rejection of overdetermined reason. God, according to Beatrice, is not to be experienced through an empirical use of language. Consequently, at the end of the story, when Belacqua is confronted with the horror of seeing a live lobster placed into a cooking pot, he falls back on a platitude, 'it's a quick death, God help us all', that rationalises what he sees. The last words though, 'it is not' (Beckett 1993: 21), besides being an early example of Beckett's mordant irony, originate from an invisible and God-like point of view. The lobster's sacrifice, which Belacqua shies away from understanding, demonstrates Beatrice's claim that divine power is not to be understood in human terms, although the pity which is extended to the lobster counteracts the remorselessness of cosmic justice.

Beckett's characters, then, are condemned to live in a universe beyond their comprehension, since their only means of understanding their existence is through a language that is overdetermined and overrational. For Beckett, like avant-garde writers before him, the pursuit of writing is an undoing of language itself. This process is not to be confused with transplanting language for something else since, in Beckett's thinking, the transcendent possibility of meaning would decentre all other meanings, effectively producing a series of absences. Almost in anticipation of deconstructionists such as Jacques Derrida, Beckett's later prose recovers the tracery of meanings within language. Beginning with the novel *How It Is* (1961), Beckett devised a simple prose style that, like Stein's, was hypnotically repetitive and eschewed all ornamentation, for example in 'Lessness' (1969):

> Figment light never was but grey air timeless no sound. Blank planes touch close sheer white all gone from mind. Little body ash grey locked rigid heart beating face to endlessness. On him will rain again as in the blessed days of blue the passing cloud. Four square true refuge long last four walls over backwards no sound. (Beckett 1995: 197)

Signifiers such as 'blessed', suggesting a theological key to the text, are denied by their subsequent lack of development. Instead, like other potential reference-points such as the Jewish Holocaust, these signifiers are shorn of meaning and reduced to an instrumental role. Beckett's later texts are characteristically colourless:

> All known all white bare white body fixed one yard legs joined like sewn. Light heat white floor one square yard never seen. White walls one yard by two white ceiling one square yard never seen. Bare white body fixed only the eyes only just. Traces blurs light grey almost white on white. (Beckett 1995: 193)

The whitening-out of meaning in texts such as 'Ping' (1966) amounts to a kind of silence that aspires to 'an ideal plenitude to which the audience can add nothing':

> A person who becomes silent becomes opaque for the other; somebody's silence opens up an array of possibilities for interpreting that silence, for imputing speech to it. (Sontag 1994: 16)

In what is, in effect, a radical extension of Edgar Allan Poe's claim that all parts of a short story should contribute to the overall sum, Beckett produces a short prose fiction in which everything is potentially meaningful, but which rebuffs the reader's desire for interpretation, so that it also appears to be devoid of significance. Yet, Beckett's opacity is also curiously transparent – his writing is what it is – insofar as it 'fizzles' (the title of a prose sequence from 1973 to 1975) with its own exhilarated sense of dying. Indeed, despite Beckett's ideal of absolute silence, one of the recurring tropes in his writing is that of the body. Exposed and bereft but for memories that might also be hallucinations, the body is presented as the victim of either fate or circumstance, for example the solitary figure in 'Stirrings Still' (1988):

> One night or day then as he sat at his table head on hands he saw himself rise and go. First rise and stand clinging to the table. Then sit again. Then rise again and stand clinging to the table again. Then go. Start to go. On unseen feet start to go. (Beckett 1995: 259)

Beckett's fiction, then, appears at the outer edge of the avant-garde ethos. He extends the pursuit of non-meaning to a point at which writing begins to dissolve into silence, an array of signifiers that may indicate nothing but themselves. Instead of achieving this ideal, though, Beckett's writing, suffused with its own melancholic imagination, reinscribes what cannot be left behind: the body as an instrument, rather than an originating source, of language.

The same can also be said for William Burroughs. *Exterminator!* (1973), deliberately and confusingly described as a novel, distils many of his major themes. Burroughs was celebrated for his use of the 'cut-up', the cutting and splicing of pre-existing texts, which had its roots in Dada, in particular Tristan Tzara's 'To Make a Dadaist Poem' (1924). The cut-up not only disarranges language, creating new combinations of meaning by collage and surreal juxtaposition, but it also acts as an inoculation against words (Porush 1985: 100–4). For Burroughs, language is akin to a parasite that controls our thought and behaviour. Whereas Beckett desires to create a condition of 'lessness', Burroughs' response is to add more information to the system so that his writing amounts to a form of positive feedback. Like the Dadaists, Burroughs is opposed to all types of system: 'As soon as you work for any organization you have rules and it's a rule that anyone working for any organization cannot be allowed to know the reason for the rules' (Burroughs 1979: 165). In this paranoid world of hyper-bureaucracy where identity, like Burroughs' nameless secret agents, is interchangeable, the only solution is to negate its influence by exposing its working methods, in particular by disassembling meaning at the most fundamental levels of language. Consequently, Burroughs extends the avant-garde aesthetic of negation, but whereas other writers pursue silence by creating stasis or inertia, Burroughs pursues silence by countering noise with more noise. The feedback loop of Burroughs' fiction relays signals in a constant and ultimately entropic exchange, so that not only do characters reappear during the course of *Exterminator!* as if in a kind of mosaic, but the stories also intersect with other characters from Burroughs' fiction: A. J. Cohen and Dutch Schultz, for example. In distilling the body of his writing into a series of short stories that defy generic classification, Burroughs performs another act of cutting and editing the printed page – the very form and layout of which seems to imply a mystical authority – so all that is left are fragments or ruins, the 'Cold Lost Marbles' of the final story composed from words and phrases not only of the text but also inevitably its intertexts. Like Beckett, Burroughs appears at the end-point of the classical avant-garde, but whereas Beckett's prose has largely proved inimitable, Burroughs' use of linguistic noise – the pastiches of popular culture colliding with the aggressive imagery of sex and violence resolving into melancholic prose-poetry – has played an integral role within the rise of postmodern fiction.

Further Reading

For theories of the avant-garde, see Peter Bürger (1984) and Renato Poggioli (1968). On the interaction between avant-garde art and literature in the modernist period, see Shari Benstock (1987), Christopher Butler (1994) and Peter Nicholls (1995). Despite the schematic distinction between 'short story' and 'short fiction', Clare Hanson (1985) affords useful insights on the role of experiment among short story-writers. On the work of individual writers, see Marianne DeKoven on Gertrude Stein (1983), Deborah Parsons (2003) on Djuna Barnes, and John Pilling (1994) on Samuel Beckett.

18

Postmodernism and the Short Story

Despite J. G. Ballard's contention that postmodernism was invented by academics in order to justify their continued existence (Ballard 1991: 329), the concept has not only informed critical reading but also creative writing in the postwar period. Yet, to attempt to periodise the postmodern is threatened by the word itself, literally meaning 'after' (post) 'the now' (from the Latin *modo*). To be always coming after and, therefore, in a continual state of transit rather than rest disturbs notions of linearity, causality and chronology. Insofar as the preceding chapters have tended to pursue a thematic and cross-sectional approach, in which the short story has been situated in terms of paradox, ambiguity and fragmentation, this book can also be said to be indebted to postmodern thought. Or, alternatively, that the short story has acted at various times as a resource for writers to contest the dominant beliefs in social progress and formal cohesion. As the complex timing of the word 'postmodern' suggests, it is impossible to locate the concept in a single or agreed body of knowledge. This undefinable quality is shared by both postmodernism and the short story. I shall not attempt to define postmodernism, as I have also avoided doing with the short story, but to propose a series of statements in which we can think about their mutual relationship (see also Bennett and Royle 2004: 248–57).

The postmodern is . . . undecidable

Modernist narratives privilege the indeterminate ending, for example, in Katherine Mansfield's 'Bliss' (1918) Bertha Young gains a pessimistic yet also mature insight into herself, which can either be read positively or negatively. To say that a narrative is indeterminate, though, is still to determine that there is a meaning to be uncovered.

The New Critics, discussed in Chapter 8, privileged the uses of ambiguity insofar as they enriched the final formal unity of the text. To say, by contrast, that the meaning of a text is undecidable is not to decide for or against the presence of meaning but to suspend the very act of deciding. The postmodern does not begin from a decision having already been made but instead proceeds by deferring the moment of decision into an indefinite future. This is not to say that postmodernism is against judgement but that it is against the overdetermination of a founding principle. In suspending judgement, the postmodern celebrates the multiple options within the act of judging.

Vladimir Nabokov's 'Signs and Symbols' (1948), for example, describes a psychiatric patient for whom 'everything is a cipher and of everything he is the theme' (Nabokov 1958: 50). Like Jorge Luis Borges' 'Funes the Memorious' (1942), Nabokov's protagonist is unable to ignore any detail since every experience is potentially meaningful. Yet, the result of his obsession is that transcendent meaning, which would 'tear a hole in his world' and allow him to 'escape' (Nabokov 1958: 49), is endlessly deferred. At the same time, though, he experiences a contentment that is lost upon his parents, so that the story also questions the definition of madness. Other postmodern writers, for example Robert Coover in 'Morris in Chains' (1969), blur the distinction of what is and isn't rational so that the reader's judgement is suspended. Instead, to quote the title of John Barth's 1967 story, readers are 'lost in the funhouse' of mirrors and distorted reflections, in which reality is conceived not only as a fiction but also as a *metafiction*: a commentary upon the writing of fiction itself. A key theme, then, of postmodern literature is how we establish an idea of truth while options multiply around us.

The postmodern is . . . decentred

To suspend judgement and to decide in favour of textual play is to reject all forms of received authority, whether that is God, patriarchy, the Empire or literature. Undecidability not only dissolves specific meanings within a text but it also throws the text off-balance: it becomes decentred. This is not necessarily to propose new centres of meaning, so for instance the study of women's history (*her story*) replaces men's history (*his story*), but to show that meaning is in a constant process of re- and decentring. For instance, Angela Carter's 'The Loves of Lady Purple' (1974) rejects historical narrative as a succession of causes and effects and presents it, instead, as a performance that is constantly replayed. One of the most influential critiques of historical origin is offered by Jean-François Lyotard in *The Postmodern Condition* (1979), where Enlightenment reason is presented as an example of what he terms a 'grand narrative': an underlying pattern that resolves histori-cal change into a single, totalising framework. William Gibson's 'The Gernsback Continuum' (1981) effectively illustrates Lyotard's argu-ment in its tale of a photographer hired to catalogue the remnants of futuristic designs from the 1930s, 'an architecture of broken dreams' from when 'what the public wanted was the future' (Gibson 1988: 40–1). In the photographer's mind, these fragments mesh not only with the technological visions of pulp science fiction but also with the Nazi architecture of the same period: 'The Thirties dreamed white marble and slipstream chrome . . . but the rockets on the covers of the Gernsback pulps had fallen on London in the dead of night, scream-ing' (Gibson 1988: 41). Eventually, the photographer's thoughts become so intermingled that he is haunted by 'semiotic phantoms' (Gibson 1988: 44):

> They were white, blond, and they probably had blue eyes . . . Here, we'd gone on and on, in a dream logic that knew nothing of pollution, the finite bounds of fossil fuel, or foreign wars it was possible to lose . . . It had all the sinister fruitiness of Hitler Youth propaganda. (Gibson 1988: 47)

Gibson's explicit link between fascism and technological progress decentres the grand narrative of scientific optimism by arguing that it conceals a covert totalitarianism. However, Gibson's protagonist only drowns out his ghosts by submitting to another kind of dystopia: the 'really bad media' of contemporary culture (Gibson 1988: 48).

In undermining narrative logic, postmodernism questions the constraints of systematised knowledge. Red Scharlach, the master-criminal of Borges' 'Death and the Compass' (1942), traps his enemy, Lönnrot, by making a study of the detective's apparently random methods of deduction. In 'Harrison Bergeron' (1961), Kurt Vonnegut imagines a future society where equality is ensured by the Handicapper General, who systematically disables everyone so that nobody is more intelligent, more attractive or more physically fit than anyone else. As the General's title suggests, there are echoes of witch hunts and persecutions, both from the Puritan context of the seventeenth century and during the paranoia of the Cold War. In his story 'Entropy' (1960), Thomas Pynchon uses the principle of thermodynamics to show how order will inevitably be engulfed by chaos.

It is in this respect that the short story's tendency towards idea and situation lends the form most effectively to the needs of postmodernism. J. G. Ballard's 'Notes Towards a Mental Breakdown' (1976), presented as a series of footnotes to an eighteen-word synopsis, reveals that a psychiatric explanation is less a key to the text than part of the problem. In 'The Largest Theme Park in the World' (1989), Ballard moves convincingly from the reasonable proposition of free trade and traffic between nations to an international fascism based upon the cult of leisure. Similarly, in his story 'Scale' (1994), Will Self offers a series of viewpoints in order to prove his narrator's claim that it is possible to lose a sense of scale but retain proportion. At one point, the drugged narrator takes delight as his pet lizard runs amok through a model village like a miniature dinosaur. Yet, these flights of fancy are grounded in Self's critiques of contemporary boredom, for instance in 'Understanding the Ur-Bororo' (1991), where two representatives of the world's most boring tribe are easily integrated into middle-class English society, or in 'Between the Conceits' (1994), where it is revealed that London is inhabited by only eight real people who control the rest of the population, but do nothing with their seemingly God-like powers.

The drift from logic to illogic recalls also the short story's tendency towards mutability and the legacy of oral and romantic traditions. Borges' 'Death and the Compass' and Iain Sinclair's 'The Griffin's Egg' (1996) are quest narratives which loop back upon themselves. Angela Carter's *The Bloody Chamber* (1979) not only draws upon the allegorical structures of fairy tale but also scatters the tradition amid other cultural debris so that the fairy tale no longer functions solely as an explanatory tool. Donald Barthelme's fiction not only makes explicit uses of transformation, for example in 'The Balloon' (1968), but also implicitly insofar as the highly fragmented structures of stories such as 'Will You Tell Me?' (1964) invite the reader to piece the text together sentence by sentence. Each break in the narrative invites the possibility of a reading that will transform the whole. Yet, as the title of William Gass' 'In the Heart of the Heart of the Country' (1968) suggests, the centre is always elsewhere. As Alasdair Gray acknowledges in the prefatory note that accompanies *Ten Tales Tall & True* (1993), 'this book contains more tales than ten so the title is a tall tale too. I would spoil my book by shortening it, spoil the title if I made it true' (Gray 1993: 8–9).

The postmodern is . . . simulation

In decentring narrative as the site of original meaning, postmodernism also calls into question the relationship between the narrative account and the world that it describes. Since at least the time of Plato, Western aesthetics have turned upon the notion of *mimesis*: the making of a copy that reproduces the original but is distinct from the real. At various times, for example, during the controversy that surrounded Samuel Richardson's romantic novel *Pamela* (1740), critics have been alarmed by readers' apparent inability to distinguish between the real and the copy. In the age of mass media, though, this distinction becomes ever less tenable: 'When the age of mechanical reproduction separated art from its basis in cult, the semblance of its autonomy disappeared forever' (Benjamin 1992: 220). Instead of the production of artistic images as authentic representations of reality, they are increasingly 'designed for reproducibility' (Benjamin 1992: 218). As Walter Benjamin suggests in his essay on mechanical reproduction, copies are nowadays valued because they *are* copies and, as such, are endlessly reproducible. The authentic experience of the original correspondingly diminishes so, for example, the conspicuousness of a painting such as *The Mona Lisa* as an object of parody or travesty, as a reproduction on postcards, T-shirts, tea towels and coffee mugs, and as an inspiration in other media, is so great that the spectator's enjoyment of it cannot be isolated from these other representations. In a way, we already 'know' *The Mona Lisa* even if we have never been to the Louvre.

Building upon Benjamin's insights, Jean Baudrillard advances the notion of simulation in contrast to mimetic representation. Instead of a copy implying an original, just as a fragment might imply a whole, copies no longer signify anything other than themselves. The real or, as Baudrillard terms it, the *hyperreal* is to be experienced as an endless series of reproducible images in which the original is irrecoverable: 'simulation is no longer that of a territory, a referential being, or a substance . . . it is nevertheless the map that precedes the territory' (Baudrillard 1994: 1). In this imploded hierarchy of copies and originals, the fragment as a loose and self-sufficient form, and so consequently the short story, become ways of navigating this changed landscape.

For example, in Salman Rushdie's 'Chekov and Zulu' (1994), two Asian diplomats conduct their friendship through a *Star Trek* fantasy, so that even their official correspondence is encoded with references to the television series. William Boyd's 'Adult Video' (2004) goes further still by segmenting the non-linear narrative so that it plays, rewinds, pauses and fast forwards. The characters experience their lives as recorded with a similar detachment as the cast of Douglas Coupland's *Generation X* (1991). Employed in low-paid jobs with no career prospects or stable family support, Coupland's protagonists are enmeshed in a net of popular cultural references that they further entangle in the tales they repeat to fill their empty lives. The social and economic framework is further constituted by the series of footnotes, consisting of slogans, youthful slang and Pop Art imitations, which append the text. Similarly, in David Foster Wallace's collection *Girl with Curious Hair* (1989), there is a recurrent preoccupation with television, advertising, marketing and merchandise. In the story 'Lyndon', purportedly an insider's view of the White House, the memoir is filtered through media representations of President Johnson so that this account is no truer than any other simulated discourse. The theme park settings of George Saunders' 'CivilWarLand in Bad Decline' (1996) and 'Pastoralia' (2000) foreground the artificial concerns of the corporate world, that is to say, the world that sells itself as materially real, in its obsession with routines, performance targets and self-assessment. In Coover's 'The Babysitter' (1969), the light of the TV screen flickers across the heroine's body so that she, too, is a desirable commodity.

Nevertheless, it is in the work of J. G. Ballard where simulated reality occurs most prominently. Although simulation and simulacra have long been science fictional tropes, for example in the forms of the robot, the clone and the alien parasite, American science fiction of the 1950s, such as Philip K. Dick's 'Second Variety' (1953) and

Frederick Pohl's 'The Tunnel Under the World' (1955), developed these elements as a paranoid critique of the consumer society and the military-industrial complex. Some of Ballard's early stories, especially 'The Subliminal Man' (1963), echo his American predecessors, but increasingly Ballard viewed simulation as a virtuality to be engaged with rather than feared. Putting aside *The Atrocity Exhibition* (1970), discussed in Chapter 10, the stories that comprise *Vermilion Sands* (1971) describe a gated community in which the leisured but lonely inhabitants spend their time sculpting clouds, breeding exotic plants, dressing in psychosensitive clothes, and exploring their deepest desires. Ballard gradually stripped away the more visionary elements of his writing in order to emphasise the everyday surrealism of current technology. For example, in 'The 60 Minute Zoom' (1976), the narrator appears to be describing in the present tense his secret recording of his wife's adulterous affair. In fact, the narrator is watching back the video of how he murdered her. The switch from present to past, and the realisation that as readers we have been made complicit in the narrator's sadistic desire, makes this story one of Ballard's most shocking.

The postmodern is . . . surface

The postmodern preoccupation with multiple, shifting or interchangeable realities results in a style of writing that stays on the surface. Although Ernest Hemingway also addressed the surface appearance of things, stories such as 'Hills Like White Elephants' (1927) hint at an underlying truth that would makes sense of the whole. What makes the fiction of J. G. Ballard, or the early stories of Ian McEwan such as 'Solid Geometry' and 'Homemade' (both 1975), so disturbing is their emotional detachment. Even while describing the most taboo of material, the stories are curiously inexpressive. That is to say, the characters' words and actions do not seem to express something which is emotionally or intellectually felt; they do not seem to emanate from an inner, central or reasoning self.

Fredric Jameson has argued that during the twentieth century four depth models dominated Western thought: the Marxist analysis of the economic structures that underpin society, the psychoanalytic examination of how conscious reactions are predetermined by the unconscious, the existentialist emphasis upon an authentic self submerged by inauthentic social conventions, and lastly, the structuralist notion that thought is embedded in language (Jameson 1991: 12). In each of these models, surface reality is exposed as a mask that conceals an underlying reality. Postmodernism, however, deconstructs this opposition between surface and depth, so that the surface is shown as concealing nothing but itself. Postmodern texts are, in that sense, transparent rather than opaque. Coover's short story cycle *A Night at the Movies* (1987) refashions a network of cinematic allusions in which the text does not signify an external reality but can only be engaged with at the level of surface play. The absurdity of Barthelme's fiction, even in its more politicised guises such as 'Game' or 'The Indian Uprising' (both 1968), implies that life is absurd and that attempts at grasping the totality of meaning are doomed: although even this reading is contingent upon how the texts are formally constructed. In short, instead of posing the question 'what does it mean?', it might be better to ask of the postmodern text, 'what does it mean to do?'

The postmodern is . . . pastiche

In its depthless treatment of writing, Jameson argues that postmodern fiction tends towards pastiche. Like its counterpart, parody, pastiche relies upon mimicry for its effect, but whereas the former is written in order to satirise, pastiche is 'devoid of laughter and of any conviction that . . . some healthy linguistic normality still exists' (Jameson 1991: 17). In other words, whereas parody reinscribes the notion of a cultural order or a hierarchy of judgement, pastiche dissolves into eclecticism: the mixing of generic conventions, media, high and low art, the tragic with the comic. Postmodern pastiche is inherently *intertextual*: *The Bloody Chamber*, for example, exhibits a profusion of elite and folk culture references. Yet, Carter's characters are unaware that they are living out pre-established narrative patterns, while her readers are often unaware of all the reference points that Carter cites. Their enjoyment of the text is not diminished, however, since as Puss-in-Boots acknowledges, 'nothing to it . . . rococo's no problem' (Carter 1995: 171). Postmodern pastiche delights in its reproduction of disparate material: detective fiction in Borges' 'Death and the Compass', the ghost story in Julio Cortázar's 'House Taken Over' (1946), science fiction in Italo Calvino's *Cosmicomics* (1965). Calvino's later sequence, *The Castle of Crossed Destinies* (1969), not only pastiches medieval novellas, such as *The Canterbury Tales* and *The Decameron*, but is also based upon a system derived from tarot. The framing and pastiche of the oral tradition ultimately calls into question the arbitrariness of the system. Calvino's richly decorated text is matched most closely in the English-speaking world by Alasdair Gray, also an artist and illustrator, whose collections such as *Unlikely Stories, Mostly* (1983) and *Ten Tales Tall & True* (1993) resemble illuminated manuscripts or the movement of word and image in the work of William Blake. As with the graphic short stories of Iain Sinclair, the reader is invited to respond to the page sensually rather than mine it for information. Consequently, despite the apparently fatalistic conclusion of Borges' 'Pierre Menard, Author of the *Quixote*' (1939) that literature can only repeat itself, the effect of postmodern pastiche is to renew the experience of reading as a tactile pleasure.

The postmodern is . . . unrepresentable

The questioning of literature's claim to truth, the blurring of reality and the play of textual pleasure not only result in the disruption of representation but also that of the postmodern. Instead, postmodernism manifests itself in phenomena that defy classification, such as the abject or the sublime, and in forms that resist definition: such as the short story. To write when there are no strict rules of representation means that the writer works blind 'in order to formulate the rules of what *will have been done*' (Lyotard 1984: 81). In other words, the postmodern is always in a state of becoming so that its common characteristics are partiality, incompleteness and obscurity.

The remark made by one of John Fowles' characters, 'nothing is real. All is fiction' (Fowles 1986: 229), echoes the world-text of Borges' 'The Library of Babel' (1941). The infinite collection, for which there can be no 'true catalogue' (Borges 1970: 81), defies representation. In Ballard's 'Report on an Unidentified Space Station' (1982), the object unfolds to encompass the entire universe while, in Angela Carter's fiction, there is no escape from the dual motifs of 'flesh and the mirror' (a title from 1974) where the body itself acts as a reflective surface in the gaze of the other. Similarly, in 'The Mystery of the Young Gentleman' (1982), Joanna Russ uses both the science fictional motif of the alien visitor and a pastiche of Victorian sexual mores to suggest not only that identity is a performance but that the deconstruction of 'man' and 'woman' also throws into doubt the viability of 'human'. In *The Things They Carried* (1990), Tim O'Brien's recombining of characters and events emphasises the impossibility of telling 'a true war story'. The compositional principle of Jeff Noon's *Cobralingus* (2001) not only depicts language as musical software but also samples and edits the text, an effect not unlike hypertext although attesting to the endless variety of the printed page.

John Barth's conceptual sequence *Lost in the Funhouse* (1968) openly challenges the act of representation. In a study of Borges entitled 'The Literature of Exhaustion' (1967), Barth had argued that literature had nowhere to go but an endless recycling of its history, themes and motifs. The metafictional texts such as 'Life-Story' and the title story put this theory into practice by reproducing clichéd scenarios, 'in the movies he'd meet a beautiful young girl in the funhouse', interjecting with criticisms, '"is anything more tiresome, in fiction, than the problems of sensitive adolescents?"', and breaking off altogether, 'and it's all too long and rambling' (Barth 1968: 87–8). In aesthetic criticism, this technique is known as *mise en abyme*, literally the putting into an abyss. 'Night-Sea Journey' (1966), for example, describes the nocturnal passage of either an impossible creature or possibly a human sperm. In 'Meneliad', Barth's reworking of Homer, King Menelaus recounts the events described in *The Iliad* and *The Odyssey*, and in particular his encounter with the shape-shifting Proteus. Just as Proteus is continually changing his form, so Menelaus is constantly switching narrative positions to the extent that it becomes impossible for him to narrate his story since there is no single 'he'. Instead, a series of embedded voices speak through Menelaus, fracturing not only the tale but also the identity of the speaker(s). Yet, despite this confusing medley, an impression emerges, namely, that of love. It is the question that Menelaus poses of Helen:

""""""Speak!" Menelaus cried to Helen on the bridal bed,' I reminded Helen in her Trojan bedroom," I confessed to Eidothea on the beach,' I declared to Proteus in the cavemouth," I vouchsafed to Helen on the ship,' I told

Peisistratus at least in my Spartan hall," I say to whoever and where- I am.
And Helen answered:
""""""""Love!""""""""""
! (Barth 1968: 150)

Helen's affirmation of love returns to Menelaus as a distant echo from a different time and place. His refusal to believe that she loves him is played out in terms of temporal disjunction. The asymmetry of the text, the suspension of Menelaus as both speaking subject and spoken object, dramatises the extent to which he has never believed Helen's offer of love. In a sense, Helen's love for Menelaus has always preceded his understanding of what Helen is offering him. As Jacques Derrida has written on the nature of amity, 'The friend is the person who loves before being the person who is loved' (Derrida 1997: 9). Love and friendship are conducted, according to Derrida, across a temporal divide, since without that tear in the social fabric there could be no amity: self and other would coexist in the same space-time. The survival of friendship depends upon there being a split – a loss of presence and representation – for 'the truth of friendship . . . is found there, in darkness, and with it the truth of the political' (Derrida 1997: 16). Menelaus' failure is to understand this: the success of Barth's story is to point towards a new kind of ethics that goes beyond metafictional play.

The postmodern is . . . over?

At one point in the science fiction film *The Matrix* (1998), the character of Morpheus welcomes the hero, Neo, to 'the desert of the real'. The line directly quotes from Baudrillard, so that the resultant wasteland can either be read as an ironic *homage* to the great aphorist of postmodern banality or an overliteral imaging of his resonant phrase. Either way, the cannibalising of postmodern strategies that characterises the film raises an important question: is postmodernism over?

It is a curious feature that as the postmodern emerged from the social sciences of the 1950s, especially in American sociology, to its initial acceptance by a few cultural critics in the 1960s (again, principally American), and then to its widespread dissemination during the 1980s, the term underwent successive critical re-evaluations. When the mass culture theorist Dwight Macdonald uses the idea it has thoroughly negative connotations, but when it is used by the literary critic Ihab Hassan it denotes a positive break from the rigidities of modernism and New Criticism. Although Baudrillard and Jameson positioned themselves as critics of postmodernity, their emphases upon the disembodying of reality and the hollow spectacle of late capitalism were greeted enthusiastically by a community of academics operating in literary, cultural and media studies. In many ways, postmodernism became a shibboleth that defined the work of the humanities following the supplanting of concepts such as socialism and the class struggle on both sides of the Atlantic by neo-conservative economics, principally the rise of the free market of which postmodernism was purportedly one symptom. The general acceptance of the Baudrillardian-Jamesonian model of postmodernism, derived as it is from other socio-economic models, was less a diagnosis than a reflection of cultural change.

If one version of the postmodern was already exhausted by the end of the 1990s, for instance in the example from *The Matrix* given above, then it was largely buried beneath the rubble of the World Trade Center in 2001. Yet, as the legacies of 9/11, the anti-globalisation movement and, most recently, the panic in the international banking system have shown, there is a need for a new political discourse that would address the intersections between global terror, media and economics. Despite an emerging critical consensus that postmodernism is over, recent political events have highlighted the need for the type of ethical thinking advanced within the post-Heideggerian tradition, for example by Maurice Blanchot, Emmanuel Levinas, Jean-François Lyotard and Jacques Derrida, in order to combat manifestations of what Lyotard has termed 'the inhuman'. A key aspect of this critique is that, as indicated in the short quotation from Lyotard above, the postmodern cannot be configured in the here and now. Whereas the tendency of capitalist economics is towards the quantification of presence – the measuring of what is materially available – the postmodern is always becoming; what passes for postmodernism is only a glimpse of what the postmodern could be. The undecidable and unrepresentable qualities of the postmodern confound all attempts at its quantification.

It is a notable feature, then, the extent to which contemporary short storywriters such as China Miéville and George Saunders openly criticise the saturation of consumer and management cultures. Furthermore, it is true to say that postmodernism has become part of the literary tradition for younger writers, such as Miéville, Saunders and Ali Smith, just as modernists were once a reference-point during the heyday of postmodernism, for example Fowles' debt to Katherine Mansfield in 'The Cloud' (1974). Since postmodernism postulated itself as a new avant-garde, and since all avant-gardes eventually decay, it is no surprise that postmodernism would also wither. Yet, there is no sorry end for postmodernism becoming another co-ordinate on the map of reading, since without there being a map there could be no writing, and without writing there could be no critique. In news of its official end, postmodernism might only just be beginning . . .

Further Reading

There are several guides to postmodernism: see for example Steven Connor (1989) and Thomas Docherty's introduction to his postmodernist reader (1993). See also the relevant essays by Barth and Hassan in Bran Nicol's reader on *Postmodernism and the Contemporary Novel* (2002). Before considering postmodernism's critique of copies and imitations, see Erich Auerbach's landmark account of mimesis (2003). For the beginnings of an ethical criticism in postmodern literary theory, see Andrew Gibson (1999). On the postmodern short story, see Farhat Iftekharuddin et al. (2003), and on the work of individual writers in the context of postmodernism, Larry McCaffery's study of Barthelme, Coover and Gass (1982).

19

Minimalism/Dirty Realism/ Hyperrealism

By the mid-1970s, American postmodernism was in its heyday and the short stories of Donald Barthelme, in particular, were widely represented in creative writing programmes. Since then, and until the emergence of devotees such as Dave Eggers, David Foster Wallace and George Saunders, Barthelme's status as a role model for prospective student writers has been diminished by Raymond Carver, a writer whose early death in 1988 at the height of his creative powers has ensured a mythic stature not known since one of Carver's heroes, Ernest Hemingway. The work of Carver and his associates, most notably Richard Ford and Tobias Wolff, has often been seen as a counter-response to the influence of postmodernism. Yet, what I will show in this chapter is that their fiction often unsettles what is meant by literary realism in ways not dissimilar to their postmodern counterparts.

Part of the problem in distinguishing the characteristic features of Carver and his contemporaries has been the critical tendency to impose upon them a sufficiently resonant group identity. Wolff refers to 'Minimalists, New Realists, Dirty Realists, even Neo-Realists' (Wolff 1993: xi), while Ann-Marie Karlsson adds to that list 'K-Mart Realism' and 'Hick Chic' (Karlsson 1990: 144). Although Carver and Ford had first met in 1976, with Wolff meeting them both while Ford was living in Vermont before joining Carver as a creative writing tutor at the University of Syracuse, the group identity rapidly becomes diffuse. The tendency towards realism in American fiction at the start of the 1980s extends to writers not part of this small coterie, for example Ann Beattie, Richard Bausch, Andre Dubus, Amy Hempel, Bobbie Ann Mason, Lorrie Moore, Jayne Anne Phillips and Mary Robison. Perhaps most perplexing is the case of Frederick Barthelme, whose early fiction at the start of the 1970s is marked by the stylistic influence of his brother Donald, but who later eschewed overt experimentation for a plainer, more realistic style. Furthermore, despite the critical attention paid to postmodernism, realism had not disappeared in American fiction, most notably in the example of Grace Paley.

In Britain, this new direction was popularised by Bill Buford, the founding editor of *Granta*, as dirty realism (Buford 1983: 4–5). The techniques of Carver and his contemporaries appeared, in one sense, to be dirtying the realism associated with the stereotype of the *New Yorker* story. Despite the uses of brevity and economy, the polluting elements were primarily in terms of content rather than form: the inclusion of regional and working-class characters in a post-industrial economic context. In this sense, though, the so-called dirty realists belonged to a naturalistic tradition in American culture that included the stories of Hemingway, Sherwood Anderson's *Winesburg, Ohio* (1919) and the paintings of Edward Hopper: stark, haunting images of urban isolation and non-communication. Carver added to the description's strength by frequently citing V. S. Pritchett on the nature of the glimpse, or the snatched-at detail. Yet, the term also generalises since it does not take into account the wit and humour of writers like Beattie and Moore, the formal ingenuity of Hempel and Phillips, or Carver's moral humanism. Instead, it acts more like a marketing slogan not only for the writers but also for *Granta*, which was then still a fledgling magazine based in Cambridge. By grouping the writers together as the vanguard of contemporary American fiction, Buford was also casting *Granta* in the role of gatekeeper to this new aesthetic. In other words, the use of dirty realism is less an explanatory tool than another instance of the legitimation crisis described in Chapter 7.

In the United States, by contrast, the writers are better known as minimalists primarily because of the shortness of their texts and their avoidance of descriptive language. In Carver's early stories, despite his admiration of Anton Chekhov and James Joyce, the expected epiphany fails to arrive:

> He said, 'I just want to say one more thing.'
> But then he could not think what it could possibly be. (Carver 1995: 122)

As with the use of impressionism to describe writers such as Stephen Crane, minimalism is borrowed from other art-forms. In music, the term is associated with composers such as John Adams, Philip Glass, Steve Reich and Terry Riley, who use a limited musical vocabulary to construct a repetitive and hypnotic effect with subtle variations of pitch. Minimalism marks a break from the discordance of modernist composition and a return to tonality and harmony. The inexpressiveness of minimalist music is complemented in the visual arts by the conceptual pieces of Carl Andre and Richard Long, and in architecture by simple and elegant designs often derived from Oriental models. As these examples suggest, however, minimalism indicates rather more than economy and compactness. Furthermore, although musical minimalism returned to formal constraints broken by modernist techniques such as serialism, it did not return to the earlier conventions of Western classical music (except in Adams' adaptation of the nineteenth-century symphony orchestra). Minimalism, therefore, was not a reactive movement – as Carver might be seen to react against postmodernism in favour of earlier models such as Chekhov and Hemingway – while art-works, such as Andre's formal arrangement of firebricks, *Equivalent VIII* (1966), resembled the alleged gimmickry of postmodern writers such as John Barth. Consequently, minimalism as a term is not sufficiently precise enough to distinguish Carver and his contemporaries.

What did the writers themselves have to say on the subject of realism? Carver, who was always keen to separate Donald Barthelme from his imitators ('He's his own man'), attacked postmodern writing as 'nutty', 'silly', 'trivial' and 'boring'. For Carver, 'the best art has its reference points in real life. Even Donald Barthelme's work, his best work, has some things that connect up.' By contrast, Carver regarded many contemporary writers as having lost their 'bearings, moral bearings, either for the work of art or in their lives' (Carver 1990: 17–18). He continued: 'there's no value system at work, no moral grounding . . . art is *not* self-expression, it is communication' (Carver 1990: 58). It is no surprise, then, that some of Carver's reviewers saw his fiction as a return to common-sense reality:

> In the 1960s and the early 1970s, some of our more ingenious fiction writers
> . . . translated the clamor of those years into fictional worlds spinning
> weirdly out of control . . . who can understand the world? they asked. Life
> is lunacy.

> The stories of Raymond Carver tell us that we don't live like that any longer
> . . . in the small struggles of individual lives, Carver touches a large human
> note . . . life in Carver's America isn't incomprehensible. It's merely very
> difficult. (quoted in Carver 1990: 87–8)

Wolff, although denying claims of a 'renaissance' in the American short story, nevertheless sets up a divide when he contends that 'the dominant impulse of American literature has been realistic', a contention that glosses the non-realistic tendencies of much nineteenth-century American fiction. Into one camp Wolff places writers from the first half of the twentieth century, who 'were storytellers rather than scholars': 'their work was impelled not by formal preoccupations but by their interest in the human' (Wolff 1993: viii). In the other camp, Wolff places writers from the 1960s, who were 'self-consciously literary, scholastic . . . and indifferent if not hostile to the short story's traditional interests in character and dramatic development' (Wolff 1993: viii–ix). Wolff goes on to argue that their 'impatience' with realism 'amounts to ferocity' (he seems mainly to be thinking of Barth) and to question whether it reveals 'culpable innocence' if 'we can freely and with pleasure lose ourselves in a contrived, artful world?' His defences of realism and the willing suspension of disbelief take on a larger dimension, though, when he associates 'this gift' with a 'democratic nature' as opposed to the 'mandarin scorn' of 'the Postmodern ironist' (Wolff 1993: ix–x). Realism, according to Wolff, is not only the keynote of American literature but is also grounded in the democratic impetus of the Constitution. The work of Wolff's contemporaries is 'inextricable from time and place': the 'gaze typically goes outward' and is driven by an 'unembarrassed faith in the power of stories to clarify our sense of reality' (Wolff 1993: xi). Postmodernism, by contrast, is depicted as a self-regarding oligarchy which behaves not unlike a colonial power.

Ford tends towards a middle course between Carver and Wolff. He writes how he found the postmodern writing of the 1960s to be 'thrilling, but so was the old, and as a reader I didn't see a need to choose'. Ford's critique is mainly directed against the hyperbole that surrounded experimental fiction rather than the writing itself. He envisions that 'change, even *refinement* could occur' when these 'extremes of form . . . could be made by writers to accommodate one another' (Ford 1998: x). Although Ford's literary tastes tend toward non-postmodern ways of writing, he presents a pragmatic view of literary development in which traditional and experimental forms are synthesised in a revisionary and evolutionary process. While Ford appears to be more open to experiment than either Carver or Wolff, his accommodation of new forms is nevertheless a conservative position. The continuity of tradition is placed at the heart of his critique, a stance which is not dissimilar to that of either T. S. Eliot and the New Critics or Cold War commentators such as William Peden.

It is curious to note the extent to which Carver, Ford and Wolff defined themselves against postmodernism just as many of the theorists of postmodernity, such as Jean Baudrillard and Fredric Jameson, regarded themselves as critics of the postmodern. Postmodernism is advanced in both cases as a nebulous condition against which the writers define themselves. The postmodern becomes, like the title character of Robert Coover's benchmark text 'The Babysitter' (1969), an illusory object, an empty vessel for the communication of desire (the babysitter's passive consumption of televisual fantasy; her recreation as a sexual fantasy in the imaginations of the male characters). As with Coover's protagonist, the postmodern is recirculated in ways that are both vacuous and abysmal: on the one hand, in the critical discourses of Baudrillard and Jameson, and on the other hand by Carver, Ford and Wolff. Realism becomes a form of consolation for the latter writers even though the realist method that they practice is irredeemably riddled by the postmodern condition to which they are opposed.

The paradigmatic illustration of realism's consoling effect is Carver's 'A Small, Good Thing' (1983). A distressed couple, whose son has died on his birthday, are harassed by a series of telephone calls. It transpires that the mysterious caller is the baker who is annoyed that the birthday cake has not been collected. The couple confront him but, instead of a fight, the baker apologises and the scene becomes instead one of reconciliation, in which the baker confesses his loneliness and the couple's anger dissipates. Eating becomes the vehicle for healing since, 'in a time like this', it 'is a small, good thing' (Carver 1995: 332). The baker is transformed into a shaman – the couple linger into the morning listening to him – while the breaking of bread, symbolic of Christ's covenant to his disciples, is cast as a redemptive spell. Earlier in the story, the mother longs 'to talk more with' the relatives of patients 'who were in the same kind of waiting as she was in' (Carver 1995: 320). The need not only for communication but also communality is what the story's ending offers, just as the narrator of 'Feathers' (1983) remembers a moment of happiness, an episode that ironically precipitates his current discontent, but which nevertheless tempers his feelings of resignation. Carver's fiction of the early 1980s deals in a series of 'small, good things', insights into other points of view such as the epiphany that closes 'Cathedral' (also 1983), which balance the main narrative focus. Nevertheless, these are all passing moments within the general context of hardship and hopelessness.

Carver's characters, especially from this period, tend to be blue-collar families, the community hardest hit during the recession of the 1970s and who, in 1980, turned *en masse* to the Republican message of national pride and material optimism. Carver may not, ideologically, have been a Reaganite but his stories nevertheless tap into the same cultural material – the iconography of the Whitmanesque common man – that Ronald Reagan also skilfully employed. In tracing with the utmost fidelity his characters' lives and feelings, there is a tendency in Carver to present this reality as the *only* reality: a world-view that fits only too neatly with a politically conservative position and which is observable in Wolff's defence of the realist tradition. (The shifting and multiple realities of postmodernism are conversely eccentric, aberrant, 'nutty', to use Carver's description.) Carver's contemporaries tend to feature a wider social range: Ford excels in both working- and lower middle-class characters as well as urban and rural backdrops, while Wolff is as comfortable writing about academic life as he is describing friends on a hunting trip. Bobbie Ann Mason, especially in her story 'Shiloh' (1982), became identified with the economic hardship of Southern farmers and Vietnam War veterans, while Lorrie Moore has made middle-class suburbia her milieu. Despite these social differences, the recurrent tendency remains the same: the depiction of characters in circumstances beyond their control who can only aim for slight revisions that ameliorate their social condition. Put another way, the realism of Carver and his contemporaries can be viewed as a literature of lowered expectations, in which transcendence is viewed as an impossible ideal, but in which local reforms can be achieved. In this respect, their portrayal of common men and women is closer to

Robert Frost than Walt Whitman, for example in Frost's sentiments that 'home is the place where . . . they have to take you in' or that 'one could do worse than be a swinger of birches' (Frost 1973: 48, 82).

The lowering of expectation, though, accords with aspects of post-modern theory, for example Richard Rorty's re-reading of pragmatism, insofar as the totality of objective understanding – the goal of the nineteenth-century realist novel – is deemed to be unobtainable. We can only attain, according to this argument, pockets of knowledge in a logic that is otherwise unknowable. For conservative-minded readers, opposed to the political radicalism of the 1960s, this position is desirable since it places the emphasis upon the individual, and his/her ability to choose from a series of options, rather than the intervening agency of the state. The portrayal of characters struggling to make sense of their lives in confined circumstances appears, in this context, not only to be realistic but also ideologically true.

Yet, there is another side to Carver's fiction that has to be taken into account. Carver's early stories tend to be brief and quizzical, as indicated by his fondness for odd-sounding titles, often extracted from dialogue, and phrased as questions. 'What's in Alaska?' (1976), for example, captures the emotional freeze within a marriage but ends on a note of menace, 'something in the hall . . . a pair of small eyes' (Carver 1995: 67), which suggests irreducible mystery. Shorter stories from this same period, such as 'The Father', or from Carver's second collection, *What We Talk about When We Talk About Love* (1981), not only feature greater concentration but also self-conscious artistry equivalent to that of postmodern experiment. The differences between these earlier stories and the stories of Carver's middle period are apparent in 'So Much Water So Close to Home', which was substantially revised for Carver's selected stories. In the earlier version, the ending is cryptic since the wife's reactions to the dead child are registered internally. On the surface, she submits to her husband's callousness out of habit and routine. In the later version, by which time Carver's humanism has become more pronounced, she wakes up crying, 'she was only a child' (Carver 1995: 193). Either way the story works, but in its revised form an intrinsic belief in human morality is reassured by the wife's protest. In the original telling, the wife's moral agency has been subjugated by the dullness of married life so that, as in other early stories by Carver, secure identities are shown to be fragile and uncertain. Without fully committing himself to the relativism of postmodernism, the early Carver nonetheless describes the randomness of human experience.

During his middle period, in which Carver's mythic stature also began to grow, the arbitrary elements of the earlier stories are less apparent. Yet, in 'Cathedral' the potential homily is countered by the narrator's attempt to draw blindly along with the blind man. As in Jean-François Lyotard's description of the postmodern artist working without rules (see Chapter 18), the narrator works without any sense of religious conviction or artistic talent. When the blind man asks the narrator to look at the result, the narrator keeps his eyes closed: 'I was in my house. I knew that. But I didn't feel like I was inside anything' (Carver 1995: 307). The narrator's disembodiment complements his acquiescence both to his guest and to his feelings of sublime elevation. Whether or not they successfully completed drawing the inside of a cathedral is immaterial to the experience.

In his last stories, Carver's writing moves to a new level of self-consciousness. Three stories, 'Intimacy', 'Blackbird Pie' and 'Errand' (all 1988), are connected by the theme of history. In the first, a writer visits his ex-wife: is he 'hunting for material' (Carver 1995: 365) or reconciliation? The narrative is constructed so that the ex-wife's tirade is mediated simply and without comment through the narrator's voice; her anger and resentment fracture the narrative he has built up of their marriage. In 'Blackbird Pie', the narrator's passion for historical narrative and fondness for literary allusion are unsettled by the letter, purportedly written by his wife, and by the surreal events – the horses that loom out of the fog and invade his garden – on the evening that his wife abandons their home. Lastly, 'Errand' reads like a biographical account of Chekhov's final days, but its self-awareness as history is highlighted by its mediation of other accounts of Chekhov's death and by its imagining of the roles played by Chekhov's wife, Olga, and by an unknown bellboy. The dignity that Carver ascribes to one of his literary heroes and to all the participants, both real and invented, goes beyond a mere historical rendering of the events.

Although there has been a tendency to mythologise Carver and to base the quality of his writing upon the authenticity of his experience, a brief examination reveals a writer concerned with the strangeness of human existence and a desire to extend the mimetic capacity of fiction. Karlsson, building upon earlier comments made by Barth, has argued that this fiction should be called 'hyperrealist' insofar as it draws attention to its form without claiming to do so (as, for example, in metafiction) and that much of its content is derived from the unreality of consumer culture (Karlsson 1990: 149–51). While one of Ford's characters remarks, 'everything's moved out to the malls' (Ford 1989: 221), in 'Next Door' (1982), the fantasies of Wolff's narrator merge with those of the television screen. Moore's debut collection, *Self-Help* (1985), makes constant allusion to popular culture, as if sharing a common language with its readership, while also making use of other stylised techniques from the fragmentation of 'How' to the use of lists in 'How to be an Other Woman' to the pastiche of diaries and manuals. Characters, as in 'The Kid's Guide to Divorce', frequently view themselves in the third-person, a technique that Moore reinforces by her omission of pronouns and inclusion of imperatives delivered in the present tense.

Whereas writers such as Moore have made continual use of stylisation in their work, it was perhaps more surprising to find Wolff turn to similar devices in his story 'Bullet in the Brain' (1995). Anders, a bored literary critic, is shot during a bank robbery when he is unable to stop himself from laughing at the robbers' clichéd use of language. Wolff then describes in minute detail the passage of the bullet into and out of Anders' brain: a concentration of subjective time that echoes (albeit unconsciously) a similar conceit in William Sansom's 'The Wall' (1944). Although the writing borders upon the hyperreal, Wolff never loses grip of the story's realist frame. Having focused upon Anders' subjective experience of time, Wolff's narrator shifts to an objective point of view so that he can recount all the items that Anders fails to remember before stating what he does recall: a quintessentially American scene of baseball and the overhearing of a chance remark, 'they is' (Wolff 1996: 206). Whereas the jaded adult would have been infuriated by the poor grammar, the teenage Anders' delight in the phrase recuperates not only the idioms of American English but also the communality and being that go with that pleasure. The stylistic trick allows Wolff to switch from a materialistic to a transcendent register while, at the same time, his commitment to the democratisation of American idiom reaffirms Wolff in a tradition that travels at least as far back as Mark Twain.

In retrospect, the innovations of Carver, Ford, Wolff, Moore and others can be seen as an attempt to negotiate the postmodern emphasis upon the exhaustion of literature. This negotiation can be partially read, in Harold Bloom's terms, as an 'anxiety of influence' (Wolff was taught by Barth), which becomes explicitly ideological when the writers attempt to recuperate the literary tradition for themselves. In effectively proposing a canon of recent American fiction, some writers are inevitably excluded or given partial admission. One of the most interesting cases is T. Coraghessan Boyle. 'Greasy Lake' (1979), his most frequently anthologised story, can be read both as an instance of postmodernism, in its plotless and amoral account of a random event, and as a particularly dirty example of dirty realism in its description of violence and sexual threat. More clearly an admirer of Barthelme than his contemporaries, for example in his uses of absurdity, surreal juxtaposition, fragmentation and non-linearity, Boyle has nevertheless attempted to ground his postmodern sensibility in a world that, at least on the surface, is recognisably familiar. Consequently, while the work of Carver and his associates can be read as hyperrealist, it is Boyle's fiction that most successfully embodies this description.

Boyle, then, is an important transitional figure from the postmodernism of the 1960s to the writers currently associated with *McSweeney's*. Another is the Canadian Douglas Coupland, whose influential text *Generation X* (1991) shares similarities with the minimalist fiction of the 1980s. Like Moore's characters, Coupland's protagonists live in a world saturated with popular culture and who largely make sense of that world through these reference-points. Like Carver's characters, they work in lowly paid jobs while their domestic lives are insecure. Unlike the heroes of Carver, Ford and Wolff, they are young and overeducated for the work they do. Yet, like their more adult counterparts, they are striving for meaning in their lives: it is almost as if the midlife anxieties that Carver describes have arrived twenty years earlier in the case of Coupland's characters. Although Coupland's text is formally more experimental than his predecessors, for instance the use of image, footnote and episodism so as to convey the social rhythms of late modernity, the addition of brand names, celebrities and commercial centres echo earlier attempts to describe the landscape of post-industrial society. Since Coupland, it has become a commonplace for writers such as George Saunders (a student of Wolff's) to draw upon an excess of allusions to contemporary consumer culture. Yet, this tendency is also apparent in the fiction of the 1980s as a type of hyperrealist detail.

In other words, despite Dave Eggers' claim that he launched *McSweeney's* due to the inability of himself and his contemporaries to find outlets for their work, his implied critique of the overprevalence of the Carver-inspired story is slightly disingenuous. Although *McSweeney's* has sought to reconcile the postmodern legacy, the writing does not represent a complete break with the fiction of the intervening years. Instead, part of the reconciliation has involved finding ways of bridging the literary divide that emerged during the 1970s. The examples of Boyle and Coupland suggest possible models, while texts by Eggers' associates, such as Arthur Bradford's *Dogwalker* (2001), offer exciting new syntheses between a realistic apprehension of the external world and an imaginative delight in formal play. Bradford's curiously innocent world, where sexual transgressions and stereotypical images of the abject body are treated as part of everyday life, suggests less a 'Book of Grotesques' (as in *Winesburg, Ohio*) than a contented series of perversions. It is in this odd positioning in or around the subject of realism that the American short story continues to reinvent itself.

Further Reading

For critical accounts of Carver, Ford and Wolff, see respectively Randolph Paul Runyan (1992), Huey Guagliardo (2000) and James Hannah (1996). Minimalism is explored in relation to Carver, Hempel and Robison by Cynthia Whitney Hallett (1999). As a starting-point for Richard Rorty's reworking of pragmatism, see his essay 'The Priority of Democracy to Philosophy' in Douglas Tallack's *Critical Theory: A Reader* (1995).

20

Voyages Out:
The Postcolonial Short Story

E. M. Forster's *A Passage to India* (1924) is one of the seminal literary texts for postcolonial criticism, and like Forster's novel, this final chapter is less a 'rounding off' than an 'opening out' (Forster 1962: 170). It is an inescapable fact that, as David Punter has argued in *Postcolonial Imaginings* (2000), the postcolonial now underwrites both the relationship and the social conditions of East and West. Unfortunately, it is less easy to say what the postcolonial is since many academics contest the term's usefulness. Part of the reason for this anomaly is that the concept has changed its meaning. At the start of the 1970s, when 'postcolonial' first began to be widely used, it was simply a descriptive tool denoting the societies that had emerged after the process of decolonisation following World War Two. By the start of the 1980s, 'postcolonial' had become an analytical method for explaining the cultural products of either the colonial past or the liberated present. 'Postcolonial' in, for example, the work of its principal theoreticians, Homi Bhabha, Edward Said and Gayatri Chakravorty Spivak, was increasingly concerned with the analysis of discursive representation (although substantial contradictions existed between their respective positions). The phrase 'postcolonial literature' supplanted the earlier, more consensual description of 'Commonwealth literature' and emphasised conflict and tension (as, for example, in the critical anthology *The Empire Writes Back*, 1989). The subject's redefinition raised questions about its content: were the colonial experiences of former dominions with large settler populations, such as Australia, Canada, New Zealand and South Africa, the same as subject nations ruled by a small elite, as was the case elsewhere in Africa, Asia, the Caribbean and the South Pacific? In the years following the break-up of the Soviet Union and the expansion of the global economy, postcolonial studies have been further redefined so that the future of the discipline is either threatened or galvanised (depending upon the individual point of view) by theories of globalisation and neo-colonialism.

Part of the problem surrounding postcolonial studies is that, unlike the postmodern where the existence of a socio-economic reality known as postmodernity is at least debatable and is not necessarily essential for discussion of a postmodern condition (Jean-François Lyotard, for example, makes a careful delineation between a 'postmodern age' and artistic practices that can be described as postmodern), it is undeniably true that a massive political transformation occurred in the middle part of the last century, which also caused vast displacements in terms of the world's population. Against this historical backdrop, it is impossible to propose a single theory that would adequately account for such changes. It is perhaps for this reason why so much of postcolonial theory has contested the neo-Hegelian positions of pioneers such as Frantz Fanon and C. L. R. James, and furthermore, why it has been preoccupied with contesting rival theoretical positions even where such discussions have purportedly been in the name of cultural (let alone literary) criticism.

In the light of these historical realities and theoretical debates, the following analysis is necessarily tentative and provisional. As with the earlier chapter on postmodernism, it does not assume an agreed definition of the postcolonial. In many respects, the term agitates the very history from which it emerged. Yet, as with the postmodern, there are similarities with the undefinable quality of the short story that also resists categorisation. It is curious to note that although postcolonial literature has been regarded as a critique of the Western literary canon, alternately by negating, rewriting or expanding its content, comparatively little attention has been paid to postcolonial short fiction. John Marx, for example, refers to 'the novels, poems, and plays that scholars and common readers have come to recognize as postcolonial' without any mention of the short story (Marx 2004: 83). Yet, as Sabry Hafez has recently observed, the short story is drawn to 'the small fragments of the large fresco' (Hafez 2008: 38), which tends instead to be the proper business of the novel. In other words, the postcolonial short story is potentially a more dissident form than the major genres, especially with regards to rethinking the postcolonial.

Following Adrian Hunter's account of Alice Munro's colonial fictions (Hunter 2004: 219–38), it is useful to think of the short story as a form of 'minor literature', a concept proposed by Gilles Deleuze and Félix Guattari in their study of Franz Kafka. As we have already seen, Kafka's strange and alienating fictions mediate the criss-crossing fractures of geography, history and language. Deleuze and Guattari characterise Kafka's writing as a machine: a systematic assemblage of parts for the production of effect, especially desire. Kafka's writing machine is an expression of 'that which a minority constructs within a major language' (Deleuze and Guattari 1986: 16). The production of minor literature is dependent upon three elements: 'deterritorialization', whereby language is displaced and contorted by the pressure of colonisation; politicisation, whereby the limited spaces in which language can operate means that it connects 'immediately to politics'; and lastly, 'collective value' whereby, since 'the political domain has contaminated every statement', all expressions of the minority culture 'already constitutes a common action' that permits 'the conception of something other than a literature of masters' (Deleuze and Guattari 1986: 16–17). Whereas postcolonial theory has relied heavily upon Eurocentric reading models (Said and Foucault, Bhabha and Derrida), Deleuze and Guattari derive their model from the experience of a writer alienated by the shifting imperial ties of middle Europe. Although denying the essentialism of local and national identities, they do not find themselves in the same political deadlock as Spivak who, in one of her most famous essays, contended that the subaltern (the colonial subject) could not speak because of the effects of colonisation. Instead, in emphasising the 'strange and minor uses' (Deleuze and Guattari 1986: 17) to which the major language is put, Deleuze and Guattari suggest a form of *bricolage*: the generation of something new from working upon the remains of culture. As they remark elsewhere, 'the formation of territories, the vectors of deterritorialization, and the process of reterritorialization' is not only interlinked but also simultaneous (Deleuze and Guattari 1994: 68), an experience that can be compared with Jacques Derrida's notion of *dissemination*, the scattering of knowledge into new and provisional fields of meaning. This emphasis upon fragmentation not only allows Deleuze and Guattari to be read in relation to postcolonialism but also the short story: an opportunity that Hunter avails himself by citing Samuel Beckett, Elizabeth Bowen and Henry James (Hunter 2004: 221).

A further benefit of applying Deleuze and Guattari to a reading of the postcolonial short story is that they destabilise the question of authenticity. Whereas African writers such as Ngugi wa Thiong'o have argued that writing can only appear in the indigenous language, since the presence of English remains an instrument of colonial oppression, Deleuze and Guattari argue that minor literature is irredeemably polluted and that its most effective use arises from contamination. Like the folktale, there is no pure formulation. This position is not the same as Bhabha's notion of *hybridity* – the ceaseless mixing of cultural selves at the expense of class and national differences – since, for Deleuze and Guattari, desire emerges as a symptom of the oppressive system that it otherwise works to dismantle. Instead, the inauthenticity of minor literature complements the rootlessness that Roger Berger has argued characterises the Anglophone African short story (in Lounsberry et al. 1998: 77–8). As Deleuze and Guattari add, writers and artists are thinkers who 'show thought's territories', who if they stammer cause 'the whole of language [to] stammer' (Deleuze and Guattari 1994: 69).

The partition stories of Saadat Hasan Manto offer a useful starting-point. Many of Manto's short stories are no more than fragments: sometimes they have a parabolic structure, for example stories such as 'Cooperation' or 'Wages'; other times, though, they are little more than snatches of dialogue or news bulletins, their formal impoverishment attesting to the illusion of wholeness as the Indian sub-continent convulsed into separate nations, and Hindus and Muslims turned upon one another. Manto repeatedly describes the rendering of the body politic in human terms. His most celebrated story, 'Toba Tek Singh', describes the plans to exchange Hindu and Muslim mental patients. Yet, it is the new political borders rather than their sense of reality which are prone to dissolution: 'It was anybody's guess what was going to happen to Lahore, which was currently in Pakistan, but could slide into India any moment' (Manto 1997: 5). One of the patients known as Toba Tek Singh after his hometown in the Punjab, now divided between India and Pakistan, insists upon knowing its location. On the day of his forced departure, and still uncertain, he refuses to be deported. The guards eventually leave him be until the following morning when he screams and dies. Stranded in no-man's-land, between the barbed wire demarcating the two nations, Toba Tek Singh's corpse marks his dominion. The physical mutilation of the body, torn in two by the events of partition, is given shocking clarity in both 'Colder than Ice', where a lover confesses to raping what he had failed to realise was a dead woman, and 'The Return', in which a comatose girl, who has been repeatedly raped, automatically opens her thighs when she hears the doctor ask for the window to be opened. Manto's stories horrifically describe the enforcement of deterritorialisation while, at the same time, creating a new conceptual space in which it can be rethought.

As Hunter indicates in his reading of Munro, the work of postcolonial writers from the large settler populations of Australia, Canada and New Zealand has been concerned with reconceiving colonialism's foundational myths. Both Munro and Margaret Atwood have, as Chapter 12 indicated, explored Canadian frontier myths in respective stories such as 'Meneseteung' (1990) and 'Wilderness Tips' (1991), although this exploration is further affected by the neo-colonial presence just across the border of the United States. Australian writers, such as Murray Bail, have revisited colonial figures such as the drover's wife made iconic by writers such as Henry Lawson and by Australian landscape artists. Although the work of Lawson is marked by his sympathetic naturalism, his descriptions of settlers are bound to his assertion of an independent national identity founded in the experience of the Australian outback. Lawson's tendency to memorialise colonial history is critiqued by later writers such as Bail, whose fictional interventions question both the basis and the writing of that history, a scepticism that echoes postmodern critiques of historical knowledge as also seen in the prose experiments that constitute Peter Carey's debut collection, *The Fat Man in History* (1976).

A similar kind of playfulness, possibly influenced by Donald Barthelme, is evident in *Missing Persons* (1989) by the white South African writer Ivan Vladislavíc. The absurdity of stories though, such as 'The Prime Minister is Dead' or 'The Box', is embedded in the violence of apartheid, where white rule is predicated upon the abuse of the black subject, and by random events such as terrorist attacks and police crackdowns. Vladislavíc's stories mark a stylistic break with earlier writers from South Africa and Rhodesia (now Zimbabwe), such as Nadine Gordimer and Doris Lessing, yet the content of his fiction is indebted to his predecessors, in particular their exploration of the impossibility of race relations under white supremacy. In Gordimer's 'Is There Nowhere Else Where We Can Meet?' (1953), the meeting of the title consists of a struggle between a white woman and a black vagrant, whom she suspects of wanting to mug her. Her suspicions though, told in a neutral third-person, are entirely her own: she projects her fears of racial aggression, internalised since childhood, onto the black man. Instead, as the title suggests, there is no social space devoid of the racist ideology in which any other kind of meeting can take place. Fearing the police questions, the woman decides to remain silent about the incident. Lessing too opts for estranged perspectives, for example the point of view of a young girl in 'The Old Chief Mshlanga' (1951), who becomes fascinated with the displaced chieftain whose village still exists on the hinterland of her father's dominion. Sneaking away one day, she visits the village in order to see the chief. On meeting him, though, she becomes tongue-tied. All she can do is wish him well – an ironic hope since the village is later moved to a reservation – since she now realises that she too is 'a victim' (Lessing 1979: 22) and that no amount of good feeling will wash away past crimes.

The theme of physical and psychological displacement is picked-up by the Nigerian author Chinua Achebe. Whereas his first four novels, from *Things Fall Apart* (1958) through to *A Man of the People* (1966), had concentrated upon what Fredric Jameson has termed the 'national allegory', Achebe's sole collection of stories, *Girls at War* (1972), focuses upon characters marginalised from the independence movement. The title story, set during the Nigerian Civil War (1967–70), describes the changing relationship of Reginald, a Biafran official, and Gladys, whom he regards at best as a good-time girl and at worst as 'reflecting a society that had gone completely rotten and maggoty at the centre' (Achebe 1972: 114). Achebe's use in the story, though, of free indirect speech allows him to question Reginald's position since, although Reginald would like to see himself as a moral centre, his stance has been undermined by the circumstances of the War: the seizure of power by successive military coups and the division of Nigeria by the secession of Biafra. Instead, it is the marginal figure of Gladys, whom Reginald dismisses as a 'girl at war', tooling herself 'with shoes, wigs, pants, bras, cosmetics and what have you' and arming herself with 'some well-placed gentleman, one of those piling up money out of the war' (Achebe 1972: 104, 109), who is ultimately more at the centre of events. It is Gladys, not Reginald, who dies attempting to protect an injured soldier. Throughout the collection, then, Achebe concentrates upon figures that have fallen out of the national narrative but whose lives, nevertheless, become intermingled with the story as the dream of independent unity begins to dissolve.

By contrast, the Kenyan writer Ngugi wa Thiong'o attempts to give shape to the disillusionment of the independence movement by structuring his collection *Secret Lives* (1975) into three sections: stories set before the so-called Mau Mau Emergency of 1952, stories that take place during the struggle for liberation, and stories set after independence and the failures of the new state. Consequently, although Ngugi is drawn to the lives of characters caught up with the national narrative (similar, in this respect, to Achebe), he attempts to set these events into an account that rationalises their experience. Ngugi's protagonists are repeatedly confronted with decisions that, although personal, are analogous with the political and moral life of the nation:

> This was a moment of trial; the moment rarely given to us to prove our worth as human beings. The moment is rare. It comes and if not taken goes by, leaving us forever regretful. (Ngugi 1975: 12)

Like Lawson's depictions of the Australian outback, Ngugi's style is naturalistic and he is prone to idealise Kenyan rural life in contrast with the alien influences of Empire, commerce and the city. The exiled South African writer Bessie Head counters this tendency in her descriptions of a Botswana village. In her collection *The Collector of Treasures* (1977), Head shows little sympathy for modern (that is to say, Western-influenced) ways of living but neither does she mythologise traditional culture. Her detachment arises from her own status as a subject woman within African society. In the essay-like passage that punctuates the title story, Head dissects African patriarchy, arguing that men had traditionally been allotted a superior role to women, but that this opposition had been exacerbated by the effects of Empire, in which men 'became "the boy" of the white man and a machine-tool of the South African mines.' Having not only lost their recourse to the traditional social hierarchy but also their own sense of individuality, most African men are now, post-independence, 'a broken wreck with no inner resources at all' (Head 1977: 92). In these circumstances, Dikeledi's murder of her immoral husband, although shattering the civilising bonds embodied by her altruistic neighbour, Paul, is necessarily expedient. The prison to which Dikeledi is sentenced, however, extends her marginalisation within African society, confirming her as the abject opposite that upholds the illusion of male autonomy.

The theme of modernity is also evident in the work of the Ghanaian author Ama Ata Aidoo and the Nigerian Ben Okri. Aidoo's collection *No Sweetness Here* (1970) is framed by stories that focus upon Western-educated Africans who are equally privileged and disadvantaged within their communities. In-between these stories, the effects of modernity are shown to be uneven. Western-educated leaders are depicted as corrupt and exploitative while the underprivileged local population, such as Zirigu in 'For Whom Things Did Not Change', are deprived of modern amenities. Generational gaps, which also hinge upon class and education, fracture the community further, for example between Zirigu and his younger counterpart Kobina. Several of the stories, for instance the experience of Sissie in 'Everything Counts', explore the unfulfilled desires of women in the context of a sexist ideology that has been reinforced rather than diminished by the imbalances within wealth and privilege. Yet, Aidoo also draws upon the African oral tradition, including the performance-based medium known as *fefewo*, in order to contextualise these changes within an earlier culture, and thereby to place them into perspective. The medley of voices that begin 'The Message' reintroduces the community as a ghostly presence, while in 'Certain Winds from the South', M'ma Asana's monologue gives voice to a host of characters that not only elides past and present but also the disruptive effects of modernity. Okri too, in 'The Dream Vendor's August' (from *Incidents at the Shrine*, 1986) and the stories that compose *Stars of the New Curfew* (1988), draws upon indigenous traditions surrounding animism, witchcraft and the transmigration of souls as a means of critically framing the importation of Western modernity into Africa.

The importance of folk culture to African writers, such as Aidoo and Okri, surfaces again among Caribbean short storywriters. Although the presence of an active series of little magazines from the end of the

1920s, and of the BBC's overseas service in the postwar period, were significant factors in developing the Caribbean short story, writers also drew upon the folk tradition of trickster tales and ballads, including the role of calypso as an immediate form of reportage. Unlike Africa, where the vision of Pan-Africanism has frequently been sundered by the internecine struggles and economic calamities that are themselves a legacy of Empire, the Caribbean has a paradoxical sense of identity: on the one hand, regarding itself as a coherent unit, and on the other hand, as a loose assemblage of islands divided furthermore by racial, economic and social tensions. Not only does the short story connect with the oral tradition but it also offers a sufficiently reflexive medium in which to convey this ambiguous island self. V. S. Naipaul's influential cycle *Miguel Street* (1959) finds a ready model not only in James Joyce's *Dubliners* (1914) and its evocation of place but also Sherwood Anderson's *Winesburg, Ohio* (1919), with its description of a young man's maturation through his experience of the failures and illusions of his seniors. The cycle's self-reflexive commentary upon its overall coherence and the relationship to its individual parts mirrors Naipaul's observation from the same period that 'there was no community . . . we had somehow found ourselves on the same small island' (Naipaul 1969: 45). Yet, despite the underlying desperation of the protagonist to leave Trinidad, he still takes pride in what the tourist fails to see: 'But we, who lived there, saw our street as a world, where everybody was quite different from everybody else' (Naipaul 1964: 79). As with other short story cycles, such as Sandra Cisneros' *The House on Mango Street* (1984), although the mature narrator can now see the limitations of his childhood heroes, he nevertheless returns to the island of his memories with a renewed sense of perspective.

Both *Miguel Street* and Samuel Selvon's *Ways of Sunlight* (1957), with its divided structure between stories set in Trinidad and London, were instrumental not only in evoking a sense of place but also in commenting upon the postwar diaspora. Nevertheless, the focus of these collections is upon men and tends to romanticise the immigrant as a wanderer rather than an outcast. The collections of women writers, among them Angela Barry (*Endangered Species*, 2002), Pauline Melville (*Shape-Shifter*, 1990; *The Migration of Ghosts*, 1998) and Olive Senior (*Summer Lightning*, 1986), have rectified this imbalance; in particular, they tend to emphasise the importance of social relations even when familial and communal ties have been broken or strained by migration. Whereas Barry and Senior tend toward naturalism (the former focusing upon themes of rootlessness and exile, the latter concentrating upon displaced persons or estranged perspectives set against a Jamaican backdrop), Melville's interests in metamorphosis and spiritualism introduce a more mixed set of literary registers that critically reflect upon her own status as a white Creole living in the United Kingdom. Without quite aligning herself to the kinds of postmodern experiment evident, for example, in Noel Williams' *The Crying of Rainbirds* (1992), Melville nonetheless enriches the language in a further act of reterritorialisation.

The yearning expressed by Caribbean writers, such as Melville, for a new social arrangement counterpoints the work of Black and Asian organisations which formed in London during the 1970s and 1980s. The Asian Women Writers' Collective, which produced two anthologies including the short story collection *Flaming Spirit* (1994), began life in 1984. As its history shows, however, such bodies are prone to contradiction. On the one hand, the Collective provided a valuable forum for women to express themselves and to communicate with one another. On the other hand, however, the Collective was dependent upon external funding and the pressures of central government upon local authorities: financial cuts effectively spelt the end for the Collective. Furthermore, the Collective was also affected by the identity politics that became a feature of the late 1980s as the large mass movements of the Left – socialism and feminism – splintered under the successful political domination of the New Right in both the United Kingdom and the United States. Both sexual and racial categories were called into question as lesbians, women of mixed race and Chinese and Middle Eastern women enlarged the Collective. Although the object of a writing group, working primarily in English, meant that the members were predominantly middle class, such distinctions were undercut by realities such as racism and poverty that linked the women to the working classes. This discrepancy between social aspiration and economic condition compares with the female characters in Aidoo's fiction. Religion, in particular the controversy surrounding Salman Rushdie's novel, *The Satanic Verses* (1988), also played a factor in diversifying the group. Consequently, the stories that appear in *Flaming Spirit* are distinguished by their mix of uniformity and heterogeneity: the result also of balancing the collaborative, workshop ethos with the editors' need for a coherent – and marketable – collection. Like other anthologies of its type (see Chapter 6), *Flaming Spirit* bears witness to a particular moment in terms of cultural change. Its internal contradictions express the paradoxes inherent to its historical period, one of these being that, despite their communal production, the stories tend to emphasise the importance of affective relationships, such as friendships, rather than familial or institutional relations. Like other examples from the Black and Asian diasporas, such as Courttia Newland's *Society Within* (1999), it is these relationships in the context of a deprived and unforgiving urban environment that are ultimately most significant.

In Salman Rushdie's *East, West* (1994), the friendship of 'Chekov and Zulu' counterpoints the lack of connection elsewhere in the anthology. Structured in three sections, the collection's trajectory seems pointed towards reconciliation and yet the single comma – the pause or hesitancy – remains tantalisingly poised between the two regions. At this point of Rushdie's writing life, when he was still in hiding from the Ayatollah's *fatwa* (or death sentence), the short story is admirably suited to the themes of identity, migration, history and myth that pervade his major novels. Whereas the longer fictions allow Rushdie to layer his writing and to go into more depth, the short story encourages him to go to the heart of the idea. Although geographically arranged, the stories are concerned with the passage of time and the rewriting of historical narrative as if to say that spatial regions such as East and West that, as in 'The Courter', pull the characters in opposite directions are no more than discursive constructs. Consequently, Rushdie revisits the consummation of Christopher Columbus and Queen Isabella not only as an imagined sexual relationship but also as a crucial moment in the making of East and West. The roles of fantasy and imagination occur in the other historical stories, 'The Free Radio' and 'The Prophet's Hair', while 'Yorick' performs a drastic rewrite of *Hamlet*'s genealogy in the style of Laurence Sterne's *Tristram Shandy* (1759–67). Picking up on the central character's fascination with cinema and stardom in 'The Free Radio', 'At the Auction of the Ruby Slippers' projects a dystopian vision in which not only film memorabilia can be sold off but also the dreams and illusions associated with them. Against this nightmare the final stories in the volume, most notably 'The Courter', proffer a notion of love and amity that might elide differences in race, language and status.

A similar promise is noticeably absent in the stories of the Egyptian-born Ahdaf Soueif. 'Sandpiper' (1994), for example, is narrated from the point of view of an anonymous, foreign woman married to an Egyptian. The estrangement from her home is mirrored by her 'inability to remember names, to follow the minutiae of politics, my struggles with his language' (Soueif 1997: 33). Unable to integrate with her surroundings, she is largely confined to the domestic space, a confinement that is reinforced by her desire to write 'my Africa story' (Soueif 1997: 29) by the accumulated notes that she is unable to transform into a narrative, and by the lack of an audience except for her daughter, 'my treasure, my trap' (Soueif 1997: 36). In many respects, 'Sandpiper' is a reworking of nineteenth-century stories such as Charlotte Perkins Gilman's 'The Yellow Wallpaper' (1892), where the narrator's inability to tell her story expresses her isolation; the blank page symbolising the inescapability of her situation: 'I was on the edge, the very edge of Africa' but 'my mind could not grasp a world that was not present to my senses' (Soueif 1997: 26). Yet, despite her indebtedness to nineteenth-century forms, Soueif nevertheless constructs a convincing portrayal of women suspended either in the East or the West through a recurrent use of metaphors associated with dislocation and imprisonment as well as contrasting dreams of flight and security.

The desire for a new social contract that emerges from this brief overview, in which the acknowledgement of all the members that constitute the territory will revise its shape, returns us to the affective relationships that the short story has traditionally represented. Whereas, in their novels, postcolonial writers such as Rushdie and Soueif mimic the panoramic scale of James Joyce and George Eliot, another approach, embodied by R. K. Narayan's tales of Malgudi, has been to concentrate upon the local and the microcosmic. Although the enclosed island community, as in the stories of V. S. Naipaul, might enhance this tendency, both Vikram Chandra and Rohinton Mistry have produced short story cycles set within urban districts (see Chapter 13). Similarly, M. G. Vassanji's *Uhuru Street* (1991) concentrates primarily upon a small area of Dar es Salaam in Tanzania but focuses upon the Asian community: a mix of Muslims, Hindus and Goans whose 'daily associations' are a 'crazy world . . . of Arabs, Africans, Asians and assorted half-castes' (Vassanji 1991: 35). Because of their displaced condition, there is nothing pure and intact about this community beyond observed customs and rituals. Instead, they have to coexist with other members of the city so that their territory is constantly being penetrated and reshaped just as emigrants to Canada in turn remodel their new home: 'Slowly, Toronto, their Toronto became like Dar' (Vassanji 1991: 112). By attending to the local, Vassanji addresses the extent to which self-containment is no longer possible either in Tanzania or elsewhere: home and away are not divisible concepts. For those who leave, Uhuru Street remains a nostalgic ideal; for those who return, they are destined towards an 'empty reclamation of the streets' (Vassanji 191: 141). In other words, the territory may no longer exist as a central locus but it can still be remapped either in the imaginative possibilities of language or in the historical movements of submerged populations.

As Rushdie has observed, the postcolonial writer 'is obliged to deal in broken mirrors, some of whose fragments have been irretrievably lost' but that what remains acquires 'greater status, greater resonance' (Rushdie 1991: 11–12). The short story as fragment elegantly corresponds with this condition of memory and desire. Furthermore, as stories such as 'A House in the Country' and 'Captives' demonstrate in Romesh Gunesekera's *Monkfish Moon* (1992), the short story is not only effective in dramatising the immediacy of internecine conflicts (in this instance, Sri Lanka) but also in historically contextualising the reasons for such conflicts; not through a detailed analysis of cause and effect but by focusing upon the human casualties of such events. While I have been unable to offer here a more detailed account of the relationship between the short story and the postcolonial moment, I hope to have shown over the course of this introduction the patterns by which the short story has more than survived in the interstices of culture, has afforded writers in different places and times the means of reshaping that culture, and has aided the articulation of the exiled imagination. At the very least, I hope to have substantiated Virginia Woolf's claim that we should 'not take it for granted that life exists more in what is commonly thought big than in what is commonly thought small' (Woolf 1988: 34).

Further Reading

There are several introductions and readers to postcolonial criticism: see in particular Ania Loomba (1998) as well as Patrick Williams and Laura Chrisman (1993). For a further account of Deleuze and Guattari, see the special issues of *Cultural Critique* (1987). On the postcolonial short story, see Jacqueline Bardolph (2001). For individual authors, see several of the entries in *A Reader's Companion to the Short Story in English*, edited by Erin Fallon et al. (2001). Louis James' *Caribbean Literature in English* (1999) is useful for setting the short story into context. Only a lack of space has prevented me from saying more on Alice Munro and Ben Okri: see respectively Ailsa Cox (2004) and Robert Fraser (2002).

Bibliography

Primary Sources

Achebe, Chinua. 1972. *Girls at War and Other Stories*. London: Heinemann.
— and C. L. Innes, eds. 1985. *African Short Stories*. London: Heinemann.
— and C. L. Innes, eds. 1992. *The Heinemann Book of African Short Stories*. London: Heinemann.
Acker, Kathy. 1993. 'The Language of the Body', in *The Penguin Book of Lesbian Short Stories*, ed. Margaret Reynolds. London: Penguin.
Adams, Bronte and Trudi Tate, eds. 1991. *That Kind of Woman*. London: Virago.
Adams, Jessica et al., eds. 2000. *Girls' Night In*. London: HarperCollins.
Aesop. 1998. *The Complete Fables*, trans. Olivia and Robert Temple. London: Penguin.
Ahmad, Rukhsana and Rahila Gupta, eds. 1994. *Flaming Spirit*. London: Virago.
Aidoo, Ama Ata. 1995. *No Sweetness Here and Other Stories*. New York: Feminist Press.
Akutagawa, Ryunosuke. 2006. *Rashomon and Seventeen Other Stories*, trans. Jay Rubin. London: Penguin.
Allen, Woody. 1997. *Complete Prose*. London: Picador.
Alvarez, Julia. 1991. *How the García Girls Lost Their Accents*. London: Bloomsbury.
Andersen, Hans Christian. 2004. *Fairy Tales*, trans. Tiina Nunnally, ed. Jackie Wullschlager. London: Penguin.
Anderson, Sherwood. 1976. *Winesburg, Ohio*. 2nd edn. London: Penguin.
— 1998. *The Egg and Other Stories*, ed. Charles E. Modlin. New York and London: Penguin.
Apuleius. 1998. *The Golden Ass*, trans. E. J. Kenney. London: Penguin.
Atwood, Margaret. 1991. *Wilderness Tips*. London: Bloomsbury.
Babel, Isaac. 2002. *The Complete Works of Isaac Babel*, trans. Peter Constantine, ed. Nathalie Babel. London: Picador.

Bail, Murray. 1996. 'The Drover's Wife', in *The Arnold Anthology of Post-Colonial Literatures in English*, ed. John Thieme. London: Edward Arnold.

Baldwin, Dean, ed. 1998. *The Riverside Anthology of Short Fiction*. Boston: Houghton Mifflin.

Baldwin, James. 1991. *Going to Meet the Man*. London: Penguin.

Ballard, J. G. 1991. 'A Response to an Invitation to Respond', *Science Fiction Studies* 18:3.

— 1993. *The Atrocity Exhibition*. London: Flamingo.

— 2001. *The Complete Short Stories*. London: Flamingo.

Balzac, Honoré de. 2001. *The Unknown Masterpiece*, trans. Richard Howard. New York: NYRB Classics.

Bambara, Toni Cade. 1984. *Gorilla, My Love*. London: Women's Press.

Barnes, Djuna. 1996. *Collected Stories*, ed. Phillip Herring. Los Angeles: Sun and Moon.

Barry, Angela. 2002. *Endangered Species and Other Stories*. Leeds: Peepal Tree Press.

Barth, John. 1968. *Lost in the Funhouse*. New York: Doubleday.

Barthelme, Donald. 1989. *Forty Stories*. New York: Penguin.

— *Sixty Stories*. 1993. New York: Penguin.

Baudelaire, Charles. 1991. *The Prose Poems and La Fanfarlo*, trans. Rosemary Lloyd. Oxford: Oxford World's Classics.

— 1995. *The Painter of Modern Life and Other Essays*, trans. and ed. Jonathan Mayne. 2nd edn. London: Phaidon Press.

Beckett, Samuel. 1965. *Proust and Three Dialogues*. London: John Calder.

— 1993. *More Pricks than Kicks*. London: John Calder.

— 1995. *The Complete Short Prose, 1929–1989*, ed. S. E. Gontarski. New York: Grove Press.

Berger, John. 2005. *and our faces, my heart, brief as photos*. London: Bloomsbury.

Blair, David, ed. 2002. *Gothic Short Stories*. Ware: Wordsworth Classics.

Blincoe, Nicholas and Matt Thorne, eds. 2001. *All Hail the New Puritans*. London: Fourth Estate.

Boccaccio, Giovanni. 2003. *The Decameron*, trans. G. H. McWilliam. 2nd edn. London: Penguin.

Bolger, Dermot, ed. 1997. *Finbar's Hotel*. London: Picador.

Borges, Jorge Luis. 1970. *Labyrinths*, ed. Donald A. Yates and James E. Irby. London: Penguin.

— 2003. 'Prologue' to Adolfo Bioy Casares, *The Invention of Morel*, trans. Ruth L. C. Simms. New York: NYRB Classics.

Bowen, Elizabeth. 1999. *Collected Stories*. London: Vintage.

Boyd, William. 2004. *Fascination*. London: Hamish Hamilton.

— 2006. *Bamboo*. London: Penguin.

Boyle, T. Coraghessan. 1998. *The Collected Stories of T. Coraghessan Boyle*. London: Granta.

Bradford, Arthur. 2002. *Dogwalker*. London: Penguin.

Brecht, Bertolt. 1983. *Short Stories, 1921–1946*, ed. John Willett and Ralph Mannhein. London: Methuen.

Burroughs, William. 1979. *Exterminator!* New York: Penguin.

— 1989. *Interzone*, ed. James Grauerholz. New York: Viking Penguin.

Butler, Robert Olen. 1992. *A Good Scent from a Strange Mountain*. New York: Grove Press.

Butts, Mary. 1991. *With and Without Buttons, and Other Stories*, ed. Nathalie Blondel. Manchester: Carcanet.

Byatt, A. S., ed. 1999. *The Oxford Book of English Short Stories*. Oxford: Oxford University Press.

Calvino, Italo. 1969. *Cosmicomics*, trans. William Weaver. London: Jonathan Cape.

— 1978. *The Castle of Crossed Destinies*, trans. William Weaver. London: Pan.

Carey, Peter. 1990. *The Fat Man in History*. London: Faber.

Carleton, William. 1990. *Traits and Stories of the Irish Peasantry*. Gerrards Cross: Colin Smythe.

Carrington, Leonora. 1988. *The House of Fear: Notes from Down Below*. New York: E. P. Dutton.

Carter, Angela. 1995. *Burning Your Boats: Collected Short Stories*. London: Chatto and Windus.

— 1997. *Shaking a Leg: Journalism and Writings*, ed. Jenny Uglow. London: Chatto and Windus.

— ed. 1986. *Wayward Girls and Wicked Women*. London: Virago.

Carver, Raymond. 1990. *Conversations with Raymond Carver*, ed. Marshall Bruce Gentry and William L. Stull. Jackson: University Press of Mississippi.

— 1995. *Where I'm Calling From: The Selected Stories*. London: Harvill.

— 1996. *What We Talk about When We Talk About Love*. London: Harvill.

— 2003. *Will You Please be Quiet, Please?* London: Vintage.

Cassini, Marco and Martina Testa, eds. 2003. *Zadie Smith introduces The Burned Children of America*. London: Hamish Hamilton.

Cervantes. 1972. *Exemplary Stories*, trans. C. A. Jones. Harmondsworth: Penguin.

Champion, Sarah, ed. 1997. *Disco Biscuits*. London: Sceptre.

Chandra, Vikram. 2000. *Love and Longing in Bombay*. 2nd edn. London: Faber.

Charters, Ann, ed. 1983. *The Story and Its Writer: An Introduction to Short Fiction*. New York: St Martin's Press.

Chaucer, Geoffrey. 1988. *The Riverside Chaucer*, ed. Larry D. Benson. Oxford: Oxford University Press.

Chávez, Denise. 2004. *The Last of the Menu Girls*. New York: Vintage.

Cheever, John. 1978. *The Stories of John Cheever*. London: Vintage.

Chekhov, Anton. 2004. *About Love and Other Stories*, trans. and ed. Rosamund Bartlett. Oxford: Oxford World's Classics.

Chesterton, G. K. 1906. *Charles Dickens*. London: Methuen.

— 2007. *The Club of Queer Trades*. London: Hesperus.

Chopin, Kate. 1984. *The Awakening and Selected Stories*, ed. Sandra M. Gilbert. New York and London: Penguin.

Cioran, E. M. 1993. *The Trouble with Being Born*, trans. Richard Howard. London: Quartet.

Cisneros, Sandra. 1991. *The House on Mango Street*. New York: Vintage.

— 2004. *Woman Hollering Creek*. London: Bloomsbury.

Colette. 1984. *The Collected Stories of Colette*, ed. Robert Phelps. London: Secker and Warburg.

Collins, Wilkie. 1994. *Mad Monkton and Other Stories*, ed. Norman Page. Oxford: Oxford World's Classics.

Conrad, Joseph, 1978. *Within the Tides*. London: Penguin.

— 1986. *The Collected Letters of Joseph Conrad, vol. 2*, ed. Frederic R. Karl and Laurence Davies. Cambridge: Cambridge University Press.

— 1997. *Selected Short Stories*, ed. Keith Carabine. Ware: Wordsworth Classics.

Coover, Robert. 1971. *Pricksongs and Descants*. London: Jonathan Cape.

— 1987. *A Night at the Movies*. London: Heinemann.

Cortázar, Julio. 1978. *End of the Game and Other Stories*, trans. Paul Blackburn. New York: Harper Colophon.

Coupland, Douglas. 1992. *Generation X: Tales for an Accelerated Culture*. London: Abacus.

Cox, Michael and R. A. Gilbert, ed. 1986. *The Oxford Book of English Ghost Stories*. Oxford: Oxford University Press.

Craig, Patricia, ed. 1994. *The Oxford Book of Modern Women's Stories*. Oxford: Oxford University Press.

Crane, Stephen. 1993. *The Open Boat and Other Stories*, ed. Philip Smith. New York: Dover.

Dahl, Roald. 2006. *Collected Stories*, ed. Jeremy Treglown. London: Dent.

Dalby, Richard, ed. 1988. *The Virago Book of Victorian Ghost Stories*. London: Virago.

Díaz, Junot. 1996. *Drown*. New York: Riverhead.

Dick, Philip K. 1990. *Second Variety*. London: Grafton.

— 1991. *We Can Remember It for You Wholesale*. London: HarperCollins.

Dickens, Charles. 1976. *Selected Short Fiction*, ed. D. A. Thomas. Harmondsworth: Penguin.

— 2005. *Mugby Junction*. London: Hesperus.

Dowson, Ernest. 1993. 'The Dying of Francis Donne', in *The Dedalus Book of Decadence: Moral Ruins*, ed. Brian Stableford. 2nd edn. Sawtry: Dedalus.

Doyle, Arthur Conan. 1981. *The Adventures of Sherlock Holmes*. Harmondsworth: Penguin.

Egerton, George. 1932. 'A Keynote on *Keynotes*', in *Ten Contemporaries: Notes Toward Their Definitive Bibliography*, ed. John Gawsworth. London: Ernest Benn.

— 1993. 'A Cross Line', in *Daughters of Decadence: Women Writers of the Fin-de-Siècle*, ed. Elaine Showalter. London: Virago.

Eggers, Dave, ed. 2004. *The Best of McSweeney's, vol. 1*. London: Hamish Hamilton.

Eisenberg, Deborah. 2006. *Twilight of the Superheroes*. London: Picador.

The Epic of Gilgamesh, trans. N. K. Sandars. 1960. London: Penguin.

Erdrich, Louise. 2005. *Love Medicine*. 2nd edn. New York: HarperPerennial.

Faulkner, William. 1963. *As I Lay Dying*. London: Penguin.

— 1985. *The Collected Stories of William Faulkner*. Harmondsworth: Penguin.

Fitzgerald, F. Scott. 1996. *The Diamond as Big as the Ritz and Other Stories*. London: Penguin.

Flaubert, Gustave. 1954. *The Selected Letters of Gustave Flaubert*, trans. and ed. Francis Steegmuller. London: Hamish Hamilton.

— 2005. *Three Tales*, trans. Roger Whitehouse. London: Penguin.

Ford, Richard. 1989. *Rock Springs*. London: Flamingo.

— ed. 1998. *The Granta Book of the American Short Story*. 2nd edn. London: Granta.

Forster, E. M. 1954. *Collected Short Stories*. London: Penguin.

— 1962. *Aspects of the Novel*. Harmondsworth: Penguin.

Fowles, John. 1986. *The Ebony Tower*. London: Pan.

Frame, Janet. 1983. *You Are Now Entering the Human Heart*. Wellington: Victoria University Press.

Futrelle, Jacques. 1907. 'The Problem of Cell 13'. http://gaslight.mtroyal.ca

Garland, Hamlin. 1956. *Main-Travelled Roads*. New York: Harper & Row.

Gibson, William. 1988. *Burning Chrome*. London: Grafton.

— 1992. 'Agrippa (A Book of the Dead)'. http://www.williamgibsonbooks. com/source/agrippa.asp

Gogol, Nikolai. 2003. *The Collected Tales of Nikolai Gogol*, trans. Richard Pevear and Larissa Volokhonsky. London: Granta.

Gordimer, Nadine. 1975. *Selected Stories*. London: Jonathan Cape.

Gray, Alasdair. 1984. *Unlikely Stories, Mostly*. London: Penguin.

— 1993. *Ten Tales Tall & True*. London: Bloomsbury.

Green, Jen and Sarah Lefanu, eds. 1985. *Despatches from the Frontiers of the Female Mind*. London: Women's Press.

Greene, Graham. 1972. *Collected Stories*. London: Bodley Head.

Gunesekera, Romesh. 1998. *Monkfish Moon*. London: Granta.

Hammett, Dashiell. 2001. *Crime Stories and Other Writings*, ed. Steven Marcus. New York: Library of America.

Hardy, Thomas. 1991. *Wessex Tales*. Oxford: Oxford World's Classics.

— 1996. *Life's Little Ironies*. Oxford: Oxford World's Classics.

Hawthorne, Nathaniel. 1987. *Young Goodman Brown and Other Tales*, ed. Brian Harding. Oxford: Oxford World's Classics.

— 1990. *The Scarlet Letter*. Oxford: Oxford World's Classics.

Head, Bessie. 1977. *The Collector of Treasures*. London: Heinemann.

Hebel, J. P. 1995. *The Treasure Chest*, trans. John Hibberd. London: Penguin.

Heinlein, Robert A. 1973. *The Best of Robert Heinlein*. London: Sphere.

Hemingway, Ernest. 1932. *Death in the Afternoon*. London: Jonathan Cape.

— 1993. *The First Forty-Nine Stories*. London: Arrow.

— 2005. *A Farewell to Arms*. 2nd edn. London: Vintage.

Henry, O. 1995. *100 Selected Stories*. Ware: Wordsworth Classics.

Highsmith, Patricia. 2005. *Nothing that Meets the Eye: The Uncollected Stories*. London: Bloomsbury.

Hill, Susan, ed. 1995. *The Penguin Book of Contemporary Stories by Women*. London: Penguin.

Hoffmann, E. T. A. 1982. *Tales of Hoffmann*, trans. and ed. R. J. Hollingdale. Harmondsworth: Penguin.

Homer. 1946. *The Odyssey*, trans. E. V. Rieu. Harmondsworth: Penguin.

Hornby, Nick, ed. 2000. *Speaking with the Angel*. London: Penguin.

Isherwood, Christopher. 2004. *Goodbye to Berlin*. 2nd edn. London: Vintage.

James, Henry. 1986. *The Figure in the Carpet and Other Stories*, ed. Frank Kermode. London: Penguin.

— 1987. *The Critical Muse: Selected Literary Criticism*, ed. Roger Gard. London: Penguin.

— 1990. *The Jolly Corner and Other Tales*, ed. Roger Gard. London: Penguin.

Jin, Ha. 1998. *Ocean of Words*. New York: Vintage.

Joyce, James. 1991. *Stephen Hero*. London: Paladin.

— 2000. *Dubliners*. Oxford: Oxford World's Classics.

Joyce, Michael. 1987. *Afternoon: A Story*. CD: Eastgate Systems.

— 1995. *Of Two Minds: Hypertext, Pedagogy and Poetics*. Ann Arbor: University of Michigan Press.

Kafka, Franz. 2005. *The Complete Short Stories*, ed. Nahum N. Glatzer. 2nd edn. London: Vintage.

Keillor, Garrison. 1985. *Lake Wobegon Days*. London: Faber.

Kelman, James. 1988. *Greyhound for Breakfast*. London: Picador.

— 1989. *Not Not While the Giro and Other Stories*. London: Mandarin.

King James Bible. http://etext.virginia.edu/kjv.browse.html

Kipling, Rudyard. 1937. *Something of Myself*. London: Macmillan.

— 1987a. *Debits and Credits*. London: Penguin.

— 1987b. *Limits and Renewals*. London: Penguin.

— 1987c. *The Man who would be King and Other Stories*, ed. Louis L. Cornell. Oxford: Oxford World's Classics.

— 1987d. *Traffics and Discoveries*. London: Penguin.

— 1996. *The Letters of Rudyard Kipling, vol. 3*, ed. Thomas Pinney. London: Macmillan.

— 2007. *The Mark of the Beast and Other Fantastical Tales*, ed. Stephen Jones. London: Orion.

Kneale, Matthew. 2005. *Small Crimes in an Age of Abundance*. London: Picador.

Lahiri, Jhumpa. 2000. *The Interpreter of Maladies*. London: Flamingo.

Lasdun, James. 2005. 'An Anxious Man', *The Paris Review* 173.

Lawrence, D. H. 1981. *The Letters of D. H. Lawrence*, ed. George J. Zytaruk and James T. Boulton. Cambridge: Cambridge University Press.

— 1982. *Selected Short Stories*, ed. Brian Finney. London: Penguin.

Lawson, Henry. 1976. *The Portable Henry Lawson*, ed. Brian Kiernan. St Lucia: University of Queensland Press.

Leacock, Stephen. 1923. *Over the Footlights and Other Fancies*. London: Bodley Head.

Leavitt, David. 2005. *The Stories of David Leavitt*. London: Bloomsbury.

Lee, Hermione, ed. 1985. *The Secret Self: Short Stories by Women*. London: Dent.

Le Fanu, Sheridan. 1993. *In a Glass Darkly*. Oxford: Oxford World's Classics.

Lessing, Doris. 1979. *This Was the Old Chief's Country*. London: Triad Grafton.

Lewis, Wyndham. 2004. *The Wild Body*. London: Penguin.

London, Jack. 2001. *Klondike Tales*. New York: Modern Library.

McEwan, Ian. 1995. *The Short Stories*. London: Jonathan Cape.

Machen, Arthur. 1995. 'The Bowmen', in *Women, Men and the Great War*, ed. Trudi Tate. Manchester: Manchester University Press.

Mack, Robert L., ed. 1992. *Oriental Tales*. Oxford: Oxford World's Classics.

Maclaren-Ross, Julian. 2004. *Selected Stories*, ed. Paul Willetts. Stockport: Dewi Lewis.

Malamud, Bernard. 2003. *The Magic Barrel*. New York: Farrar, Straus and Giroux.

Mansfield, Katherine. 1984. *The Stories of Katherine Mansfield*, ed. Antony Alpers. Auckland, Melbourne and Oxford: Oxford University Press.

— 1987. *The Critical Writings of Katherine Mansfield*, ed. Clare Hanson. London: Macmillan.

Manto, Saadat Hasan. 1997. *Mottled Dawn: Fifty Sketches and Stories of Partition*, trans. Khalid Hasan. New Delhi: Penguin.

Mars-Jones, Adam and Edmund White. 1987. *The Darker Proof*. London: Faber.

Mason, Bobbie Ann. 2001. *Shiloh and Other Stories*. New York: Random House.

Maupassant, Guy de. 1971. *Selected Short Stories*, trans. Roger Colet. London: Penguin.

Melville, Herman. 1997. *Billy Budd, Sailor and Selected Tales*, ed. Robert Milder. Oxford: Oxford World's Classics.

Melville, Pauline. 1990. *Shape-Shifter*. London: Women's Press.

— 1999. *The Migration of Ghosts*. London: Bloomsbury.

Menéndez, Ana. 2001. *In Cuba I Was a German Shepherd*. London: Review.

Mérimée, Prosper. 1989. *Carmen and Other Stories*, trans. and ed. Nicholas Jotcham. Oxford: Oxford World's Classics.

Míeville, China. 2006. *Looking for Jake and Other Stories*. London: Pan.

Mistry, Rohinton. 1992. *Tales from Firozsha Baag*. London: Faber.

Mitford, Mary Russell. 1904. *Our Village*. London: Dent.

Moore, George. 1990. *The Untilled Field*. Gloucester: Alan Sutton.

Moore, Lorrie. 1987. *Self-Help*. London: Faber.

Morrison, Arthur. 1912. *Tales of Mean Streets*. London: Methuen.

Morrow, Bradford and Patrick McGrath, ed. 1992. *The Picador Book of the New Gothic*. London: Picador.

Mukherjee, Bharati. 1989. *The Middleman and Other Stories*. London: Virago.

Munro, Alice. 1996. *Selected Stories*. London: Chatto and Windus.

Murakami, Haruki. 2003. *after the quake*, trans. Jay Rubin. London: Vintage.

Nabokov, Vladimir. 1958. *Nabokov's Dozen*. New York: Popular Library.

Naipaul, V. S. 1964. *Miguel Street*. 2nd edn. London: Andre Deutsch.

— 1969. *The Middle Passage*. London: Penguin.

Narayan, R. K. 2006. *Malgudi Days*. 2nd edn. London: Penguin.

Newland, Courttia. 2000. *Society Within*. London: Abacus.

Ngugi wa Thiong'o. 1975. *Secret Lives*. London: Heinemann.

Noon, Jeff. 2001. *Cobralingus*. Hove: Codex.

Oates, Joyce Carol. 1976. *Crossing the Border*. New York: Vanguard Press.

— ed. 1992. *The Oxford Book of American Short Stories*. Oxford: Oxford University Press.

O'Brien, Tim. 1991. *The Things They Carried*. London: Flamingo.

O'Connor, Flannery. 1990. *The Complete Stories*. London: Faber.

Okri, Ben. 1986. *Incidents at the Shrine*. London: Heinemann.

— 1989. *Stars of the New Curfew*. London: Penguin.

Ovid. 2004. *Metamorphoses*, trans. David Raeburn. London: Penguin.

Paley, Grace. 1999. *The Collected Stories*. London: Virago.

Perelman, S. J. 1959. *The Most of S. J. Perelman*. London: Heinemann.

Pirandello, Luigi. 1987. *Short Stories*, trans. Frederick May. London: Quartet.

Poe, Edgar Allan. 1948. *The Letters of Edgar Allan Poe, vol. 1*, ed. John Ward Ostron. Cambridge, MA: Harvard University Press.

— 1965. *Literary Criticism of Edgar Allan Poe*, ed. Robert L. Hough. Lincoln: University of Nebraska Press.

— 1976. *The Science Fiction of Edgar Allan Poe*, ed. Harold Beaver. Harmondsworth: Penguin.

— 1998. *Selected Tales*, ed. David Van Leer. Oxford: Oxford World's Classics.

Porter, Katherine Anne. 1964. *Collected Stories*. London: Jonathan Cape.

Pronzini, Bill and Jack Adrian, eds. 1995. *Hard-Boiled: An Anthology of American Crime Stories*. Oxford: Oxford University Press.

Proulx, Annie. 2006. *Close Range: Brokeback Mountain and Other Stories*. London: HarperPerennial.

Pushkin, Alexander. 1997. *The Queen of Spades and Other Stories*, trans. Alan Myers. Oxford: Oxford World's Classics.

Pynchon, Thomas. 1985. *Slow Learner: Early Stories*. London: Jonathan Cape.

Rhys, Jean. 1972. *Tigers are Better-Looking*. London: Penguin.

Richardson, Angelique, ed. 2005. *Women Who Did: Stories by Men and Women, 1890–1914*. 2nd edn. London: Penguin.

Richardson, Dorothy. 1989. *Journey to Paradise*, ed. Trudi Tate. London: Virago.

Rook, Clarence. 1979. *The Hooligan Nights*. Oxford: Oxford University Press.

Rosten, Leo. 1988. *The Education of H*Y*M*A*N K*A*P*L*A*N*. 2nd edn. London: Penguin.

Roth, Philip. 1986. *Goodbye Columbus, and Five Short Stories*. London: Penguin.

Rothenberg, Jerome and Pierre Joris, eds. 1994. *Poems for the Millennium*. Berkeley: University of California Press.

Rushdie, Salman. 1991. *Imaginary Homelands: Essays and Criticism 1981–1991*. London: Granta.

— 1995. *East, West*. London: Vintage.

Russ, Joanna. 1985. *Extra(ordinary) People*. London: Women's Press.

Saki. 1930. *The Short Stories of Saki*, ed. Christopher Morley. London: Bodley Head.

Sansom, William. 1982. 'The Wall', in *Short Stories from the Second World War*, ed. Dan Davin. Oxford: Oxford University Press.

Sargent, Pamela, ed. 1978. *Women of Wonder: Science Fiction Stories by Women about Women*. Harmondsworth: Penguin.

Saunders, George. 1997. *CivilWarLand in Bad Decline*. London: Vintage.

— 2000. *Pastoralia*. London: Bloomsbury.

— 2006. *The Brief and Frightening Reign of Phil, and In Persuasion Nation*. London: Bloomsbury.

Self, Will. 2006a. *Grey Area*. 2nd edn. London: Bloomsbury.

— 2006b. *The Quantity Theory of Insanity*. 2nd edn. London: Bloomsbury.

Selvon, Samuel. 1957. *Ways of Sunlight*. London: MacGibbon & Kee.

Senior, Olive. 1986. *Summer Lightning and Other Stories*. Harlow: Longman.

Shalamov, Varlam. 1994. *Kolyma Tales*, trans. John Glad. Harmondsworth: Penguin.

Shapard, Robert and James Thomas, eds. 1988. *Sudden Fiction: American Short-Short Stories*. London: Penguin.

Shippey, Tom, ed. 1992. *The Oxford Book of Science Fiction Stories*. Oxford: Oxford University Press.

Silko, Leslie Marmon. 1981. *Storyteller*. New York: Arcade.

Simpson, Helen. 2001. *Hey Yeah Right, Get a Life*. London: Vintage.

Sinclair, Iain and Dave McKean. 1996. 'The Griffin's Egg', in *It's Dark in London*, ed. Oscar Zarate. London: Serpent's Tail.

Singer, Isaac Bashevis. 1982. *The Collected Stories of Isaac Bashevis Singer*. London: Jonathan Cape.

Somerville, Edith and Martin Ross. 1944. *Experiences of an Irish RM*. London: Dent.

Soueif, Ahdaf. 1997. *Sandpiper*. London: Bloomsbury.

Stein, Gertrude. 1990. *Three Lives*. New York: Penguin.

— 1993. *A Gertrude Stein Reader*, ed. Ulla E. Dydo. Evanston: Northwestern University Press.

Sterling, Bruce, ed. 1986. *Mirrorshades: The Cyberpunk Anthology*. London: Paladin.

Stern, Jerome, ed. 1996. *Micro Fiction: An Anthology of Really Short Stories*. New York: Norton.

Stevenson, Robert Louis. 1995. *The Letters of Robert Louis Stevenson, vol. 7*, ed. Bradford A. Booth and Ernest Mehew. New Haven, CT: Yale University Press.

— 2006. *The Strange Case of Dr Jekyll and Mr Hyde and Other Tales*, ed. Roger Luckhurst. Oxford: Oxford World's Classics.

Stockton, Frank R. 1882. 'The Lady or the Tiger'. www.classicshorts.com

Tales from the Thousand and One Nights, trans. N. J. Darwood. 1973. 2nd edn. London: Penguin.

Tan, Amy. 1998. *The Joy Luck Club*. London: Vintage.

Tertz, Abram [Andrei Sinyavsky]. 1960. *On Socialist Realism*, trans. George Dennis. New York: Pantheon.

— 1987. *Fantastic Stories*. Evanston: Northwestern University Press.

Thomas, Dylan. 1983. *The Collected Stories*. London: Dent.

Thomas, James et al., eds. 1992. *Flash Fiction: Very Short Stories*. New York: Norton.

Toomer, Jean. 1969. *Cane*. New York: Harper & Row.

Trevor, William. 1992. *The Collected Stories*. London: Penguin.

— 2007. *Cheating at Canasta*. London: Penguin.

Turgenev, Ivan. 1967. *Sketches from a Hunter's Album*, trans. Richard Freeborn. Harmondsworth: Penguin.

Twain, Mark. 1993. *Short Stories and Tall Tales*. Philadelphia: Courage Classics.

Updike, John. 1987. *Forty Stories*. Harmondsworth: Penguin.

Upward, Edward. 1972. *The Railway Accident and Other Stories*. London: Penguin.

Vassanji, M. G. 1991. *Uhuru Street*. London: Heinemann.

Verga, Giovanni. 1999. *Cavalleria Rusticana and Other Stories*, trans. G. H. McWilliam. London: Penguin.

Vladíslavic, Ivan. 1989. *Missing Persons*. London: David Phillips.

Vonnegut, Kurt. 1968. *Welcome to the Monkey House*. New York: Dell.

Wallace, David Foster. 1997. *Girl with Curious Hair*. London: Abacus.

Ward, Candace, ed. 1996. *Great Short Stories by American Women*. New York: Dover.

Webber, Andrew J., ed. 1997. *Eight German Novellas*, trans. Michael Fleming. Oxford: Oxford World's Classics.

Wells, H. G. 1914. *The Country of the Blind and Other Stories*. London: Thomas Nelson.

Welty, Eudora. 1993. *Thirteen Stories*, ed. Ruth M. Vande Kieft. New York: Harcourt Brace.

Wilde, Oscar. 1980. *Complete Shorter Fiction*, ed. Isobel Murray. Oxford: Oxford World's Classics.

Williams, Noel. 1992. *The Crying of Rainbirds*. Leeds: Peepal Tree Press.

Wodehouse, P. G. 2001. *What Ho! The Best of P. G. Wodehouse*. London: Penguin.

Wolff, Tobias. 1996. *The Night in Question*. London: Bloomsbury.

— 1997. *The Stories of Tobias Wolff*. London: Bloomsbury.

— ed. 1993. *The Picador Book of Contemporary American Stories*. London: Picador.

Woolf, Virginia. 1935. *The Common Reader, Second Series*. 2nd edn. London: Hogarth Press.

— 1976. *The Question of Things Happening: The Letters of Virginia Woolf, vol. 2*, ed. Nigel Nicolson. London: Hogarth Press.

— 1988. *The Essays of Virginia Woolf, vol. 3*, ed. Andrew McNeillie. London: Hogarth Press.

— 2003. *A Haunted House: The Complete Shorter Fiction*, ed. Susan Dick. London: Vintage.

Zipes, Jack, ed. 2001. *The Great Fairy Tale Tradition: From Straparola and Basile to the Brothers Grimm*. New York: Norton.

Zoline, Pamela. 1983. 'The Heat Death of the Universe', in *New Worlds: An Anthology*, ed. Michael Moorcock. London: Flamingo.

Secondary Sources

Abraham, Nicolas and Maria Torok. 1994. *The Shell and the Kernel: Renewals of Psychoanalysis*, trans. and ed. Nicholas T. Rand. Chicago: University of Chicago Press.

Adorno, Theodor W. 1967. *Prisms*, trans. Samuel and Shierry Weber. London: Neville Spearman.

— 1991/2. *Notes to Literature, vols 1 and 2*, trans. Shierry Weber Nicholson, ed. Rolf Tiedemann. New York: Columbia University Press.

— and Walter Benjamin. 1999. *The Complete Correspondence*, trans. Nicholas Walker, ed. Henri Lonitz. Cambridge: Polity Press.

Allen, Walter. 1981. *The Short Story in English*. Oxford: Clarendon Press.

Amis, Kingsley. 1960. *New Maps of Hell*. London: Victor Gollancz.

Anderson, Graham. 2000. *Fairytale in the Ancient World*. London: Routledge.

Aristotle. 1954. *The Rhetoric and the Poetics*, trans. W. Rhys Roberts and Ingram Bywater. New York: Random House.

Armstrong, Tim. 1998. *Modernism, Technology and the Body: A Cultural Study*. Cambridge: Cambridge University Press.

Ashley, Mike. 2000. *The Time Machines: The Story of the Science-Fiction Pulp Magazines from the Beginning to 1950*. Liverpool: Liverpool University Press.

Auerbach, Erich. 2003. *Mimesis: The Representation of Reality in Western Literature*, trans. Willard R. Trask. 2nd edn. Princeton: Princeton University Press.

Austen, Jane. 2003. *Northanger Abbey*. 2nd edn. London: Penguin.

Ayers, David. 1992. *Wyndham Lewis and Western Man*. Basingstoke: Macmillan.

Baker, Brian. 2007. *Iain Sinclair*. Manchester: Manchester University Press.

Baldwin, Dean. 1993. 'The Tardy Evolution of the British Short Story', *Studies in Short Fiction* 30:1.

Ballaster, Ros. 2005. *Fabulous Orients: Fictions of the East in England, 1662–1785*. Oxford: Oxford University Press.

Bardolph, Jacqueline, ed. 2001. *Telling Stories: Postcolonial Short Fiction in English*. Amsterdam: Rodopi.

Barr, Robert et al. 1897. 'How to Write a Short Story: A Symposium'. http://gaslight.mtroyal.ab.ca

Barthes, Roland. 1977. *Image Music Text*, trans. and ed. Stephen Heath. London: Fontana.

— 1995. *Roland Barthes*, trans. Richard Howard. London: Papermac.

Baudrillard, Jean. 1994. *Simulacra and Simulation*, trans. Sheila Faria Glaser. Ann Arbor: University of Michigan Press.

Belsey, Catherine. 1980. *Critical Practice*. London: Methuen.

Benjamin, Walter. 1983. *Charles Baudelaire: A Lyric Poet in the Era of High Capitalism*, trans. Harry Zohn. London: Verso.

— 1992. *Illuminations*, trans. Harry Zohn, ed. Hannah Arendt. 2nd edn. London: Fontana.

Bennett, Andrew and Nicholas Royle. 2004. *Introduction to Literature, Criticism and Theory*. 3rd edn. Harlow: Pearson.

Bennington, Geoffrey. 1988. *Lyotard: Writing the Event*. Manchester: Manchester University Press.

Benstock, Shari. 1987. *Women of the Left Bank, Paris 1900–1940*. London: Virago.

Bercovitch, Sacvan. 1975. *The Puritan Origins of the American Self*. New Haven, CT: Yale University Press.

Bettelheim, Bruno. 1976. *The Meaning and Importance of Fairy Tales*. London: Thames and Hudson.

Bishop, Edward. 1996. 'Re:Covering Modernism – Format and Function in the Little Magazines', in *Modernist Writers and the Marketplace*, ed. Ian Willison et al. Basingstoke: Macmillan.

Blanchot, Maurice. 1995. *The Writing of the Disaster*, trans. Ann Smock. Lincoln: University of Nebraska Press.

Bolter, Jay David. 1991. *Writing Space: The Computer, Hypertext, and the History of Writing*. Hillsdale: Lawrence Erlbaum.

Bonney, William. 1980. *Thorns and Arabesques: Contexts for Conrad's Fiction*. Baltimore: Johns Hopkins University Press.

Botting, Fred. 1996. *Gothic*. London: Routledge.

Bourdieu, Pierre. 1984. *Distinction: A Social Critique of the Judgement of Taste*, trans. Richard Nice. London: Routledge and Kegan Paul.

Boyce, Benjamin. 1968. 'English Short Fiction in the Eighteenth Century: A Preliminary View', *Studies in Short Fiction* 5.

Bradbury, Malcolm and James McFarlane, eds. 1976. *Modernism*. Harmondsworth: Penguin.

Briggs, Julia. 1977. *Night Visitors: The Rise and Fall of the English Ghost Story*. London: Faber.

Brooks, Cleanth and Robert Penn Warren. 1959. *Understanding Fiction*. 2nd edn. London: Prentice Hall.

Buford, Bill. 1983. 'Editorial', *Granta* 8.

Bürger, Peter. 1984. *Theory of the Avant-Garde*, trans. Michael Shaw. Manchester: Manchester University Press.

Burroway, Janet. 2003. *Writing Fiction: A Guide to Narrative Craft*. 6th edn. New York: Longman.

Butler, Christopher S. 1994. *Early Modernism: Literature, Music and Painting in Europe, 1900–1916*. Oxford: Clarendon Press.

Carabine, Keith. 1992. '"Irreconcilable Differences": England as an "Undiscovered Country" in Conrad's "Amy Foster"', in *The Ends of the Earth: 1876–1918*, ed. Simon Gatrell. London: Ashfield Press.

Cawelti, J. G. 1976. *Adventure, Mystery and Romance: Formula Stories as Art and Popular Culture*. Chicago: Chicago University Press.

Certeau, Michel de. 1984. *The Practice of Everyday Life, vol. 1*, trans. Steven Rendall. Berkeley: University of California Press.

Cixous, Hélène. 1974. 'The Character of Character', *New Literary History* 5.

Clark, Robert. 1984. *History, Ideology and Myth in American Fiction, 1823–52.* London: Macmillan.

Clark, Timothy and Nicholas Royle, eds. 2004. 'The Blind Short Story', *Oxford Literary Review* 26.

Clements, Robert J. and Joseph Gibaldi. 1977. *Anatomy of the Novella: The European Tale Collection from Boccaccio and Chaucer to Cervantes.* New York: New York University Press.

Connor, Steven. 1989. *Postmodernist Culture: An Introduction to Theories of the Contemporary.* Oxford: Basil Blackwell.

Cooper, James Fenimore. 1963. *Notions of the Americans, vol. 2.* New York: Frederick Ungar.

Cox, Ailsa. 2004. *Alice Munro.* Tavistock: Northcote House.

— 2005. *Writing Short Stories.* London: Routledge.

Culler, Jonathan. 1985. *Flaubert: The Uses of Uncertainty.* 2nd edn. Ithaca, NY: Cornell University Press.

Cultural Critique. 1987. Special issue, 6/7.

Current-García, Eugene. 1965. *O. Henry (William Sydney Porter).* Boston: Twayne.

— and Walton R. Patrick, eds. 1974. *What is the Short Story?* 2nd edn. Glenview: Scott, Foresman.

Davis, Erik. 1999. *Techgnosis: Myth, Magic and Mysticism in the Age of Information.* London: Serpent's Tail.

Deane, Seamus. 1985. *Celtic Revivals: Essays in Modern Irish Literature 1880–1980.* London: Faber.

DeKoven, Marianne. 1983. *A Different Language: Gertrude Stein's Experimental Writing.* Madison: University of Wisconsin Press.

Deleuze, Gilles and Félix Guattari. 1986. *Kafka: Toward a Minor Literature,* trans. Dana Polan. Minneapolis: University of Minnesota Press.

— 1994. *What is Philosophy?,* trans. Graham Burchell and Hugh Tomlinson. London: Verso.

Derrida, Jacques. 1992. *Acts of Literature,* ed. Derek Attridge. London: Routledge.

— 1994. *Specters of Marx: The State of the Debt, the Work of Mourning, and the New International,* trans. Peggy Kamuf. London: Routledge.

— 1997. *Politics of Friendship,* trans. George Collins. London: Verso.

Docherty, Thomas, ed. 1993. *Postmodernism: A Reader.* Hemel Hempstead: Harvester Wheatsheaf.

Dollimore, Jonathan. 1991. *Sexual Dissidence: Augustine to Wilde, Freud to Foucault.* Oxford: Clarendon Press.

Donald, James. 1999. *Imagining the Modern City.* London: Athlone Press.

Dunn, Maggie and Ann Morris. 1995. *The Composite Novel: The Short Story Cycle in Transition*. New York: Twayne.

Eagleton, Mary. 1989. 'Genre and Gender', in *Re-Reading the Short Story*, ed. Clare Hanson. Basingstoke: Macmillan.

Eagleton, Terry. 1978. *Criticism and Ideology: A Study in Marxist Literary Theory*. London: Verso.

Elias, Camelia. 2004. *The Fragment: Towards a History and a Poetics of a Performative Genre*. Bern and New York: Peter Lang.

Elmer, Jonathan. 1995. *Reading at the Social Limit: Affect, Mass Culture, and Edgar Allan Poe*. Stanford: Stanford University Press.

Erdinast-Vulcan, Daphna. 1999. *The Strange Short Fiction of Joseph Conrad*. Oxford: Oxford University Press.

Fallon, Erin et al. 2001. *A Reader's Companion to the Short Story in English*. Westport: Greenwood Press.

Farrell, James T. 1948. *The League of Frightened Philistines*. London: Routledge.

Ferber, Michael, ed. 2005. *A Companion to European Romanticism*. Oxford: Basil Blackwell.

Fletcher, Ian, ed. 1979. *Decadence and the 1890s*. London: Edward Arnold.

Ford, Ford Madox. 1964. *Critical Writings of Ford Madox Ford*, ed. Frank MacShane. Lincoln: University of Nebraska Press.

Fraser, Gail. 1996. 'The Short Fiction', in *The Cambridge Companion to Joseph Conrad*, ed. J. H. Stape. Cambridge: Cambridge University Press.

Fraser, Robert. 2002. *Ben Okri: Towards the Invisible City*. Tavistock: Northcote House.

Freud, Sigmund. 1984. *On Metapsychology*, ed. Angela Richards. Harmondsworth: Penguin.

— 1985. *Art and Literature*, ed. Albert Dickson. Harmondsworth: Penguin.

Freund, Elizabeth. 1987. *The Return of the Reader: Reader-Response Criticism*. London: Methuen.

Frisby, David. 1985. *Fragments of Modernity: Theories of Modernity in the Work of Simmel, Kracauer and Benjamin*. Cambridge: Polity.

Frost, Robert. 1973. *Selected Poems*, ed. Ian Hamilton. Harmondsworth: Penguin.

Fuchs, Barbara. 2003. *Romance*. London: Routledge.

Fullbrook, Kate. 1986. *Katherine Mansfield*. Brighton. Harvester Press.

Fusco, Richard. 1994. *Maupassant and the American Short Story: The Influence of Form at the Turn of the Century*. University Park, PA: Pennsylvania State University Press.

Fussell, Paul. 1975. *The Great War and Modern Memory*. Oxford: Oxford University Press.

Gasiorek, Andrzej. 2001. 'Ford Madox Ford's Modernism and the Question of Tradition', *English Literature in Transition* 44:1.

Gelfant, Blanche, ed. 2000. *The Columbia Companion to the Twentieth-Century American Short Story*. New York: Columbia University Press.

Gerlach, John. 1985. *Toward the End: Closure and Structure in the American Short Story*. Alabama: University of Alabama Press.

Gibson, Andrew. 1999. *Postmodernity, Ethics and the Novel: From Leavis to Levinas*. London: Routledge.

Gioia, Dana and R. S. Gwynn, ed. 2006. *The Art of the Short Story*. New York: Longman.

Gottlieb, Erika. 2001. *Dystopian Fiction East and West: Universe of Terror and Trial*. Montreal: McGill-Queen's University Press.

Greaney, Michael. 2002. *Conrad, Language and Narrative*. Cambridge: Cambridge University Press.

Gross, Ruth V. 2002. 'Kafka's Short Fiction', in *The Cambridge Companion to Franz Kafka*, ed. Julian Preece. Cambridge: Cambridge University Press.

Guagliardo, Huey, ed. 2000. *Perspectives on Richard Ford*. Jackson: University Press of Mississippi.

Hafez, Sabry. 2008. *The Quest for Identities: The Development of the Modern Arabic Short Story*. London: Saqi Press.

Hallett, Cynthia Whitney. 1999. *Minimalism and the Short Story: Raymond Carver, Amy Hempel and Mary Robison*. Lampeter: Edwin Mellen Press.

Hannah, James. 1996. *Tobias Wolff: A Study of the Short Fiction*. New York: Twayne.

Hanscombe, Gillian and Virginia L. Smyers. 1987. *Writing for Their Lives: The Modernist Women, 1910–1940*. London: Women's Press.

Hanson, Clare. 1985. *Short Stories and Short Fictions, 1880–1980*. London: Macmillan.

Harris, Janice Hubbard. 1984. *The Short Fiction of D. H. Lawrence*. Rutgers: Rutgers University Press.

Harris, Wendell V. 1979. *British Short Fiction in the Nineteenth Century*. Detroit: Wayne State University Press.

Hayes, Kevin J. 2000. *Poe and the Printed Word*. Cambridge: Cambridge University Press.

Head, Dominic. 1992. *The Modernist Short Story: A Study in Theory and Practice*. Cambridge: Cambridge University Press.

Hewison, Robert. 1977. *Under Siege: Literary Life in London 1939–1945*. London: Weidenfeld and Nicolson.

Hoffman, Frederick et al., eds. 1946. *The Little Magazine: A History and Bibliography*. New York: Klaus Reprint.

Hogle, Jerrold E., ed. 2002. *The Cambridge Companion to Gothic Fiction.* Cambridge: Cambridge University Press.

Hughes, Linda K. and Michel Lund. 1991. *The Victorian Serial.* Charlottesville: University Press of Virginia.

Hunter, Adrian. 2004. 'Story into History: Alice Munro's Minor Literature', *English* 207.

Huyssen, Andreas. 1986. *After the Great Divide: Modernism, Mass Culture, Postmodernism.* Bloomington: Indiana University Press.

Iftekharuddin, Farhat et al., eds. 2003. *The Postmodern Short Story: Forms and Issues.* London: Praeger.

Ingram, Forrest L. 1971. *Representative Short Story Cycles of the Twentieth Century.* The Hague: Mouton.

Jack, Ian. 2003. 'Introduction', *Granta* 81.

Jackson, Rosemary. 1981. *Fantasy: The Literature of Subversion.* London: Methuen.

James, Edward and Farah Mendlesohn, eds. 2003. *The Cambridge Companion to Science Fiction.* Cambridge: Cambridge University Press.

James Joyce Quarterly. 1991. *Dubliners* issue, 28:2.

James, Louis. 1999. *Caribbean Literature in English.* London: Longman.

Jameson, Fredric. 1991. *Postmodernism, or the Cultural Logic of Late Capitalism.* London: Verso.

Jenny Brown Associates and Book Marketing Limited. 2004. 'The Short Story in the UK'. www.theshortstory.org.uk/aboutus/history.php4

Jouve, Nicole Ward. 1991. *White Woman Speaks with Forked Tongue: Criticism as Autobiography.* London: Routledge.

Kaplan, Sydney Janet. 1991. *Katherine Mansfield and the Origins of Modernist Fiction.* Ithaca, NY: Cornell University Press.

Karlsson, Ann-Marie. 1990. 'The Hyperrealistic Short Story: A Postmodern Twilight Zone', in *Criticism in the Twilight Zone: Postmodern Perspectives on Literature and Politics*, ed. Danuta Zadworna-Fjellestad and Lennart Björk. Stockholm: Almqvist and Wiksell International.

Keating, Peter. 1989. *The Haunted Study: A Social History of the English Novel, 1875–1914.* London: Secker and Warburg.

Kelley, Margot. 1997. 'A Minor Revolution: Chicano/a Composite Novels and the Limits of Genre', in *Ethnicity and the American Short Story*, ed. Julie Brown. New York and London: Garland.

Kemp, Sandra. 1988. *Kipling's Hidden Narratives.* Oxford: Basil Blackwell.

Kennedy, J. Gerald, ed. 1995. *Modern American Short Story Sequences: Composite Fictions and Fictive Communities.* Cambridge: Cambridge University Press.

Kilroy, J. F., ed. 1984. *The Irish Short Story: A Critical History*. Boston: Twayne.

Klaus, H. Gustav. 2004. *James Kelman*. Tavistock: Northcote House.

Kolocotroni, Vassiliki et al., eds. 1998. *Modernism*. Edinburgh: Edinburgh University Press.

Kristeva, Julia. 1982. *Powers of Horror: An Essay on Abjection*, trans. Leon S. Roudiez. New York: Columbia University Press.

Leavis, Q. D. 1932. *Fiction and the Reading Public*. London: Chatto and Windus.

Ledger, Sally. 1997. *The New Woman: Fiction and Feminism at the Fin de Siècle*. Manchester: Manchester University Press.

— and Roger Luckhurst, eds. 2000. *The Fin de Siècle: A Reader in Cultural History, c. 1880–1900*. Oxford: Oxford University Press.

Levenson, Michael. 1984. *A Genealogy of Modernism: A Study of English Literary Doctrine, 1908–1922*. Cambridge: Cambridge University Press.

Levy, Andrew. 1993. *The Culture and Commerce of the American Short Story*. Cambridge: Cambridge University Press.

Litz, A. Walton et al., eds. 2000. *The Cambridge History of Literary Criticism, vol. 7: Modernism and the New Criticism*. Cambridge: Cambridge University Press.

Lodge, David. 1990. *After Bakhtin: Essays on Fiction and Criticism*. London: Routledge.

Lohafer, Susan. 1983. *Coming to Terms with the Short Story*. Baton Rouge: Louisiana State University Press.

— and Jo Ellyn Clary, eds. 1989. *Short Story Theory at a Crossroads*. Baton Rouge: Louisiana State University Press.

Loomba, Ania. 1998. *Colonialism/Postcolonialism*. London: Routledge.

Lounsberry, Barbara et al., eds. 1998. *The Tales We Tell: Perspectives on the Short Story*. Westport: Greenwood Press.

Luckhurst, Roger. 1997. *The Angle Between Two Walls: The Fiction of J. G. Ballard*. Liverpool: Liverpool University Press.

— 2005. *Science Fiction*. Cambridge: Polity.

Lukács, Georg. 1969. *The Historical Novel*, trans. Hannah and Stanley Mitchell. Harmondsworth: Penguin.

— 1971. *The Theory of the Novel*, trans. Anna Bostock. London: Merlin Press.

Lyotard, Jean-François. 1984. *The Postmodern Condition: A Report on Knowledge*, trans. Geoffrey Bennington and Brian Massumi. Manchester: Manchester University Press.

— 1993. *The Inhuman: Reflections on Time*, trans. Geoffrey Bennington and Rachel Bowlby. Cambridge: Polity.

McCaffery, Larry. 1982. *The Metafictional Muse: The Works of Robert Coover, Donald Barthelme and William H. Gass*. London: Feffer and Simons.

Macdonald, Dwight. 1998. 'A Theory of Mass Culture', in *Cultural Theory and Popular Culture: A Reader*, ed. John Storey. 2nd edn. London: Prentice Hall.

Mann, Susan Garland. 1989. *The Short Story Cycle*. New York: Greenwood Press.

March-Russell, Paul. 2006. '"Close, but without touching": Hearing, Seeing and Believing in Conrad's "The Tale"', *Conradiana* 38:3.

Marx, John. 2004. 'Postcolonial Literature and the Western Literary Canon', in *The Cambridge Companion to Postcolonial Literary Studies*, ed. Neil Lazarus. Cambridge: Cambridge University Press.

Matthews, Brander. 1901. *The Philosophy of the Short-Story*. New York and London: Longmans, Green and Co.

Matthiessen, F. O. 1941. *American Renaissance: Art and Expression in the Age of Emerson and Whitman*. New York and Oxford: Oxford University Press.

Matz, Jesse. 2001. *Literary Impressionism and Modernist Aesthetics*. Cambridge: Cambridge University Press.

May, Charles E. 1995. *The Short Story: The Reality of Artifice*. New York: Twayne.

— ed. 1994. *The New Short Story Theories*. Athens: Ohio University Press.

Miller, Karl. 1987. *Doubles: Studies in Literary History*. Oxford: Oxford University Press.

Mix, Katharine Lyon. 1960. *A Study in Yellow: The Yellow Book and Its Contributors*. Lawrence: University of Kansas Press.

Montefiore, Jan. 2007. *Rudyard Kipling*. Tavistock: Northcote House.

Nagel, James. 1980. *Stephen Crane and Literary Impressionism*. University Park, PA: Pennsylvania State University Press.

— 2001. *The Contemporary American Short-Story Cycle: The Ethnic Resonance of Genre*. Baton Rouge: Louisiana State University Press.

Nicholls, Peter. 1995. *Modernisms: A Literary Guide*. Basingstoke: Macmillan.

— 2004. 'Surrealism in England', in *The Cambridge History of Twentieth-Century English Literature*, ed. Laura Marcus and Peter Nicholls. Cambridge: Cambridge University Press.

Nicol, Bran, ed. 2002. *Postmodernism and the Contemporary Novel: A Reader*. Edinburgh: Edinburgh University Press.

Nochlin, Linda. 1994. *The Body in Pieces: The Fragment as a Metaphor of Modernity*. London: Thames and Hudson.

O'Brien, Edward J. 1931. *The Advance of the American Short Story*. 2nd edn. New York: Dodd, Meal.

280 The Short Story

O'Connor, Frank. 2004. *The Lonely Voice: A Study of the Short Story*. Hoboken, NJ: Melville House.

O'Flinn, Paul. 1995. 'Production and Reproduction: The Case of *Frankenstein*', in *Frankenstein: Mary Shelley*, ed. Fred Botting. Basingstoke: Macmillan.

Ong, Walter J. 1982. *Orality and Literacy: The Technologizing of the Word*. London: Methuen.

Orel, Harold. 1986. *The Victorian Short Story: The Development and Triumph of a Literary Genre*. Oxford: Oxford University Press.

Osborne, Peter. 1992. 'Modernity is a Qualitative, Not a Chronological Category', *New Left Review* 192.

The Oxford English Dictionary. www.oed.com

Pain, Barry. 1916. *The Short Story*. London: Martin Secker.

Parsons, Deborah. 2000. *Streetwalking the Metropolis: Women, The City, and Modernity*. Oxford: Oxford University Press.

— 2003. *Djuna Barnes*. Tavistock: Northcote House.

Pater, Walter. 1912. *The Renaissance: Studies in Art and Poetry*. 7th edn. London: Macmillan.

Pattee, F. L. 1975. *The Development of the American Short Story*. New York: Biblo and Tannen.

Pease, Donald E. 1985. '*Moby Dick* and the Cold War', in *The American Renaissance Reconsidered*, ed. Walter Benn Michaels and Donald E. Pease. Baltimore: Johns Hopkins University Press.

Peden, William. 1975. *The American Short Story: Continuity and Change 1940–1975*. 2nd edn. Boston: Houghton Mifflin.

Perry, Bliss. 1920. *A Study of Prose Fiction*. 2nd edn. Cambridge, MA: Riverside Press.

Pilling, John, ed. 1994. *The Cambridge Companion to Samuel Beckett*. Cambridge: Cambridge University Press.

Poggioli, Renato. 1968. *Theory of the Avant-Garde*, trans. Gerald Fitzgerald. Cambridge, MA: Belknap Press.

Pope, Rob. 2005. *Creativity: Theory, History, Practice*. Abingdon: Routledge.

Porush, David. 1985. *The Soft Machine: Cybernetic Fiction*. London: Methuen.

Priestman, Martin, ed. 2003. *The Cambridge Companion to Crime Fiction*. Cambridge: Cambridge University Press.

Propp, Vladimir. 1968. *Morphology of the Folktale*, trans. Laurence Scott. 2nd edn. Austin: University of Texas Press.

Punter, David. 2000. *Postcolonial Imaginings: Fictions of a New World Order*. Edinburgh: Edinburgh University Press.

Rabaté, Jean-Michel. 1996. *The Ghosts of Modernity*. Gainesville: University Press of Florida.

Readings, Bill. 1996. *The University in Ruins*. Cambridge, MA: Harvard University Press.

Reid, Ian. 1977. *The Short Story*. London: Methuen.

Royle, Nicholas. 2003. *The Uncanny: An Introduction*. Manchester: Manchester University Press.

Runyan, Randolph Paul. 1992. *Reading Raymond Carver*. Syracuse: Syracuse University Press.

Sadler, Simon. 1998. *The Situationist City*. Cambridge, MA: MIT Press.

Schor, Naomi. 1987. *Reading in Detail: Aesthetics and the Feminine*. London: Methuen.

Scofield, Martin. 2006. *The Cambridge Companion to the American Short Story*. Cambridge: Cambridge University Press.

Shaw, Valerie. 1983. *The Short Story: A Critical Introduction*. London: Longman.

Sinfield, Alan. 1992. *Faultlines: Cultural Materialism and the Politics of Dissident Reading*. Oxford: Clarendon Press.

Sontag, Susan. 1994. *Styles of Radical Will*. London: Vintage.

Spangler, Jacquelyn. 2001. 'A Democracy of Letters: Best Short Stories and the Literary Aesthetic of Edward J. O'Brien', *Short Story* 9:1.

Springhall, John. 1998. *Youth, Popular Culture and Moral Panics: Penny Gaffs to Gangsta-Rap, 1830–1996*. Basingstoke: Macmillan.

Steger, Manfred B. 2003. *Globalization: A Very Short Introduction*. Oxford: Oxford University Press.

Stevenson, Lionel. 1972. 'The Short Story in Embryo', *English Literature in Transition* 15.

Stevenson, Randall. 1998. *Modernist Fiction: An Introduction*. 2nd edn. London: Prentice Hall.

Sullivan, Jack. 1978. *Elegant Nightmares: The English Ghost Story from Le Fanu to Blackwood*. Athens: Ohio University Press.

Suvin, Darko. 1979. *Metamorphoses of Science Fiction: On the Poetics and History of a Literary Genre*. New Haven, CT: Yale University Press.

Tallack, Douglas. 1993. *The Nineteenth-Century American Short Story*. London: Routledge.

— ed. 1995. *Critical Theory: A Reader*. London: Harvester Wheatsheaf.

Taylor, Debbie. 2003. 'Endangered Species', *Mslexia* 16.

Thompson, J. A. 1979. *Progressivism*. Durham: BAAS.

Todorov, Tzvetan. 1977. *The Poetics of Prose*, trans. Richard Howard. Ithaca, NY: Cornell University Press.

Tönnies, Ferdinand. 1955. *Community and Association*, trans. Charles P. Loomis. London: Routledge and Paul.

Trollope, Anthony. 1950. *An Autobiography*. London: Oxford University Press.

Turner, Frederick Jackson. 1962. *The Frontier in American History*. 3rd edn. New York: Holt, Rinehart and Winston.

von Trier, Lars and Thomas Vinterberg. 1995. 'The Vow of Chastity'. http://www.dogme95.dk/

Waugh, Patricia, ed. 2006. *Literary Theory and Criticism*. Oxford: Oxford University Press.

Wharton, Edith. 1997. *The Writing of Fiction*. New York: Touchstone.

Wheeler, Kathleen M., ed. 1984. *German Aesthetic and Literary Criticism: The Romantic Ironists and Goethe*. Cambridge: Cambridge University Press.

Williams, Patrick and Laura Chrisman, ed. 1993. *Colonial Discourse and Post-Colonial Theory: A Reader*. Hemel Hempstead: Harvester Wheatsheaf.

Williams, Raymond. 1973. *The Country and the City*. London: Chatto and Windus.

— 1976. *Keywords: A Vocabulary of Culture and Society*. London: Fontana.

— 1989. *The Politics of Modernism*, ed. Tony Pinkney. London: Verso.

Williams, William Carlos. 2001. *The Collected Poems, vol. 1*, ed. A. Walton Litz and Christopher J. MacGowan. Manchester: Carcanet.

Winship, Janice. 1987. *Inside Women's Magazines*. London: Pandora.

Winther, Pers et al., eds. 2004. *The Art of Brevity: Excursions in Short Fiction Theory and Analysis*. Columbia, SC: University of South Carolina Press.

Wolff, Janet. 1990. *Feminine Sentences: Essays on Women and Culture*. Cambridge: Polity.

Wolmark, Jenny. 1993. *Aliens and Others: Science Fiction, Feminism and Postmodernism*. London: Harvester Wheatsheaf.

Wonham, Henry B. 1993. *Mark Twain and the Art of the Tall Tale*. Oxford: Oxford University Press.

Wordsworth, William. 1995. *The Prelude: The Four Texts*, ed. Jonathan Wordsworth London: Penguin.

Yagoda, Ben. 2000. *About Town: The New Yorker and the World It Made*. London: Duckworth.

Zola, Emile. 1963. 'The Experimental Novel', in *Documents of Modern Literary Realism*, ed. George J. Becker. Princeton: Princeton University Press.

Index